Palgrave Studies in Global Higher Education

Series Editors
Roger King
School of Management
University of Bath
Bath, UK

Jenny Lee
Centre for the Study of Higher Education
University of Arizona
Tucson, AZ, USA

Simon Marginson
UCL Institute of Education
University College London
London, UK

Rajani Naidoo
School of Management
University of Bath
Bath, UK

This series aims to explore the globalization of higher education and the impact this has had on education systems around the world including East Asia, Africa, the Middle East, Europe and the US. Analyzing HE systems and policy this series will provide a comprehensive overview of how HE within different nations and/or regions is responding to the new age of universal mass higher education.

More information about this series at
http://www.palgrave.com/gp/series/14624

Catherine Yuan Gao

Measuring University Internationalization

Indicators across National Contexts

Catherine Yuan Gao
Centre for International Research on Education
Victoria University
Melbourne, VIC, Australia

ISSN 2662-4214   ISSN 2662-4222 (electronic)
Palgrave Studies in Global Higher Education
ISBN 978-3-030-21464-7   ISBN 978-3-030-21465-4 (eBook)
https://doi.org/10.1007/978-3-030-21465-4

© The Editor(s) (if applicable) and The Author(s), under exclusive licence to Springer Nature Switzerland AG 2019
This work is subject to copyright. All rights are solely and exclusively licensed by the Publisher, whether the whole or part of the material is concerned, specifically the rights of translation, reprinting, reuse of illustrations, recitation, broadcasting, reproduction on microfilms or in any other physical way, and transmission or information storage and retrieval, electronic adaptation, computer software, or by similar or dissimilar methodology now known or hereafter developed.
The use of general descriptive names, registered names, trademarks, service marks, etc. in this publication does not imply, even in the absence of a specific statement, that such names are exempt from the relevant protective laws and regulations and therefore free for general use.
The publisher, the authors and the editors are safe to assume that the advice and information in this book are believed to be true and accurate at the date of publication. Neither the publisher nor the authors or the editors give a warranty, express or implied, with respect to the material contained herein or for any errors or omissions that may have been made. The publisher remains neutral with regard to jurisdictional claims in published maps and institutional affiliations.

This Palgrave Macmillan imprint is published by the registered company Springer Nature Switzerland AG
The registered company address is: Gewerbestrasse 11, 6330 Cham, Switzerland

I would like to dedicate this book to my Parents, Husband, and Son.

Preface

Researching the internationalization of higher education is my fate. The same day that I was writing this preface, I received approval of my Australian citizenship. What a wonderful coincidence! I witness, experience, participate in, implement, and study internationalization of higher education, and ultimately, I benefit from it. It is no exaggeration to say that internationalization changed my life trajectory. I became interested in the subject during the last year of my secondary education. As a Chinese high school student who had never travelled abroad, I learned that, rather than taking the University Entrance Examination in China, there is another option—to study at universities overseas. I learned this in 2002, when self-financed study overseas began to be prevalent in China. Before that, among the small number of students who studied overseas, the Chinese government selected and supported the majority. At that time, I had little idea what it meant to study overseas, and did not even know what it was like to live abroad. The only incentive for me to go overseas was a picture in my mind: a girl standing at a crossroads in a country other than China, holding a pile of books, and looking into the distance while the wind blew her shoulder-length hair. As you can guess, the girl was me.

I will not describe all of the dramatic incidents in the story, but will skip to the most important. After I received an offer from a university in Australia, my parents decided that they still wanted me to take the University Entrance Examination, as in their view, I was highly likely to be admitted into the best universities in China, and they preferred that I attend Peking University (PKU) or Tsinghua rather than study overseas. As it happened, I performed very well on the examination and enrolled in PKU. At that point, it seemed that studying overseas was just a shining dream in my life that never would become a reality, although the seed had been planted and continued to grow. On my first day at university, fate arranged another opportunity for me to make my overseas dream come true. However, overwhelmed by the great excitement of being accepted at PKU, I rejected the offer without a second thought. That was the first year that universities in Hong Kong (HK) were allowed to recruit students from mainland China. In this first pilot year, two universities there made irresistible offers to students who were accepted by PKU and Tsinghua. As long as they relinquished their places in these two universities, they were welcome to choose any major in the two universities in HK and were offered a HK$500,000 scholarship for the four years. If I received this offer today, I would take it immediately, as I know that universities in HK could provide me with more internationalized learning experiences and serve as a bridge for my overseas dream, which students in the top two universities in China share commonly. However, 16 years ago, I knew little about those universities or the difference between them and their counterparts in mainland China. Instead, my experiences shaped my views. As I knew nothing about the 'outside world,' to me, PKU seemed unparalleled in the world. Thus, the story ended with me spending four years at PKU.

However, fate is generous. Although I rejected my first two opportunities to experience overseas study, I was offered a third when I completed my studies at PKU, and went to the UK as a postgraduate. Since then, internationalization has become part of my life. I worked in the International Office of Nankai University after I completed my Master's, and the challenges I encountered in my work inspired me to pursue the field of international education policy studies further, which led me to enter the Ph.D. program at the University of Melbourne.

Preface

With great passion and gratitude for internationalization, I devoted four years of doctoral research to develop a set of indicators to measure universities' performance in internationalization, on which this book is based.

I believe in the value of internationalization. Without my international and intercultural experiences, I would not be the person I am today. Internationalization opened my mind, extended my vision, and gave me an appreciation of the best of mankind's wisdom across national, cultural, and language boundaries. Had I not studied in the UK, I would not be interested in European history or understand the origin of modern civilization and its profound influences on human society. Had I not trained academically in the UK and Australia, I would have been unable to engage in another type of scholarship, one that differs completely from that with which I was familiar, and that instilled my lifelong interest in philosophy and sociology. Without a profound understanding of both Oriental and Western scholarship and culture, I would not believe cross-cultural education and research are so fascinating. Because of internationalization, my life has been enriched significantly. More importantly, internationalization has given me the confidence, courage, and skills to live in any country in the world. New places never cause me uncertainty or fear, but excitement. Internationalization gives me the freedom to live anywhere I like and appreciate the values with which I agree. Thus, I owe my thanks to internationalization. Without it, my material and spiritual life would be much more monotonous than it is now. I hope that internationalization prospers and flourishes, and that its benefits reach more people. Therefore, I wrote this book to make my small contribution to understanding and measuring university internationalization better so that it can develop properly and achieve desirable outcomes.

Melbourne, Australia Dr. Catherine Yuan Gao
March 2019

Acknowledgements

This project would not have been possible without the generous support of eighteen policymakers from seventeen leading universities in Australia, Singapore, and China. I would like to thank each of them sincerely for their valuable time and insightful ideas about university internationalization. They showed me the real picture of internationalization as it is taking place in different institutions and helped me achieve an integrated understanding of the process. Without their kind support, internationalization would always be an abstract concept to me. I am also grateful to the 182 administrative staff in those universities who participated in the online survey and shared their views about the appropriate indicators to measure internationalization. Without them, I would not have had the opportunity to understand the complexity of measurement.

Throughout my doctoral study at the University of Melbourne, the support offered by my supervisors, Professor Simon Marginson at Oxford University, and Dr. Chi Baik, and Professor Richard James at the Melbourne Centre for the Study of Higher Education (MCSHE), has been invaluable. I thank Chi for being engaged and supportive during every stage of my study. I also thank Richard for his critical comments and vivid explanation of the 'argument highway,' which helped me understand what academic writing is and its key criteria. Special thanks go to Simon, who used to be my principal supervisor. Although he left after one year of my candidature, he helped me shape and design the entire study, and his hard work set an example for me and always encouraged me to do my best. I cannot express adequately my gratitude to him for all the nurturing and mentoring he provided. I am truly proud to have had him as my supervisor, and he will continue to be a role model for me.

I would also like to thank Professor Rui Yang, who is based in Hong Kong, for his support overall throughout the four years. His profound understanding of China and higher education there has helped me understand the puzzle of internationalization in Chinese universities.

Finally, I thank my family. My parents have always provided unconditional support for me, and my husband, Bruce, has sacrificed much to be fully supportive of my career. Although I know that he has little interest in the internationalization of higher education or the various measurement tools, he has always been patient with me and made his best efforts to contribute intellectually.

Praise for *Measuring University Internationalization*

"People in higher education often find internationalization high-sounding and cannot make head or tail of it. This timely volume provides them with a convenient yet well-grounded grip. It is essential reading for both theorists and practitioners."
—Professor Rui Yang, *The University of Hong Kong, China*

"This book is a highly relevant study on why and how universities should embrace the internationalization agenda. The author represents the best of the new generation of international higher education scholars, challenging and developing existing research on internationalization in higher education."
—Hans de Wit, *Director of the Center for International Higher Education at Boston College, USA*

"This original and insightful study of university internationalization brings a new rigour to the discussion. Focused on key countries in the Asia-Pacific region, we can expect it to be widely read."
—Professor Simon Marginson, *University of Oxford, UK*

Contents

1	An Overview of the Project	1
2	Conceptualizing University Internationalization	21
3	Measuring University Internationalization	73
4	China	111
5	Singapore	135
6	Australia	155
7	An Integrated Understanding of University Internationalization Across Nations	185
8	An Indicator Set for Benchmarking University Internationalization Performance Across Nations	211
9	The Future of University Internationalization	273

Appendix A: Data Collection Instruments Used in This Project 295

Appendix B: A Summary of the Characteristics of Existing Instruments 309

Appendix C: Descriptive Statistics of Respondents' Perceptions of the Draft Indicators 317

Appendix D: Review Form for the Project 'A Set of Indicators for Measuring University Internationalization Across National Boundaries' 329

Index 331

Abbreviations

ACE	American Council on Education
ARWU	Academic Ranking of World Universities
ASEAN	Association of Southeast Asian Nations
CCP	The Chinese Communist Party
CeQuInt	Certificate for Quality in Internationalization
CHE	Center for Higher Education Development
CIC	Committee on Institutional Cooperation
DAAD	German Academic Exchange Service
EMQT	Erasmus Mobility Quality Tools
ESF	European Science Foundation
EU	European Union
FTE	Full-Time Equivalent
GS	Global School
HEI(s)	Higher Education Institution(s)
ICTs	Information and Computer Technologies
IMPI	Indicators for Mapping and Profiling Internationalization
IMS 2020	International Medical School 2020
IQRP	International Quality Review Programme
MINT	Mapping Internationalization Tool
NPM	New Public Management
NTU	Nanyang Technological University

Nuffic	Netherlands Organisation for International Cooperation in Higher Education
NUS	National University of Singapore
NVAO	Netherlands Flemish Accrediting Association
PVC(s)	Pro Vice-Chancellor(s)
R&D	Research and Development

List of Tables

Table 2.1	Definitions of university internationalization	35
Table 2.2	Key components of institutional internationalization strategies	50
Table 3.1	Dimensions and components measured by indicators	91
Table 3.2	A short list of available indicators for university internationalization	98
Table 4.1	Final indicators for measuring university internationalization performance (China)	128
Table 5.1	Final indicators for measuring university internationalization performance (Singapore)	148
Table 6.1	Final indicators for measuring university internationalization performance (Australia)	178
Table 7.1	Key dimensions and components of internationalization in flagship universities	187
Table 8.1	Distribution of responses by institution	212
Table 8.2	Distribution of respondents by demographic and professional background	214
Table 8.3	Importance of listed indicators in the research dimension by nation	217
Table 8.4	Importance of listed indicators in the student dimension by nation	219

Table 8.5	Importance of listed indicators in the faculty dimension by nation	220
Table 8.6	Importance of listed indicators in the curriculum dimension by nation	222
Table 8.7	Importance of listed indicators in the engagement dimension by nation	224
Table 8.8	Importance of listed indicators in the governance dimension by nation	225
Table 8.9	Indicators cited by most respondents as 'very important' for each component	227
Table 8.10	Draft final indicator set	229
Table 8.11	Feasibility of the 17 draft indicators	231
Table 8.12	The final set of indicators for measuring university internationalization	239
Table 8.13	Perceptions of the importance of the seven identified indicators by nation	242
Table 8.14	Perceptions of the feasibility of the 15 indicators	247
Table 8.15	Importance of six dimensions by nation	249

1

An Overview of the Project

The new global context is compelling universities to reconsider their missions, goals, and responsibilities, as well as to develop innovative strategies to improve their relevance and competitiveness. For over three decades by now internationalization of higher education has attracted increasing attention in the policy arena, at institutional, national, regional, or international level. It is a global phenomenon affecting almost all countries in the world and has come to be recognized as a key reform strategy by institutions as well as governments. The goals and purposes of the national strategies may vary from country to country and can be different from the institutional goals. But the significance of internationalization to national prosperity, competitiveness, and cultural diversity has been widely acknowledged. Governments and higher education institutions (HEIs) around the world have assumed a wide variety of strategies and activities to achieve internationalization.

In the past three decades, the scope and scale of internationalization have expanded from what, for many countries, was limited essentially to the mobility of students and scholars, to a more comprehensive and inclusive strategy, including the internationalization of curricula, research, university governance, and engagement with local communities and industries (Georghiou & Larédo, 2015; Jenkins-Deas, 2009; Take & Shoraku, 2018; van den Besselaar, Inzelt, Reale, de Turckheim, & Vercesi, 2012). As internationalizing a university requires a substantial and long-term investment of an institution's financial and human resources, assessment and quality control are critical to ensure that internationalization contributes to the relevance and quality of higher education and produces desirable outcomes (Coelen, 2009; Hudzik & Stohl, 2009; Knight, 2004; Taylor, 2004).

Demand for Better Measurement of University Internationalization

There are a number of reasons why measuring internationalization should be a priority. First, as Knight (2008) argued, 'institutions need a way to monitor internationalization and collect information on an ongoing basis. They often spend too much time describing in very vague terms the status of the internationalization' (p. 48). In this respect, universities require reliable and concrete information to demonstrate to what extent, and in what aspects, they are internationalized, in order to avoid defining themselves vaguely as an internationalized university or a global university. Effective measurements can help universities to distinguish between strategic aspirations and strategic reality, and to recognize that, for some, there is a 'gap' between the two (Foskett, 2010; Graham, Faiyaz, & John, 2005). Understanding the difference between current and desired levels of performance is a powerful aid to systematic decision-making where investment in people and programs is concerned. There has also been greater acceptance among university leadership that measurement and evaluation are early steps on a route to performance improvement against their own individual missions and goals (Sowter, 2013). Measurements of explicit achievements will help provide the information necessary to analyze an institution's strengths and identify the areas in need of improvement (Knight, 2008; Maringe, 2010). The results of assessment can be used as leverage by university policymakers in allocating resources to maintain their strengths, improve areas of weakness, and ensure that institutional goals and objectives are met. This is, in turn, a precursor to analyzing the outcomes of internationalization efforts.

Further, because of the intensified competition and increasing importance of rankings and league tables, there is greater demand than ever for comparative information on universities. This demand comes from the institutions themselves, governments, students, and the wider public (Sowter, 2013). International ranking of universities is a widely debated example of how measurement has influenced institutional management and operation in ways that differ from those in the past (Marginson, 2011; Marginson & van der Wende, 2009). HEIs need information to assess their competitive position in terms of their efforts to achieve internationalization, to show the international effects of their research, as well as their popularity with international students. Using a similar set of performance indicators allows HEIs to observe changes over time and comparison between peers, making it an effective method of controlling (Graham et al., 2005). Moreover, benchmarking one's performance with that of peer institutions enables universities to differentiate themselves from the competition and identify their comparative advantage, which helps them establish their brand or profile in the international arena (Beerkens et al., 2010; Green, 2012).

Finally, the emergence in higher education of a culture of accountability that is based on evaluation has also advanced the agenda. Since the 1980s, accountability has been on the higher education policy agenda in many systems (Huisman & Currie, 2004). General change in the direction of 'entrepreneurial university' increases the focus on the economic aspects of the business activities of universities. Consequently, it is necessary not only to develop sources of income and methods of controlling costs, but also expand financial reporting for universities. The answer to these challenges is to establish the concept of accountability, serving to govern universities (Łukasz, 2016). Accountability increases transparency of universities and produces an increment of trust in society toward university. There are two main components in accountability: the response of a university to social needs and efficiency in resources management (Michavila & Martinez, 2018). The trend for greater transparency and accountability has been supplemented by an increasing need to demonstrate value for money and (public) investor confidence (Hazelkorn, 2013). As a result, HEIs have been called upon to increasingly account for their expenditures and to demonstrate their effectiveness. As internationalization begins to cost more, both in terms of monetary and human resources, knowing objectively, and in measurable terms, that it produces the value intended becomes critical in garnering support beyond rhetoric (Hudzik & Stohl, 2009; Jenkins-Deas, 2009). Only with empirical data can universities demonstrate their achievements in internationalization to both internal stakeholders and the public. Governments and policymakers ask HEIs to provide evidence that they have a clear strategy, use their resources wisely, and are successful in their efforts to achieve internationalization (Green, 2012). Further, there is increasing pressure for accountability from international and domestic students, as well as faculty and academic leaders, to ensure the provision of appropriate quality internationalization programs (de Wit, 2010; Hudzik & Stohl, 2009). Therefore, it is not surprising that university leaders are expecting that institutions take the lead in demonstrating accountability and providing clear information to the public and policymakers about their institution's performance, rather than waiting for rules and procedures to be established by others (Green, 2012).

More than two decades ago, Knight (1994) identified six stages to the process of internationalization: awareness; commitment; planning; operating; review, and reinforcement. As internationalization comes of age, measuring university performance in internationalization has become a priority in both research and practice (Dewey & Duff, 2009; de Wit, 2011; Knight, 2001, 2008; van den Besselaar et al., 2012). More sophisticated information and useful tools would assist with the exercise of mapping and measuring this phenomenon, especially in a comparative manner. In general, assessing university performance in internationalization is critical to its sustainability, credibility, and accountability.

A range of instruments has been developed in the past two decades to measure internationalization performance. The first endeavor was the International Quality Review Program (IQRP) developed by the Institutional Management in Higher Education, OECD, together with the Academic Cooperation Association (Knight & de Wit, 1999).

Following this effort, there was a considerable increase in the number of studies and projects that attempted to construct appropriate indicators of internationalization. Not surprisingly, the first tools that were developed came from countries where internationalization had gained more importance because of an increasing flow of foreign students, including the United States (e.g., Green, 2005; Horn, Hendel, & Fry, 2007), UK (e.g., Ayoubi & Massoud, 2007), Australia (e.g., Krause, Coates, & James, 2005), and some European countries (e.g., Brandenburg & Federkeil, 2007; DAAD, 2010; de Wit, 2009). In addition, there has been increasing interest in internationalization indicators in Asia, including the projects conducted by Osaka University (Furushiro, 2006) and by Paige (2005) for Japan, by Chin and Ching (2009) for Taiwan, and by Chen, Zeng, Wen, Weng, and Yu (2009) for universities in mainland China. As an important part of the IRIS project, indicators were developed to measure internationalization level of universities in Israel ('Providing Support Services for International Activity,' 2014).

Most recently, cross-border instruments have been established to serve a variety of HEIs in different regions. For example, the Indicators for Mapping and Profiling Internationalization (IMPI) project (Beerkens et al., 2010), the Erasmus Mobility Quality Tools (EMQT) (Managing Committee of the EMQT project, 2011), the Certificate for Quality in Internationalization (CeQuInt) project (Aerden & Weber, 2013), and the International Medical School 2020 (IMS 2020) project (Gajowniczek & Schlabs, 2013) focused on the European context. In 2016, UNESCO Office in Bangkok in collaboration with the University of Tokyo initiated a project to develop internationalization indicators of higher education in the Association of Southeast Asian Nations (ASEAN) plus 6 countries (Preciousa & Blueboard, 2017). A comprehensive review of these existing instruments can be found in Chapter 3.

Thanks to the efforts of many researchers, HEIs have diverse choices in the tools that they can use to monitor and assess their internationalization performance. These instruments may serve the purposes of self-evaluation, benchmarking, accreditation, ranking or a mix of these. Despite the various tools available, however, an efficient instrument has yet to be developed that includes a manageable number of indicators to help universities measure their internationalization performance systematically as well as generate valid information to make comparisons between institutions in different parts of the world. Previous studies on the development of measurements for university internationalization have provided valuable lessons for further efforts in the field. More importantly, the weaknesses of current instruments indicate the need for a better understanding of university internationalization and its measurement, as well as the need for new instruments.

The majority of existing measures have been framed based on a Western dominant perception of internationalization. As measuring internationalization has become a concern for universities in different parts of the world, it would be problematic if the instrument were devised from a biased perspective. Emerging conceptualizations of the phenomenon have challenged earlier definitions that focused on Western or European concepts and approaches (Cross, Mhlanga, & Ojo, 2011; Gao, 2015). A conceptual framework developed for the West could be less relevant to university internationalization practices in other parts of the world. In order to develop valid, effective, and comparable measurements for university internationalization, it is important to understand the phenomenon in different national and cultural contexts.

Further, there is no consensus on the components that should be included in measuring university internationalization, implying a lack of a clear construct. The instruments developed in previous studies have shown both similarities and differences in the components of university internationalization that are included and the way in which these components are grouped. The premise of developing measurements is to identify which components should be taken into account when assessing university internationalization, and which can be assessed by a particular type of measurement.

In addition, existing instruments have been developed to a large extent by researchers without engaging university practitioners in the procedure. Only some recent projects, such as MINT, IMPI, and EMQT, have incorporated practitioners proactively. The internationalization of universities is seen as a socially constructed phenomenon with 'historic and cultural locatedness' (Scott & Usher, 1996, p. 13), and conceptual questions, such as the meaning of internationalization and key components of its strategies are understood through the eyes of the participants (Chan & Dimmock, 2008). Because international activities take place largely in individual universities, university practitioners, as the participants who are involved with internationalization most directly, should be engaged to conceptualize the phenomenon and to develop measurements, in order to ensure that the conceptual framework on which an instrument is based is relevant to the practice. A particular measurement may or may not make sense depending on the view of the user (Coelen, 2009). As the audience of the measurement will be individual universities, practitioners' voices should be carefully taken into account. As van den Besselaar et al. (2012) argued, if measurements are developed without interaction with users, the design phase will be faster; however, in such cases, the consensus on the usefulness and the requirements for data collection would take much more time. University practitioners are clear about the need for measuring tools, and their involvement will assist in ensuring the utility and acceptance of measurements.

Moreover, a systemic and well-established instrument that can be used in different institutional and national contexts has not been developed (de Wit, 2010; Jenkins-Deas, 2009). Those measurements available are generally national and regional in scope and cannot normally be transferred between countries because of cultural differences and varying understandings of internationalization.

Finally, in some prior instruments, there is evidence of the 'mushrooming effect' (Beerkens et al., 2010), which reveals continuous growth in the number of indicators. It is not useful to propose a measurement that will be burdensome or unaffordable in terms of time or money, and mushrooming leads to a very complex indicator system that is less likely to be usable. Comprehensive indicator sets at any level would be very costly and would impose substantial burdens on those supplying data. Indicators, as a means of measurement, are favored by practitioners and researchers due to their simple and operable features. In the literature, simplicity of an indicator set is often advocated, even if initially it may seem less attractive technically (Ewell & Jones, 1994). Many scholars have argued that an extensive indicator set is unmanageable (James, 2003; Shavelson, McDonnell, & Oakes, 1989), too complex (Blank, 1993), and lacks utility (Porter, 1991). As equipment, funding, time, and human resources are required to collect, analyze, and report data, a comprehensive set of indicators would be very costly to develop and maintain (Oakes, 1986; Pollard, 1989) and might take so long to collect and analyze that the information would lose its relevance.

Research Questions

The imperative to measure university internationalization, on the one hand, and the limitation with the existing instruments, on the other hand, has prompted this project. The primary goal of the project was to develop a set of internationally applicable indicators that will provide universities with insights into their internationalization performance and also offer options for comparison. In doing so, a better understanding of university internationalization in different national contexts could be achieved. Three questions steered the investigation:

- What does university internationalization mean in different national contexts? What are its key dimensions and components?
- What are appropriate indicators to measure a university's internationalization performance?
- To what extent are data for the indicators presently available?

The use of some key concepts in this project needs to be clarified at the beginning. Finding a workable terminology is not an exercise in determining the correct use of a given word; rather, it is an attempt to select a particular lexicon that is as clear and consistent as possible. It is necessary to realize that any choice of terminology is somewhat arbitrary when words have multiple meanings and varied uses. This is particularly true in the area of internationalization, where the concepts are complex and the language is potentially confusing. There are two key terms that needed to be defined in this study: *university internationalization* and *indicators*. There is no simple, unique, or universally agreed upon definition of university internationalization (de Wit, 2002). Over the years, there has been a great diversity of interpretations of the concept. Due to the lack of a universally accepted definition, there seems to be a general trend in studies of university internationalization to define it 'in the context of' or 'for the purpose of' a specific study. This study was designed to develop a measurement for university internationalization, which is required to outline the key dimensions of the phenomenon. Given this, the use of the term internationalization in this research aligns with Knight's (1994, p. 7) definition of a 'process of integrating an international or intercultural dimension into the teaching, research, and service functions of the institution.' This definition assists in addressing the broad aspects to be internationalized in a particular HEI.

Another critical concept in this study is 'indicators.' Indeed, the term 'indicator' tends to be misused and includes many forms of descriptive information in different studies. Various definitions of indicators have been proposed by different scholars across different educational settings (e.g., Dickson & Lim, 1991; Lashway, 2001; Oakes, 1986; Ogawa & Collom, 1998; Selden, 1985; Shavelson, 1991) and have resulted in a consensus on the quantitative nature of indicators. Qualitative information, such as perceptions collected through surveying and demonstrative data, and specific examples that represent standards are more likely to be regarded as complementary to indicators (Jongbloed & Westerheijden, 1994) The working definition of the term 'indicators' in this project is consistent with Taylor, Meyerson, and Massy's (1993, p. 10) definition of 'ratios, percentages, or other quantitative values that allow an institution to compare its position in key strategic areas to peers, to past performance, or to previously set goals.' This definition highlights the agreed upon quantitative nature of indicators and also implies that internationalization, if not in its entirety, at least in some part, is understood, measurable, and able to be represented by data.

Indicators can be produced for a variety of audiences and to meet diverse purposes. The purposes that an indicator set aim to serve, determine the selection of indicators included in a particular set. Specifically, the indicator set developed in this project was expected to:

- *Report the status of institutional internationalization*, providing a snapshot of what is happening at a given moment in time.
- *Monitor changes over time*, used on a longitudinal basis; it can make a time series assessment and illustrate shifts and trends.
- *Profile the (comparative) strengths and weaknesses of internationalization practice*, reflecting different patterns in internationalization evolution.
- *Inform policy and decision makers*, providing information about what generic types of internationalization strategies are being implemented in various countries and what general types of subsequent changes seem to be associated with them through the comparison with peers.

Research Design

This project employed both qualitative and quantitative methods in a multi-stage investigation. In the first phase, literature review and interviews with university policymakers were conducted to understand university internationalization from both the researchers and practitioners' perspectives. The analysis of the literature and interviews together resulted in a conceptual framework of university internationalization for developing the indicator set. With this framework, the study moved onto select the appropriate indicators to be included in the final set. This process was aided significantly by university administrative staff engaged with international activities. An online questionnaire was administrated to these staff to survey their perceptions of the appropriateness of a short list of indicators.

Sampling the Research Site and Participants

Ideally, an internationally applicable set of indicators is expected to serve any types of universities. However, the indicator set developed in this project is more compatible with research-intensive universities.

The focus on research universities is because they are the most active and powerful players in the process of internationalization compared with other types of universities (Geuna, 1998). Geographically, this project focused on three countries: Australia, Singapore, and China. These three countries were included because they provide distinctive national contexts in which to examine university internationalization. Australia represents the dominant English-speaking context and has the highest proportion of overseas student among the OECD countries (OECD, 2011). In contrast, China provides the context of a non-English-speaking country in the initial phase of internationalization. It sends out the largest number of students to other countries and has become an increasingly popular destination for overseas study. Specific to its national context, China is a country with a long-established civilization and centralized education system (Huang, 2007; Yang, 2014). The city-state of Singapore was used in this study because it lies between the other two. First, it has a diverse linguistic environment, in which both English and Chinese are official languages. Second, the government has played a strong role in the development of education in Singapore. As a result of the 'education hub' strategy, it has achieved a more balanced two-way flow of students than have the other two countries (Gopinathan, 2007). Exploring internationalization and the needs to measure it in these three distinctive contexts lends the instrument developed in this study considerable potential to transcend national boundaries and cultures, being applied to research-intensive universities in different parts of the world.

Given the focus of the project, the *Academic Ranking of World Universities* (ARWU) was used to identify the research-intensive universities in the three countries. The selection of the ARWU was because its ranking places particular attention to the research capacity of universities. Since the indicator set developed in the current study is expected to serve a comparison purpose, it is necessary to assure a 'like' to 'like' comparison. It means the sample universities are required to possess similar traits or characteristics. Taking this into account, homogeneous sampling technique (see Kemper, Stringfield, & Teddlie, 2003;

Morse & Niehaus, 2009) was used to select the universities to secure the largest degree of similarity. According to the ARWU 2012, among the top 300, nine universities in Australia, two in Singapore and seven in China were identified and formed the sample of research sites. All these 18 universities had similar international reputations and could be regarded as flagship universities in their own countries, which suggested they were likely to share similar missions and objectives in terms of internationalization. The Pro-Vice-Chancellors (PVC) of International in the selected were invited for an interview. In the case that there was no PVC (international) in the university, the Vice-Chancellor was contacted. The final sample of interviewees consisted of 18 participants from 17 universities. Following the interview, all administrative staff who were responsible for institutional international activities in the 17 participating universities were invited to participate in a survey to help identify the appropriate indicators.

Data Collection and Analysis

Semi-structured interviews were conducted either face-to-face or over the phone with the 18 university leaders in their native languages. Online questionnaires were developed in both English and Chinese for administrative staff to indicate their views of the appropriateness of a list of draft indicators. A four-point Likert rating scale was used to ask respondents to specify their degree of agreement to both the importance and feasibility of 57 draft indicator. The questionnaire was also designed to explore other appropriate indicators that might be missing from the draft list. In this case, open-ended questions were used to probe the possibilities. The interview protocol and the questionnaire are presented in Appendix A. Thematic analysis was undertaken once the qualitative data had been collected through interviews. Descriptive analyses were conducted to identify the indicators to be included in the final set from the survey responses. Kruskal–Wallis and Mann–Whitney U tests were performed to explore any divergences between respondents from different countries in relation to their perceptions of the indicators.

Summary

This project was a response to the demand for internationally applicable measurements of university internationalization. To order to develop the indicator set needed to measure universities' performance in internationalization, it required a re-examination of the phenomenon to gain a complete understanding of its nature and characteristics. Although a large number of studies have discussed the definitions of, and rationales and strategies for university internationalization extensively, many researchers have argued that the meaning of internationalization remains ambiguous and unclear (Mok, 2007; Stier & Borjesson, 2010; Yang, 2002). The majority of existing studies on the phenomenon are case studies or those that focus on the divergence of institutional motives and strategies, and unfortunately, university internationalization has yet to be guided by a well-established theory. Thus, a clear and robust construct of the phenomenon is still lacking. Internationalization has been used as an umbrella term without a clear idea of what is included in that definition. By identifying the key dimensions and components of common university internationalization practice, and developing a shared understanding, this study moves us a step closer to a systematic theory of the phenomenon.

With the indicator set developed, this project augments the choices that universities can make to fulfill their diverse needs in measuring internationalization performance. This does not imply that the instrument developed in this project is the best one or that it provides a 'one-fits-in-all' solution, but it may be seen as complementary to existing tools. The assessment of internationalization has to move beyond national borders so that a common currency for performance measurement at the global level can be identified (Gacel-Avila, 2005). The indicator set developed in this project is an example of attempts to design those common currencies. By taking into account various national and institutional contexts, the conceptual framework and indicators were constructed to capture the generic aspects of university internationalization, which guarantee their relevance to the practice of research universities in most countries, not restrained to the three nations sampled in this project.

References

Aerden, A., & Weber, M. (2013). *Frameworks for the assessment of quality in internationalisation* (Occasional Paper). Certificate for Quality in Internationalisation: European Consortium for Accreditation in Higher Education (ECA).

Ayoubi, R. M., & Massoud, H. K. (2007). The strategy of internationalization in universities: A quantitative evaluation of the intent and implementation in UK universities. *International Journal of Educational Management, 21*(4), 329–349.

Beerkens, E., Brandenburg, U., Evers, N., van Gaalen, A., Leichsenring, H., & Zimmermann, V. (2010). *Indicator projects on internationalisation: Approaches, methods and findings: A report in the context of the European project 'Indicators for Mapping & Profiling Internationalisation' (IMPI)*. Gütersloh: CHE Consult GmbH.

Blank, R. K. (1993). Developing a system of education indicators: Selecting, implementing, and reporting indicators. *Educational Evaluation and Policy Analysis, 15*(1), 65–80.

Brandenburg, U., & Federkeil, G. (2007). *How to measure internationality and internationalisation of higher education institutions! Indicators and key figures*. Gütersloh: Centre for Higher Education Development.

Chan, W. W. Y., & Dimmock, C. (2008). The internationalization of universities: Globalist, internationalist and translocalist models. *Journal of Research in International Education, 7*(2), 184–204.

Chen, C.-G., Zeng, M.-C., Wen, D.-M., Weng, L.-X., & Yu, Z. (2009). The establishment of indicator system for the evaluation of internationalisation of reserch universities in China. *Peking University Education Review, 7*(4), 116–135 (in Chinese).

Chin, J. M.-C., & Ching, G. S. (2009). Trends and indicators of Taiwan's higher education internationalization. *Asia-Pacific Education Researcher, 18*(2), 185–203.

Coelen, R. J. (2009). Ranking and the measurement of success in internationalisation: Are they related? In H. de Wit (Ed.), *Measuring success in the internationalisation of higher education* (EAIE Occasional Paper No. 22, pp. 39–47). Amsterdam: European Association for International Education.

Cross, M., Mhlanga, E., & Ojo, E. (2011). Emerging concept of internationalisation in South African higher education: Conversations on local and global exposure at the University of the Witwatersrand (Wits). *Journal of Studies in International Education, 15*(1), 75–92.

DAAD. (2010). *Internationality at German universities: Concepts and collecting profile data*. Bonn, Germany: German Academic Exchange Service (DAAD).

Dewey, P., & Duff, S. (2009). Reason before passion: Faculty views on internationalization in higher education. *Higher Education, 58*(4), 491–504.

de Wit, H. (2002). *Internationalization of higher education in the United States of America and Europe: A historical, comparative, and conceptual analysis*. Westport, CT: Greenwood Press.

de Wit, H. (2009). Measuring success in the internationalisation of higher education: An introduction. In H. de Wit (Ed.), *Measuring success in the internationalisation of higher education* (EAIE Occasional Paper No. 22, pp. 1–8). Amsterdam: European Association for International Education.

de Wit, H. (2010). *Internationalisation of higher education in Europe and its assessment, trends and issues*. The Hague, The Netherlands: NVAO.

de Wit, H. (2011). Internationalisation of higher education in Europe and its Assessment: Towards a European certificate. In H. de Wit (Ed.), *Trends, issues and challenges in internationalisation of higher education* (pp. 39–43). Amsterdam: Centre for Applied Research on Economics and Management Hogeschool van Amsterdam.

Dickson, G. S., & Lim, S. (1991). *The development and use of indicators of performance in educational leadership*. Paper presented at the International Congress for School Effectiveness and Improvement, Cardiff, Wales.

Ewell, P. T., & Jones, D. P. (1994). Pointing the way: Indicators as policy tools in higher education. In S. Rupert (Ed.), *Charting higher education accountability: A sourcebook on state-level performance indicators* (pp. 6–16). Denver, CO: Education Commission of the States.

Foskett, N. (2010). Global markets, national challenges, local strategies: The strategic challenge of internationalization. In F. Maringe & N. Foskett (Eds.), *Globalisation and internationalisation in higher education: Theoretical, strategic and management perspectives* (pp. 35–50). London: Continuum.

Furushiro, N. (2006). *Developing evaluation criteria to assess the internationalization of universities final report grant-in-aid for scientific research*. Osaka: Osaka University.

Gacel-Avila, J. (2005). The internationalisation of higher education: A paradigm for global citizenry. *Journal of Studies in International Education, 9*(2), 121–136.

Gajowniczek, J., & Schlabs, T. (2013). *International medical school label methodology*. Retrieved 20 May 2014, from http://www.ims-2020.eu/downloads/FC_IMS_label_methodology.pdf.

Gao, Y. (2015). Constructing internationalisation in flagship universities from the policy-maker's perspective. *Higher Education, 70*(3), 359–373. https://doi.org/10.1007/s10734-014-9834-x.

Georghiou, L., & Larédo, P. (2015). *Dimensions of internationalisation— Universities at home and abroad*. Retrieved from https://hal-upec-upem.archives-ouvertes.fr/hal-01275905/document.

Geuna, A. (1998). The internationalisation of European universities: A return to medieval roots. *Minerva: A Review of Science, Learning and Policy, 36*(3), 253–270.

Gopinathan, S. (2007). Globalisation, the Singapore developmental state and education policy: A thesis revisited. *Globalisation, Societies and Education, 5*(1), 53–70.

Graham, E., Faiyaz, D., & John, F. (2005). Visualising the "internationalisation" of universities. *International Journal of Educational Management, 19*(4), 318–329. https://doi.org/10.1108/09513540510599644.

Green, M. F. (2005). *Measuring internationalization at research universities*. Washington, DC: American Council on Education.

Green, M. F. (2012). *Measuring and assessing internationalization*. Retrieved 21 June 2014, from http://www.nafsa.org/uploadedFiles/NAFSA_Home/Resource_Library_Assets/Publications_Library/MeasuringandAssessing Internationalization.pdf.

Hazelkorn, E. (2013). World-class universities or world-class systems? Rankings and higher education policy choices. In P. T. M. Marope, P. J. Wells, & E. Hazelkorn (Eds.), *Rankings and accountability in higher education: Uses and misuses* (pp. 71–94). Paris: UNESCO.

Horn, A. S., Hendel, D. D., & Fry, G. W. (2007). Ranking the international dimension of top research universities in the United States. *Journal of Studies in International Education, 11*(3–4), 330–358.

Huang, F. (2007). Internationalisation of higher education in the era of globalisation: What have been its implications in China and Japan? *Higher Education Management and Policy, 19*(1), 47–61.

Hudzik, K. J., & Stohl, M. (2009). Modelling assessment of the outcomes and impacts of internationalisation. In H. de Wit (Ed.), *Measuring success in the internationalisation of higher education* (EAIE Occasional Paper 22, pp. 9–21). Amsterdam: European Association for International Education.

Huisman, J., & Currie, J. (2004). Accountability in higher education: Bridge over troubled water? *Higher Education, 48*(4), 529–551.

James, R. (2003). Suggestions relative to the selection of strategic system-level indicators to review the development of higher education. In A. Yonezawa & F. Kaiser (Eds.), *System-level and strategic indicators for monitoring higher education in the twenty-first century* (pp. 219–232). Bucharest: UNESCO-CEPES.

Jenkins-Deas, B. (2009). The impact of quality review on the internationalisation of Malaspina University-College, Canada: A case study. In H. de Wit (Ed.), *Measuring success in the internationalisation of higher education* (EAIE Occasional Paper 22, pp. 111–124). Amsterdam: European Association for International Education.

Jongbloed, B. W. A., & Westerheijden, D. F. (1994). Performance indicators and quality assessment in European higher education. *New Directions for Institutional Research, 1994*(82), 37–51.

Kemper, E. A., Stringfield, S., & Teddlie, C. (2003). Mixed methods sampling strategies in social science research. In C. Teddlie & A. Tashakkori (Eds.), *Handbook of mixed methods in social & behavioral research* (pp. 273–296). Thousand Oaks, CA: Sage.

Knight, J. (1994). *Internationalisation: Elements and checkpoints* (CBIE Research No. 7). Ottawa: CBIE.

Knight, J. (2001). Monitoring the quality and progress of internationalization. *Journal of Studies in International Education, 5*(3), 228–243.

Knight, J. (2004). Internationalization remodeled: Definition, approaches, and rationales. *Journal of Studies in International Education, 8*(1), 5–31.

Knight, J. (2008). *Higher education in turmoil: The changing world of internationalization*. Rotterdam: Sense Publishers.

Knight, J., & de Wit, H. (1999). *Quality and internationalisation in higher education/Programme on institutional management in higher education*. Paris: Organisation for Economic Co-operation and Development.

Krause, K.-L., Coates, H., & James, R. (2005). Monitoring the internationalisation of higher education: Are there useful quantitative performance indicators? In M. Tight (Ed.), *International relations*. International Perspectives on Higher Education Research (Vol. 3., pp. 233–253). Bingley: Emerald Group.

Lashway, L. (2001). *Educational indicators*. ERIC Digest. Eugene, OR: Eric Clearinghouse on Educational Management.

Łukasz, S. (2016). Accountability of university: Transition of public higher education. *Entrepreneurial Business and Economics Review, 4*(1), 9–21. https://doi.org/10.15678/EBER.2016.040102.

Managing Committee of the EMQT Project. (2011). *The outcomes of the EMQT project*. Retrieved 20 May 2014, from http://www.emqt.org/images/stories/Outcomes_of_the_EMQT_Project_Presentation.pdf.

Marginson, S. (2011). Strategizing and ordering the global. In R. King, S. Marginson, & R. Naidoo (Eds.), *Handbook on globalization and higher education* (pp. 394–414). Cheltenham: Edward Elgar.

Marginson, S., & van der Wende, M. (2009). Europeanisation, international rankings and faculty mobility: Three cases in higher education globalisation. In OECD Research & Innovation (Ed.), *Higher education to 2030, Volume 2: Globalisation* (pp. 109–144). Paris and Washington, DC: Organisation for Economic Co-operation and Development.

Maringe, F. (2010). The meanings of globalization and internationalization in higher education: Findings from a world survey. In F. Maringe & N. Foskett (Eds.), *Globalisation and internationalisation in higher education: Theoretical, strategic and management perspectives* (pp. 17–34). London: Continuum.

Michavila, F., & Martinez, J. M. (2018). Excellence of universities versus autonomy, funding and accountability. *European Review, 26*(1), 48–56. https://doi.org/10.1017/S1062798717000539.

Mok, K. H. (2007). Questing for internationalization of universities in Asia: Critical reflections. *Journal of Studies in International Education, 11*(3–4), 433–454.

Morse, J. M., & Niehaus, L. (2009). *Mixed method design: Principles and procedures*. Walnut Creek, CA: Left Coast.

Oakes, J. (1986). *Educational indicators: A guide for policymakers*. CPRE Occasional Paper Series. Washington, DC: Center for Policy Research in Education.

OECD. (2011). *Education at a glance 2011: OECD indicators*. OECD Publishing. http://dx.doi.org/10.1787/eag-2-11-en.

Ogawa, R., & Collom, E. (1998). *Educational indicators: What are they? How can schools and school districts use them?* Riverside: University of California, Riverside, California Educational Research Cooperative.

Paige, R. M. (2005). Internationalization of higher education: Performance assessment and indicators. 名古屋高等教育研究, *5*(8), 99–122.

Pollard, J. S. (1989). *Developing useful educational indicator systems: Insights on educational policy and practice*. Austin, TX: Southwest Educational Development Lab.

Porter, A. (1991). Creating a system of school process indicators. *Educational Evaluation and Policy Analysis, 13*(1), 13–29.

Preciousa, P., & Blueboard, P. B. (2017). *Internationalization indicators of higher education in ASEAN+6: Trends, challenges, future directions*. Retrieved from http://www.ateneo.edu/news/research/internationalization-indicators-higher-education-asean6-trends-challenges-future.

Providing Support Services for International Activity. (2014). *Measuring university internationalization level*. Retrieved from Warsaw http://www.braude.ac.il/files/tempus_iris/Assts/WP4/Workshop3/Measuring_University_Internationalization_Level.pdf.

Scott, D., & Usher, R. (1996). *Understanding educational research*. London: Routledge.

Selden, R. W. (1985). *Educational indicators: What do we need to know that we don't know now?* Washington, DC: National Center for Education Statistics.

Shavelson, R. J. (1991). *What are educational indicators and indicator systems?* ERIC/TM Digest. Washington, DC: Eric Clearinghouse on Tests, Measurement Evaluation.

Shavelson, R. J., McDonnell, L. M., & Oakes, J. (1989). *Indicators for monitoring mathematics and science education: A sourcebook*. Santa Monica, CA: The RAND Corporation.

Sowter, B. (2013). Issues of transparency and applicability in global university rankings. In P. T. M. Marope, P. J. Wells, & E. Hazelkorn (Eds.), *Rankings and accountability in higher education: Uses and misuses* (pp. 55–68). Paris: UNESCO.

Stier, J., & Borjesson, M. (2010). The internationalised university as discourse: Institutional self-presentations, rhetoric and benchmarking in a global market. *International Studies in Sociology of Education, 20*(4), 335–353.

Take, H., & Shoraku, A. (2018). Universities' expectations for study-abroad programs fostering internationalization: Educational policies. *Journal of Studies in International Education, 22*(1), 37–52.

Taylor, B. E., Meyerson, J. W., & Massy, W. F. (1993). *Strategic indicators for higher education: Improving performance*. Princeton, NJ: Peterson's.

Taylor, J. (2004). Toward a strategy for internationalisation: Lessons and practice from four universities. *Journal of Studies in International Education, 8*(2), 149–171.

van den Besselaar, P., Inzelt, A., Reale, E., de Turckheim, E., & Vercesi, V. (2012). *Indicators of internationalisation for research institutions: A new approach* (A report by the ESF Member Organisation Forum on Evaluation: Indicators of Internationalisation). Strasbourg: European Science Foundation.

Yang, R. (2002). University internationalisation: Its meanings, rationales and implications. *Intercultural Education, 13*(1), 81–95.

Yang, R. (2014). China's strategy for the internationalization of higher education: An overview. *Frontiers of Education in China, 9*(2), 151–162.

2

Conceptualizing University Internationalization

Internationalization has become a major concern of universities across the globe. This chapter reviews the body of work on university internationalization, including topics such as the changing global setting and the definitions, ideologies, motives, and institutional strategies for internationalization. The review highlights the complexities, controversies, and gaps in conceptualizing university internationalization. Although internationalization has become one of the most discussed topics in higher education, a well-established conceptual framework of the phenomenon remains absent. Scholars do not share a common understanding of university internationalization or agree on the key components of institutional internationalization strategies. Moreover, most discussions on the phenomenon are drawn from a Western perspective, which may cause internationalization in other parts of the world to be misinterpreted as 'Westernization,' or a following of Anglo-Saxon standards and practices. In fact, internationalization emphasizes the dialogue between nations and institutions, which requires an awareness of different national and institutional characteristics and cultures. Given the diverse national and cultural contexts, any further attempts to conceptualize university internationalization should take into account a wider range of contexts.

Moreover, in most existing studies, university practitioners' views on internationalization are largely neglected. The majority of current literature is based on researchers' understanding of the phenomenon. Most internationalization activities occur at universities; therefore, university practitioners are directly involved in developing and putting institutional international strategies into practice. What is currently happening at individual higher education institutions (HEIs) in relation to internationalization is unclear, and in some cases, it could be a different from what is theoretically expected to happen. Therefore, university practitioners' perspectives need to be included in contextualization in order to understand how internationalization is being put into practice at universities.

The Changing Global Setting for Higher Education

A number of global forces have influenced the emergence of internationalization as a strategic priority for national higher education systems and individual HEIs. These forces include increased interdependency between nations, the new knowledge economy based on information and computer technologies (ICTs), the growing influence of global rankings, the pursuit of world-class research universities, and new models of university governance. HEIs are reconsidering their role in the global setting and reinventing their management structures and institutional systems in ways that prioritize internationalization. This reinvention process, in turn, influences the traditional cornerstones of universities—namely, research and teaching.

The current trend toward globalization touches all dimensions of society and the private sphere. For example, globalization has increased transnational movement of capital, which has resulted in increased associations between national economies and the international marketplace and new cross-border modes of cooperation (Kearns & Schofield, 1997; Moller, 2000). Electronic media and communication, mass travel, and the growing dominance of the English language have allowed diverse parts of the world to integrate in new ways. Universities are often at the forefront of this intensification of communication and technology and the movement of people and knowledge (Currie, 2014; Hertig, 2016). As Scott argues, 'Not all universities are (particularly) international, but all are subjects to the same process of globalization—partly as objects, victims even, of these processes, but partly as subjects, or key agents, of globalization' (1998, p. 122). The environment in which universities operate is characterized by finance, goods, services, knowledge, and cultural activities flowing across borders in the context of worldwide markets, multinational organizations, and competition (Georghiou & Larédo, 2015). Global higher education, which involves intensified cross-border linkage and competition, has created opportunities for HEIs to reposition themselves in global, national, and local landscapes by developing effective international strategies (Marginson & van der Wende, 2007).

A growing emphasis on cross-border linkages, networks, and mobility distinguishes contemporary academia from its past forms (Wescott, 2005). In spite of the severe competition that is common between academic institutions, universities are recognizing the need to partner with one another to better serve students, enhance research, and meet public needs (Beerkens, 2002; Kinser & Green, 2009). It is becoming clear that no institution, however strong or prestigious, can continue to be entirely successful operating on its own. Van Ginkel (1997) expresses that universities that want to be global players must focus their attention on the field(s) in which they excel and build connections with 'co-makers,' other universities, and prominent players in those field(s), in order to keep offering a variety of high-quality courses and research. Strategic partnerships in research, teaching, and transfer of knowledge between universities and industries outside national borders are the future for higher education, as they help HEIs manage the challenges of globalization (Bauman, 2002; de Wit, 2002).

Regionalization of higher education, or creating regional higher education spaces, is another emerging approach that can increase both competition and cooperation between universities across international boundaries (Verger & Hermo, 2010). Europe serves as a vivid illustration of the role that regionalization can play in increasing the visibility of a higher education system on the global map and has raised considerable interest in similar processes in other parts of the world (Beerkens, 2004; Kuroda, Yuki, & Kang, 2010; Verger & Hermo, 2010). Regionalization allows small- or medium-sized higher education systems to cooperate with each other and act as a bloc to compete with larger, more dominant systems (Marginson, Murphy, & Peters, 2010). As such, regionalization is here to stay as a feature of the global higher education landscape.

Internationalization has incited global competition between universities, particularly through the practice of ranking. As the global higher education landscape began to emerge, policymakers and the public sought comparisons between HEIs in different countries, which led to the growth of the ranking industry. The practice of university rankings dates back to the publication of *Where We Get Our Best Men* in the latter half of the 1800s in England. Though the practice was soon emulated in other countries, it was more or less met with disinterest and little debate outside of closeted academic corridors. The general disinterest in university rankings began to change in 1983 with the publication of 'America's Best Colleges' by the US News and World Report. A decade later, in 1993, the first 'Times Good University Guide' was published in the UK, prompting—as had happened previously in the United States—public debate as to which institutions fared better or worse in the guide (Marope & Wells, 2013). The expansion of the ranking industry has spurred the process of globalization and exacerbated competition between universities. Global rankings are no longer relevant only to elite institutions but have become a real concern for a wide spectrum of universities that seek to be included in, or improve their position in, various rankings (Rauhvargers, 2011).

University policymakers widely recognize and agree that rankings are an effective tool for global branding. Achieving a prominent position on major ranking tables is key for universities that have decided to go global, as a high ranking attracts high-performing students, world-class faculty, and additional funding from both public and private sources (Hertig, 2016; Morphew & Swanson, 2011). More importantly, internationalization has become increasingly important as a performance measure (or to be more precise, a set of performance measures) in its own right. This is reflected in various international ranking tables such as the Times Higher Education (THE) World University Rankings, the Academic Ranking of World Universities (ARWU), and the QS Stars rating system (Hoyler & Jöns, 2013). The QS rankings, for example, include student and faculty mobility as an indicator, and international outlook is weighted 7.5% in THE's rankings.[1] Universities are enthusiastic about attracting international students to improve their rankings as well as their financial resources, and they are encouraged to hire international 'star' faculty to enhance their reputation, establish international research networks, and increase their global rankings (Shin & Toutkoushian, 2011).

Despite the controversy surrounding rankings, there is little question that they have been a key driver for transparency and accountability among institutions and have paved the way for a rich and growing culture of performance evaluation in higher education (Marope & Wells, 2013). More and more, universities find themselves having to explain their performance to the public using criteria set by rankers and other quality-monitoring bodies. Rankings have led to a revolution in the availability of data on HEIs, which in turn guides institutional and governmental strategies for higher education (Sowter, 2013).

Accountability is important for public institutions' reliability and clarity of settlements. A specific accounting and reporting system is a prerequisite for accountability and responsibility (Sułkowski, 2016). Many systems have begun to call for universities' increased accountability. In a number of countries, accountability is institutional and commonly accepted; in some, it is a more recent phenomenon; and in still others, it is a contested issue on the higher education agenda (Huisman & Currie, 2004). Why is there an increasing global emphasis on the accountability of HEIs? Many studies indicate that the changing relationship between governments and universities is the most important factor in the rise of accountability (e.g., see Huisman & Currie, 2004; Michavila & Martinez, 2018; Ramírez & Tejada, 2018). A shift toward more institutional independence and autonomy and, to some extent,

---

[1] A university's international outlook rating is based on three elements: ratio of international to domestic students, ratio of international to domestic staff, and proportion of total research journal publications that have at least one international author.

increasing market mechanisms have induced the implementation of new and better systems of accountability (Huisman & Currie, 2004). Universities receive public funding, and in some countries, such as the United States, private donations as well. Governments require measurable value in return for their money, and the public has a right to know how funds are spent by universities. This creates pressure for universities to introduce systems and mechanisms enabling full transparency of their accounts (Huang, 2007; Kim, 2009; Marginson & van der Wende, 2007; Ng, 2012).

Paradoxically, this growth in accountability has been accompanied by a decrease in funding from governments and neoliberal governance structures, which has encouraged HEIs to adopt corporate or business ideas, principles, and strategies as they reform their operation (Healey, 2008; Kim, 2006; Yang, 2004). Corporate governance is deeply embedded within a wider set of ideas and trends in the public sector. New Public Management (NPM) evolved during the 1980s and 1990s in the OECD countries as a response to a perceived lack of focus on outcomes, efficiency, and transparency in national bureaucracies. The solution suggested by the NPM was to introduce managerial techniques borrowed from private enterprises to the public sector. These techniques most often included delegation, decentralization, and deregulation; results-based funding and accountability regarding the extent to which planned results were achieved; strategic management and planning; the adoption of contract-based relationships; and the strengthening of managerial culture (Aucoin, 1990; OECD, 1997). NPM-style reforms are profoundly affecting the governance of HEIs in an increasing number of countries as universities gain greater autonomy to manage their financial and human resources and research programs and to decide on course content and the size of student enrollment. Additionally, public funding increasingly depends on universities' achievement of targets, which are expressed as input, output, or outcome indicators (Leitner et al., 2014, p. 11). The requirement for more accountability and transparency in university governance parallels the urgent demand for valid measurements of internationalization. Measurement of a university's performance when it comes to internationalization will allow governments and other stakeholders to ensure that the university is on track and achieving what is expected.

The growing demand for accountability is one current movement in higher education; the pursuit of 'world-class universities' (WCUs) is another, influenced by the blossoming global ranking industry (Currie, 2014; Hazelkorn, 2016; Tilak, 2016; Yudkevich, Altbach, & Rumbley, 2015). The WCU concept has become common over the last decade and represents not simply an improvement in the quality of teaching and research but the capacity to compete in the global education marketplace through the acquisition and creation of advanced knowledge (Altbach, 2004; Salmi, 2009). Although there is no clear definition of a WCU and much difficulty in prescribing normative ways to reach such a level (Mohrman, 2005; Deem, Mok, & Lucas, 2008), the notion has entered the everyday language of many universities, the media, and governmental policies (Altbach, 2004). WCUs are seen as a guarantee of success in the global economy, and many countries including China, Finland, France, Germany, India, Japan, Latvia, Malaysia, Russia, Singapore, South Korea, Spain, Taiwan, and Vietnam have launched excellence initiatives to create them (Cantwell & Maldonado-Maldonado, 2009; Hazelkorn, 2013). In some emerging countries, establishing WCUs is a national strategy for narrowing the gap between the country's current quality of education and research and that of developed nations (Chan, 2008; Huang, 2007; Mok, 2007).

What exactly are WCUs? As Phillip Altbach once observed, 'Everyone wants one, no one knows what it is and no one knows how to get it.' Whether a country is interested in rankings or not, it may still be interested in having WCUs, as such universities will be able to attract and retain high-quality faculty, talented students from within and outside national borders, public and private investments and a label, which itself is a matter of prestige (Tilak, 2016). Endeavors have been made by various researchers to discover a formula for WCUs. Alden and Lin (2004), for instance, identified a set of characteristics of a WCU, including:

- An international reputation for research and teaching,
- A number of research stars, world leaders, and visitors of international standards,
- The most able students,
- The most talented staff from the international market,
- A high proportion of postgraduate students,
- Operation in a global market,
- Internationalized research and teaching,
- A very sound financial base with diversified sources of funds, including large endowments and capital funds,
- A first-class management team with a strategic vision and plans for its implementation,
- A long history of superior performance in making big contributions to society, and
- Peer recognition of other WCUs.

Salmi (2009) suggested a different set of characteristics by which to identify a WCU:

- A high concentration of talent (faculty and students),
- Abundant resources to offer a rich learning environment and conduct advanced research, and
- A favorable governance regime that encourages strategic vision, innovation, and flexibility, enabling the institution to manage resources unencumbered by bureaucracy.

No matter how a WCU is defined, it has to be internationalized in its teaching, research, and engagement. It has to possess an international reputation and meet international standards for quality higher education. It has to commit to the culture, norms, and values of international science. It must have an open and cosmopolitan outlook and respect for otherness. Last but not least, its aspiration to be the best should be placed on a global rather than national scale. With these factors in mind, global ranking tables play a key role in defining, or at least co-defining, WCUs. The global drive to develop WCUs has further intensified the process of university internationalization.

Though it is clear that global rankings have had a substantial influence on university governance and institutional strategies, the set of indicators developed in this project is by no means intended to fuel the global mania of rankings. Indeed, we need to be fully aware of the isomorphic effects that rankings have had on the development of HEIs. Given that international or cross-jurisdictional comparisons are likely to remain a constant feature of global higher education, the design and use of benchmarking tools is particularly critical to guaranteeing that the measurements and comparisons are valid and healthy. To avoid any undesirable effects, the users of this indicator set or any other measurement or benchmarking tools must understand their own needs and set their own goals for internationalization.

Internationalization as National Priority

The pace of globalization will not slow down, and global forces will continue to influence higher education. Hence, university internationalization as a means of performing successfully in the global higher education landscape will continue to be placed at a central spot in regional, national, and institutional policy and agendas. Numerous governments have already put specific, long-term strategies and plans in place for the internationalization of higher education. The European Union (EU) provides a good example of engaging national governments in internationalization. In 'European higher education in the world' (European Commission, 2013), the European Commission reiterates the importance of internationalization for Europe and attempts to put the topic firmly on the agenda for the coming years. The document presents a broad internationalization plan that identifies priority areas and strategic goals at the regional level. This plan is supported by funds secured under the EU multiannual financial framework for 2014–2020, particularly by part of the over 14 billion euros allocated to the Erasmus+ program.

Similarly, Canada has adopted an economic approach toward internationalizing higher education. Their internationalization strategy falls under the jurisdiction of the Ministry of International Trade and is a key element of the Global Markets Action Plan. International collaboration in higher education contributes to Canada's success on both domestic and global levels. The recruitment of international students and researchers creates new jobs and opportunities for Canadians, addressing labor shortages while also bringing in people with needed skills. Most importantly, internationalization of education fuels the people-to-people ties crucial to long-term success in an increasingly interconnected global economy (Foreign Affairs, Trade and Development Canada, 2014). In Australia, international education has been recognized as a key to national prosperity. It is critical to the government's plan to build a more diverse, world-class economy and unleash Australia's full economic potential. The international education sector not only generates significant economic benefits but also enriches Australia's social, cultural, and intellectual life. In order for Australia to maintain its current place as one of the top five international study destinations, the government developed a national strategy that includes:

- Creating 'an education system that stands out as the best in the world' (Australian Government, 2015),
- Raising Australia's profile as a world leader in international education,
- Improving the global connectedness of Australians,
- Improving the experience of international students in Australia, and
- Expanding Australian education and training overseas.

Internationalization of higher education has not only been a concern for Western countries, which are usually considered the 'leaders' in international education; it has also become a policy priority for the 'followers,' such as countries in Eastern Asia, Latin America, and Africa. As part of the 'global strategy' to open up Japan to the whole world and expand the flow of people, goods, money, and information between Japan and countries in Asia and other regions in the world, the Japanese government developed the 300,000 Foreign Students Plan with an aim of accepting up to 300,000 international students by the year 2020. A series of measures will be taken to strategically recruit excellent and highly capable international students while giving consideration to the balance of countries, regions, and fields of study. The plan suggests taking five specific measures to invite international students to study in Japan: providing incentives and one-stop service to international students; improving the ease of entrance examinations, enrollment, and entry into Japan; promoting globalization of universities and other educational institutions; improving the environment for accepting international students; and promoting acceptance of international students in society after their graduation or completion of courses (Ministry of Education, Culture, Sports, Science and Technology, Japan, 2010).

Malaysia, another example, is an emerging contender as a global higher education provider. Higher education has become a huge investment in the country's effort to be competitive globally. Internationalization of HEIs in Malaysia is the fifth thrust under the country's National Higher Education Strategic Plan. Malaysia aspires to be the hub of excellence for higher education internationally by 2020, with 200,000—or 10%—international student enrollment in HEIs. In line with the increasing number of international students, the number of international staff is also expected to increase by 15% by 2020. Some of the initiatives proposed under the National Higher Education Strategic Plan to accelerate internationalization include:

* Encouraging international collaboration between local and foreign HEIs, as well as between foreign institutions,
* Diversifying courses offered to cover regional studies as well as setting up regional research centers to encourage more research,
* Organizing international conferences and seminars,
* Providing globalized curriculum content,
* Intensifying marketing activities abroad, and
* Enhancing student service activities through staff training and development (Ministry of Higher Education Malaysia, 2011).

Meaning of University Internationalization

Internationalization of higher education is not a new concept.[2] Universities have always been international in character, in terms of 'the universality of knowledge' (Brown, 1950, cited in Knight & de Wit, 1995, p. 6) and being an international community of scholars and students (Altbach, 2006; Block, 1995; Maringe, 2010; van der Wende, Beerkens, & Teichler, 1999). But despite being an old phenomenon, internationalization has evolved in the past three decades. It has been perceived and conceptualized in new ways that are related to the diversity of national higher education systems and institutions, educational ideologies and social-economic and political contexts. So far, a scholarly consensus on the exact meaning of the term 'internationalization' has not been reached. One reason for this could be that there is little need for a definition, since institutions approach internationalization in different ways. The whole of higher education rarely has to perceive the concept with one accord. Also, the early period of the growth of internationalization in the higher education sector required so much energy to develop all of its many dimensions that little time was left for the difficult task of formulating a universal definition that could be generic enough to apply to all the different countries, cultures, and education systems of the world (Arum & Van de Water, 1992; Knight, 2008). The next section aims to shed light on the complexities and the controversies that surround conceptualizing university internationalization.

Globalization and Internationalization

The exploration of the meaning of university internationalization begins with two related concepts: internationalization and globalization.

---

[2]In Western society, historically, universities have been international as far back as the Middle Ages. The original universities used Latin as a common language and involved the international mobility of students and scientists (Altbach & Knight, 2007; Scott, 2000; Trondal, 2010). In China, Confucius began his teaching with the notion that he could teach all, including those who lived in the neighboring countries. With this idea in mind, he traveled to different countries to teach (Yang, 2002).

These terms are often confused or used interchangeably; however, they are separate—though closely related—concepts (de Wit, 2011a; Knight, 1997; Marginson & van der Wende, 2009; Yang, 2002).

The term 'globalization' means 'becoming global,' which in general refers to the development of increasingly integrated systems and relationships beyond a single nation (Marginson & Rhoades, 2002). Globalization is a multidimensional phenomenon that rests on the worldwide systems of communication, information, knowledge, and culture tending toward a single world community (Marginson & van der Wende, 2007). It is an economic process that increases the cross-national mobility of capital, labor, and information; it is also a social, political, and cultural process that reduces the constraints of geography on social and cultural arrangement and ultimately affects the flow of knowledge, people, values, and ideas (Blackmore, 2000; Waters, 1995).

The process of globalization is mostly beyond the control of individual HEIs and governments; internationalization is more steerable by governments and institutions (van der Wende, 2007). Based on this consideration, many researchers regard internationalization efforts as countries' or institutions' proactive response to the effects of globalization (e.g., Altbach, Reisberg, & Rumbley, 2009; de Wit, 2011a; Knight, 2008; Maringe & Foskett, 2010). However, as mentioned before, universities have had an international mission and focus since their genesis in medieval Europe long before the phenomenon of globalization was ushered in by the recent communication revolution (Altbach & Knight, 2007; Boulton & Lucas, 2008; Kerr, 1994; Marginson, 2011a; Teichler, 2004). Because of this, globalization can only be seen as one of a number of external forces that have accelerated the pace of the internationalization of higher education. Internationalization, in turn, intensifies the process of globalization.

Globalization should not be regarded simply as a higher level of internationalization or an advanced phase in the evolving process of internationalization (Bartell, 2003). In this study, globalization and internationalization are differentiated in two ways. First, internationalization reflects a world order dominated by nation-states; however, globalization implies a radical reordering and blurring of national boundaries (Scott, 2000). A key element of globalization is its reference to worldwide engagement; thus, it is distinctly different from 'internationalization,' which emphasizes relationships across borders, either between nations or single institutions situated within different national systems (Enders & Fulton, 2002; Knight, 2008; Marginson & van der Wende, 2009). Steiner (2000) describes internationalization as a different phenomenon from globalization in that its goal is not dialogue but worldwide communication, transfer and sharing of information. Second, national identity and culture are essential to internationalization, while the homogenization of culture is often cited as a critical concern or effect of globalization. According to de Wit (2000), internationalization includes both international and local elements; it has an intercultural dimension. As a process that enhances relations between nations, internationalization is a product of the modern nation-state. It presupposes cross-border relations in which nations' authority and identities are essentially unchanged (Marginson, 2011b). In contrast, globalization does not primarily refer to intercultural activity or accentuate the identity of nations; therefore, it should be seen as a different concept from internationalization (Lenn, 1999; Middlehurst, 2000; Sadlak, 2001).

Evolution of the Concept of University Internationalization

What is meant by 'university internationalization'? Over the years, there have been various interpretations of the concept. Researchers use the term in accordance with their various purposes and contexts. As the Association of Universities and Colleges of Canada has concluded, 'There is no simple, unique or all-encompassing definition of internationalization of university' (1993, cited in de Wit, 2002, p. 109). The definitions instead reflect internationalization strategies and practices at a given time and in a given context. Several representative definitions are summarized in Table 2.1. By looking at the various definitions, three phases in the evolution of the concept of university internationalization can be identified.

Early understandings of internationalization stressed a set of activities such as student and faculty mobility, international academic programs,

Table 2.1 Definitions of university internationalization

Periods	Definitions	Features
Early 1990s	'A process by which the teaching, research and service functions of a higher education system become internationally and cross-culturally compatible' (Ebuchi, 1989, p. 109) 'The multiple activities, programmes and services that fall within international studies, international educational exchange and technical cooperation' (Arum & Van de Water, 1992, p. 202) 'It is faculty with an internal commitment striving to internationalize its own course offerings. It is the presence of an obvious institution-wide positive attitude toward understanding better other cultures and societies' (Harari, 1992, p. 75)	Internationalization was understood on a program/activity basis The unit of internationalization could be diverse, including institution, faculty, and program
Mid-1990s to Early 2000s	'The process of integrating an international and intercultural dimension into teaching, research and service functions of the institution' (Knight, 1994, p. 7) 'The complex of processes whose combined effect, whether planned or not, enhances the international dimension of the experience of higher education in universities' (de Wit, 1995, p. 28) 'The process of integrating an international perspective into a college or university system. It is an ongoing, future-oriented, multidimensional, interdisciplinary, leadership-driven vision that involves many stakeholders working to change the internal dynamics of an institution to respond and adapt appropriately to an increasingly diverse, globally focused, ever-changing external environment' (Ellingboe, 1998, p. 199) 'A process of organizational change, curriculum innovation, staff development and student mobility for the purpose of attaining excellence in teaching, research and the other activities which universities undertake as part of their function' (Rubzki, 1998, p. 16)	Internationalization was seen as an ongoing process An institutional approach to internationalization was recognized

(continued)

Table 2.1 continued

Periods	Definitions	Features
Late 1990s to Mid-2000s	'Any systematic effort aimed at making higher education responsive to the requirements and challenges related to the globalization of societies, economy and labour market' (van der Wende, 1997, p. 18) 'An ongoing, counter-hegemonic educational process that occurs in an international context of knowledge and practice where societies are viewed as subsystems of a larger, inclusive world. The process of internationalization at an educational institution entails a comprehensive, multifaceted program of action that is integrated into all aspects of education' (Schoorman, 1999, p. 21) 'A change process from a national higher education institution to an international higher education institution leading to the inclusion of an international dimension in all aspects of its holistic management in order to enhance the quality of teaching and learning and to achieve the desired competencies' (Soderqvist, 2002, p. 29) 'The process of integrating an international, intercultural or global dimension into the purpose, functions or delivery of post-secondary education' (Knight, 2004, p. 11) 'The totality of substantial changes in the context and inner life of higher education relative to an increasing frequency of border-crossing activities amidst a persistence of national system' (Teichler, 2004, p. 22)	Internationalization was integrated into all aspects of university life Internationalization became a university strategy that is planned and implemented systematically

and international projects. Arum and Van de Water's (1992) and Harari's (1992) definitions are good examples. Then, a process-oriented perspective was introduced that illustrated the dynamic and changing nature of the internationalization phenomenon (e.g., see de Wit, 1995; Ellingboe, 1998; Knight, 1994; Soderqvist, 2002). Later, the focus of internationalization shifted, and the definition rapidly broadened to encompass all aspects of university life. Knight (2004) updated her definition into a more comprehensive one that is widely used today. Written the same year, the definition proposed by Teichler (2004) emphasizes the changes that internationalization brings to higher education.

As internationalization comes of age, new perspectives continue to influence its definition. Most recently, Arkoudis, Baik, Marginson, and Cassidy (2012, pp. 11–12) investigated internationalization from the perspective of student experience and made significant progress in defining it in terms of both process and outcomes:

- In terms of process, 'internationalization' means fostering a nationally and culturally diverse and interactive university community where all students have a sense of belonging.
- In terms of outcomes, 'internationalization' means graduates who are globally aware, globally competent, and able to work with culturally and linguistically diverse people either locally or anywhere in the world.

Jane Knight also discussed the question 'What is an international university?' in *The State of Higher Education 2014* by the OECD Higher Education Programme. She starts by saying that there is much confusion as to what it actually means for a university to be international. In fact, she states, the term is not important; what is important is the approach or model the university uses. She identifies three 'generations' of international universities: an internationalized university with diverse international partnerships, international students and staff and multiple collaborative activities; universities with satellite offices in the form of branch campuses, research centers, and management/project offices; and, most recent, stand-alone institutions cofounded or co-developed by two or more partner institutions from different countries. However, de Wit (2015) argues that the 'generations' of international universities actually just refer to three different types of internationalization strategy: *internationally cooperative*, *internationally active*, and *internationally operative*.

Over the years, the definitions of internationalization have become broader and more comprehensive as almost all aspects of university life have become internationalized. There is increased awareness that the meaning of internationalization is highly sensitive to context such as institution, country, and culture. Until recently, a majority of studies conceptualized the phenomenon from a Western perspective and focused on developed, English-speaking regions. It is fair to say that those regions, which include Europe, North America, and Australia, have been the leaders of contemporary higher education internationalization. When it comes to the 'followers,' such as Eastern Asia, Latin America, and Africa, however, the issue is more complicated. Recent studies exploring higher education internationalization in non-English-speaking countries—Eastern Asian countries in particular—have revealed that internationalization in emerging countries means something different from how it is understood in the West (e.g., see Mok & Yu, 2013; Palmer, Roberts, Cho, & Ching, 2011). For example, in China, internationalization of higher education means connecting China's educational practices with mainstream international trends (Yang, 2002). This could also be true for universities in Japan (e.g., see Arimoto, 2011; Le Phan, 2013), Malaysia (e.g., see Sidhu & Kaur, 2011), Taiwan (Ching & Chin, 2012), and Korea (see Kim & Choi, 2011). These emerging countries aspire to build their own WCUs, develop their capacity for research, and become a regional education hub. In this way, these nations have treated internationalization as an effective strategy for improving the competence of their universities and higher education systems.

Marginson (2011a) argues that this process could be regarded as a kind of synchrony that takes the form of imitating and following others and may result in a one-sided adaption to the educational practices in more economically advanced countries at the expense of one's own national characteristics. Compared to the 'leader' countries, the followers have to face much more of the tension between internationalization and the maintenance of their national identities. This is a major challenge for not only emerging Asian countries but also countries in Africa and Latin America (see Beigel, 2013; Jowi, 2012; Wan & Geo-JaJa, 2013), and the issue has become a much-debated point in the discourse on internationalization in non-English-speaking countries. Because of the discrepancy between leader and follower countries, researchers conceptualizing internationalization need to more carefully consider national and cultural contexts.

Drivers of University Internationalization

Just as there are a variety of ways to describe and define internationalization, there are also a number of different motivations for university leaders to increasingly strive for internationalization at their institutions. Too often, institutions are keen to internationalize simply because the policymakers believe it is the right thing to do. There is no single, absolute rationale for internationalization. Motives may overlap, combine, or differ within and between 'stakeholders' due to differences in priorities and interpretations of internationalization (Jiang, 2008). At the institutional level, there are many factors that influence motives, ranging from missions, student populations, faculty profile, geographic location, funding sources, level of resources, and orientation to local, national, and international interests (Knight, 2004).

The Changing Role of Higher Education

The rationales for internationalization cannot be separated from the role and goals of higher education. Traditionally, universities' contributions to society have primarily had to do with education and research (Boulton & Lucas, 2008). Universities have been remarkably successful in seeking practical ways to make discoveries, reinvigorating and carrying forward the inherited knowledge of earlier generations and training students to go out into the world with both general and specific skills

(Boulton & Lucas, 2008). But immediately after World War II, the role of higher education as an agent for national development became more prominent. Education came to serve the administrative and economic interests of nation-states, producing the labor force required by both the public and private sectors. Education also became essential to the development of national identify (de Wit, 1997, 1998).

Today, knowledge is a fundamental component of economic and social development. In the new brand of capitalism created by globalization, knowledge has replaced the traditional, much more locally bound resources—labor, capital goods, and natural resources—as the number-one commodity (Beck, 1999; Castells, 1996; Giddens, 1990). The ability of a society to produce and use knowledge is critical for sustained economic growth and improved living standards. This shift has redefined the role of the institutions that generate knowledge: universities. Universities play an essential role in building a strong human capital base and contributing to an efficient national innovation system. HEIs help countries build globally competitive economies by developing a skilled, productive, and flexible labor force and by creating, applying, and disseminating new ideas and technologies (Altbach & Knight, 2007; Hazelkorn, 2013; Marginson & van der Wende, 2007). Today's universities are expected to develop the capacity not simply to build alliances with other institutions but to attain equity, development, justice, and democracy as well as to shape a new generation of thinkers and influencers. Instead of meeting this new demand in the global era, however, universities have been accused of largely serving economic purposes and tending to ignore their social and cultural responsibilities (Brandenburg & de Wit, 2011; Naidoo & Jamieson, 2005; Ng, 2012; Rizvi, 2007).[3]

Hand in hand with becoming a key economic player, an instrument for assuring economic growth and national welfare, the university has transformed from being a center of democratic inquiry and intellectual

---

[3]Rizvi (2007) notes that the emphasis on teaching about ICTs in transforming educational practice does not so much enable people greater access to each other as facilitate economic growth and productivity. It does not support the core role of higher education, which is to help us understand the world and improve our dealings with it.

creativity to an institution with more corporate purposes (Dunn & Faison, 2015; Hertig, 2016). As Giroux (2007) explains,

> There exists an increasing corporate influence on higher education and the currently fashionable idea of the university as a "franchise," largely indifferent to deepening and expanding the possibilities of democratic public life and increasingly hostile to the important role the academy can play in addressing matters of public service. (p. 7)

Universities had to partially give up the traditional, admittedly not always very efficient, way of producing scientific knowledge: curiosity and 'wind blows as it will' principles. Academic traditions have been replaced by a business culture with all the standard private business instruments and management principles, from NPM to extensive control and permanent 'end-to-end' output evaluation (Marginson, 2011a). Although the core mission of a university, which has never changed, is to create (through research) and disseminate (through teaching) knowledge, the perceived purpose of creating and disseminating knowledge has become gradually less noble as an ideal and steadily more instrumental.

Motives for Being Internationalized

The existing studies on university internationalization show five categories of rationales that drive the effort toward internationalizing higher education: political, economic, academic, social/cultural, and ethical (Aigner, Nelson, & Stimpfl, 1992; Johnston & Edelstein, 1993; Kahane, 2009; Knight, 2004; Knight & de Wit, 1995; Marginson, 2011a; Maringe & Foskett, 2010). They are not mutually exclusive or distinctively different. The five categories are interrelated; indeed, one of the changes occurring is that there is more integration or blurring of these dimensions. Furthermore, a shifting emphasis on the five categories can be observed with time.

Throughout history, universities have strived to gain knowledge and understanding of other cultures (de Wit, 1998). During the process of colonial expansion, political rationales became increasingly influential in the internationalization of higher education. Higher education was seen as a tool for expressing the dominance of colonial powers.[4] After World War II, this political rationale had some new dimensions, such as supporting the economic growth of low-income, developing countries[5] and expanding the influence of the United States, the main international power in this period.[6]

Since the end of Cold War, economic imperatives, instead of political ones, have increasingly driven the internationalization agenda (Cai & Kivistö, 2013; Cantwell, 2015; de Wit, 1998; Harris, 2009; Turner & Robson, 2008; van der Wende, 2001). The pursuit in the international student market is, to a large degree, determined by a climate of 'do more with less' and the cutting off of government investment in and funding of higher education (Welch, 2002). Higher education is an expensive business, and governments that publicly subsidize universities to keep down tuition costs typically cap the number of university places available to control the overall cost to taxpayers. As tertiary participation rates have grown and governments have come under fiscal pressure from an aging population, universities have seen their support from the taxpayer lessen. In countries that have deregulated the recruitment of international students (i.e., removed both

---

[4] Between the eighteenth century and World War II, internationalization was seen as a method of exporting HE systems and was often accompanied by imperialism and colonialism. European colonial powers such as Britain, France, and Iberian Peninsula countries exported their academic system to the rest of the world. Even higher education in the United States, now often seen as the dominant model in internationalization studies, was originally based on European influences and remained so for a long time (Altbach & Selvaratnam, 1989; de Wit, 2002).

[5] The best-known example of this was the Colombo Plan, as part of which the Australian and New Zealand governments provided scholarships for top students from developing economies in the Commonwealth (Blackton, 1951). There was both an altruistic and a strategic dimension to this form of development aid. On the one hand, the Colombo Plan trained future business people, politicians, and civil servants who could return to their countries and put their studies to good use; on the other, it created an elite group in the Commonwealth Asia-Pacific that had strong professional and emotional ties to Australia and New Zealand, facilitating the promotion of commercial and political cooperation (Oakman, 2010).

[6] During this period, exchanges of faculty and students were small in number, and the objectives were more related to diplomacy than to academic and cultural cooperation. Internationalization of higher education also manifested in the form of technical assistance and development aid (de Wit, 2002, 2011a; Huang, 2007).

tuition and enrollment caps), universities have been incentivized to recruit large numbers of full-cost international students, which effectively cross-subsidizes the teaching of domestic students in high-cost courses (e.g., science and engineering) as well as research (Altbach & Knight, 2007; Harris, 2008; Jiang, 2008).[7]

The economic rationale also includes developing human resources for the international competitiveness of a nation in the global knowledge economy (Harris, 2009; Knight, 1997), which means preparing graduates who are internationally knowledgeable and competent to live and work in the global society of the twenty-first century (Coelen, 2009; Hser, 2005; Welch, 2002). For governments, the economic incentive does not merely mean the rewards generated by international dealings, such as fee revenue from foreign students; it also promises a competitive position in the world acquired through better research and greater capacity for innovation (Marginson, 2011b). A long-standing driver of internationalization is governments of developing or emerging economies who run scholarship schemes to fund study abroad programs, normally on the condition that the beneficiaries return to work in the country (Georghiou & Larédo, 2015).[8]

Economic considerations are not the only motive for countries and universities to embrace internationalization in today's world. Political rationales, although more and more bound up with the economic, factor internationalization significantly into the strengthening of national identities and the maintenance of national security and peace (Knight, 1997; Maringe, 2010). Higher education and its international dimension are still underpinned by the idea of nation-states, even in this era

---

[7] Universities in Australia, the UK, and New Zealand are heavily dependent on international tuition revenue but have flourished since deregulation (e.g., Tarling, 2012). Governments in continental Europe have noted the high global rankings of universities from the English-speaking world and some, notably Denmark, Finland, and Sweden, have concluded that charging international students full-cost tuition fees is the only way of balancing the demands on the public purse with academic quality (West, 2013).

[8] Examples of such schemes include Royal Thai Government Scholarships, provided by the country's Office of the Civil Service Commission, or, for undergraduate study, the Malaysian Public Service Department (Jabatan) scholarship scheme.

of rapid globalization (de Wit, 2011a; Marginson, 2011b).[9] As Healey (2008) claims, for much of the post-war period, many governments viewed the recruitment of foreign students to their domestic campuses as, at best, a form of international development policy or a tool of strategic foreign policy. Using export education to build strategic relationships with third countries is often now termed 'projecting soft power' (Amirbek & Ydyrys, 2014). Currently, the Chinese government is the main exponent of this approach, using government scholarships to attract young people from the West to study the Chinese language and culture in its universities, in the belief that they will return home as 'boosters' for the country of their alma maters (Nye, 2015).

Internationalization activities influence the core functions of the university: education, research, and service, which lead to the third motive for universities to incorporate internationalization: for academic reasons. Internationalization has become integral to institutional competition, worldwide reputation, and brand building (Marginson, 2011b), enhancing research quality and academic standards (Altbach & de Wit, 2015; Soria & Troisi, 2014; Taylor, 2010), contributing to the resolution of global problems (Fielden, 2006, cited in Foskett, 2010, p. 38), and alerting societies to major emerging issues (Scott, 2005). The academic competition for position or esteem is distinct from the economic competition for capital. To attract students and resources, there is a strong emphasis on the 'visibility' of universities (Stier & Borjesson, 2010). In order for a university to remain central rather than marginal, internationalization has to be integrated into the core of its academics—research in particular (McBurnie, 2000). Research plays a determinative role in defining the hierarchy of institutions in national and global

---

[9]Whether partnerships are more or less likely to be realized with certain countries; whether developing aid or competition between advanced countries is in the limelight of discussions and activities; whether 'international understanding' or 'knowledge society' is underscored more heavily; whether political activities in favor of 'convergence' of higher education play a small or substantial role; whether understanding other cultures is seen as a desirable goal in general or almost as a necessity for survival—all of these contrasting governmental viewpoints show how much the internationality of higher education is embedded in politics. In recent years, many observers have pointed out that—following some years of increased optimism after the end of the Cold War—international political tensions and 'international misunderstanding' are on the rise again (Teichler, 2017).

systems of status rankings. Hence, a university's position in global circuits of knowledge matters more than resources to individual HEIs (Marginson, 2011a).[10]

Universities also strive to retain their wider social missions. For example, they act as key cultural mediators in the encounter between world culture and national cultures (Scott, 2005) and aim to build international values, cross-cultural understanding, and tolerance and create a more global mind-set in the wider community (Chan, 2008; Knight, 1997; Meiras, 2004). Educating students from abroad was viewed as an important mechanism for countries to appreciate 'what makes each other tick' and to 'build bridges and create cultural understanding, reducing the likelihood of war and terrorism and just binding people together in ways that are helpful for peace and prosperity' (Chankseliani, 2018). Another social motivation for internationalization is the willingness of some HEIs to learn the structure, challenges, and peculiarities of other societies (Lewkowicz, Young, Budrytė, & Boykin, 2018; Lumby & Foskett, 2016). The reason this knowledge is valuable is that it allows these HEIs to become advocates for social change or vanguards of reactions to change within those societies (Lotz-Sisitka, Wals, Kronlid, & McGarry, 2015; Marginson, 2016).

In addition to the above-mentioned rationales, Bottery (2005) adds another emerging motive for internationalization: the ethical motive. He argues that internationalization of higher education is also concerned with the development of human flourishing and with forging communities conducive to spiritual growth. Kreber echoes this idea, stating, 'For many educators … a key reason for internationalization is ethical: it helps student to examine their implicit and explicit beliefs about whose wellbeing matters, and to develop a more globalized sense of responsibility and citizenship' (2009, p. 49). In terms of its ethical

---

[10]Some highly prestigious universities use internationalization as a means of talent acquisition. Universities like Harvard, Cambridge, and Imperial College London recruit students globally, particularly at the postgraduate level, to attract the brightest minds and keep them ahead of their rivals in terms of their institutional research productivity and quality. The motivation is not directly commercial, in the sense that they often pay scholarships to the top students, but the universities clearly expect a long-term financial return in the form of better global rankings and higher research income (Healey, 2017).

mission, a university's internationalization goals should be to enhance international awareness, empathy, and social action as well as to address development needs identified in specific communities (Kreber, 2009).

Priorities in the motives driving university internationalization change over time and by country and region. The motives are also becoming more and more interconnected. Like the definitions of university internationalization, the rationales are highly sensitive to context; there seems to be considerable variation in motivations between countries and universities and even between different units within a single university.[11] At national versus institutional levels, the driving force for internationalization could be different or sometimes contradictory.[12] The various motives behind internationalization initiatives help explain the diversity in interpretations of the phenomenon. And both the motivations for and understandings of internationalization are influenced by the underlying ideologies of individuals, groups, or institutions.

Ideologies

It is not surprising to find arguments that link the impact of globalization not only to economic restructuring but also to the cultural and ideological spheres. Universities are guided by competing ideologies in their pursuit of internationalization. Ideology, as defined by Stier, refers to 'a set of principles, underpinnings, desired goals and strategies that structure actions and beliefs of international educators, groups, organizations or societies' (2004, p. 85). Three main ideologies that influence universities' actions and decisions on internationalization are idealism, instrumentalism, and educationalism. These three ideologies are ideal-type constructs—that is, they are to be viewed as a means of

---

[11] For example, in the United States, internationalization remains more driven by political concerns about national security and foreign policy, while in Europe, regional identity and academic competitiveness are the dominant impetuses. In emerging countries, the academic incentives are more prominent.

[12] For example, both states and universities invest in internationalization to obtain a competitive position in the world. For governments, the issue is more related to national economic growth, while universities aim to improve their local, national, and international reputation and status.

discussion on internationalization rather than mutually exclusive categories. Universities and policymakers do not adhere to one of these ideologies alone, but often vacillate between them (Stier, 2004).

Idealists believe that through international academic cooperation, higher education can contribute to the creation of a more democratic, fair, and equal world. This particular type of ideology underpins the cultural/social rationales for internationalization, which stem from the normative assumption that 'internationalization is good per se.' To learn about another culture is to increase tolerance. Idealism leads to the utopian view that education will reduce the likelihood of conflict between nations and cultures; international education is perceived by idealists as a process that will bring world peace in some blessed and dreamt-of future. The mission of universities is, among other things, to cultivate citizens who adhere to an emancipatory outlook on the world. The idealism perspective connects internationalization with the outside world rather than narrowing it within academic settings. Paradoxically, while idealists advocate for respect for all value systems, the 'better world' to be created through internationalization is mostly based on Western-biased values (Stier, 2004).

From the instrumentalist perspective, the primary objective of internationalizing higher education is to ensure a sufficient workforce to meet the demands of the capitalist world. University education is seen as a global commodity. For example, Kameoka (1996) argues that governments are increasingly looking at higher education as playing a part in their wider policy objectives, many of which now have a strong international emphasis. These government interests range from broad foreign policy concerns to more specific issues of economic development, all of which can be served by the expertise and resources found in higher education. Policymakers aim to increase the level of transparency and transference between national education systems to facilitate the mobility of the labor force and homogenize university degrees and grading systems (Stier, 2004).

Although internationalization may in some ways be a response to the labor market's demands for a globally competent workforce, for educationalists its purpose extends beyond the idealistic and professional aspirations of policymakers. Educationalists argue that being exposed to and having to adapt to an unfamiliar academic setting enriches the overall academic experience of both students and teaching staff. The focus of educationalism is personal growth and self-actualization. When universities' values are aligned with educationalism, the pursuit of academic excellence becomes the dominant motivation for them to internationalize (Stier, 2004).

Institutional Strategies

The motives for and underlying ideologies of internationalization address the 'why' of internationalization. This section focuses on the 'how,' or in other words, the strategies for integrating an international dimension into the core functions of universities. The 'why' and 'how' are (or at least should be) directly linked. The key drivers that a country or institution has identified for internationalization direct their goals and objectives, which in turn shape the strategy that is used to achieve the goals.

There are many ways to describe the initiatives undertaken to internationalize a university; the term 'strategy' refers to a planned and integrated approach toward internationalization at both institutional and national levels (Knight & de Wit, 1995). It can be applied to academic activities as well as to organizational procedures and policies.

As this project aims to develop an instrument to measure institutional internationalization performance, national-level strategies are not discussed in detail. It does not mean the nation-state is fading away from the higher education system. Indeed, it remains a powerful player in shaping internationalization strategies (Teichler, 2004; van der Wende, 2007). A great majority of institutions continue to be nationally embedded and dependent on governmental legitimation and resource support (Marginson & van der Wende, 2007). National policies significantly affect the process of internationalization and influence institutional plans and actions. There is no single format for an internationalization strategy; institutional strategies are filtered through the specific internal context of the university, the type of university it is and how the university is positioned nationally (Stockley & de Wit, 2011).

Another point worth noting is that internationalization should not be regarded as a goal in itself (de Wit, 2011b). Many other worthwhile goals flow naturally from the implementation of internationalization strategies. HEIs develop international strategies aimed at more effective performance within the global, national, and local landscape, the enhancement and richness of students' learning experiences, and improvement in the quality of education. Internationalization strategies help universities establish global connectivity, maximize institutional performance on a worldwide platform, and optimize the benefits of internationalization back home in national and local settings (Marginson & van der Wende, 2007). Internationalization is also a means for universities to achieve internationally oriented learning outcomes, preparing graduates who will be operating in increasingly internationalized workplaces. By internationalizing the teaching and learning process, universities can help students embrace the diversity, commonalities, and interdependencies of the world's nations and environmental systems. Students learn to develop effective and appropriate teamwork and communication skills to interact with people of different nationalities and cultures and build global citizenship. With these skills, students are expected to support the common good of the world community, which involves advocating for diversity, human rights and the welfare of others and sustainability of natural systems and species (Papp, 2008).

Key Components

Many studies have explored the internationalization strategies that universities have developed, and a review of the literature reveals a number of generic components that constitute internationalization strategies across institutions (see David, 1992; Dewey & Duff, 2009; Ellingboe, 1998; Graham, Faiyaz, & John, 2005; Georghiou & Larédo, 2015; Healey, 2017; Knight, 1994, 2004; Soliman, Anchor, & Taylor, 2018; Take & Shoraku, 2018; Teichler, 2017; Windham, 1996; Yesufu, 2018). These components fit into three broader themes: governance, academic, and service, which are summarized in Table 2.2. These three categories

Table 2.2 Key components of institutional internationalization strategies

Governance	A supportive policy framework/organizational structure
	International presence in leadership
	An international office
	Staff development of international awareness and skills
	Budget for internationalization initiatives
	Monitoring/evaluation system for internationalization performance/process
Academic	International institutional agreements/networks/partnerships
	Outgoing and exchange opportunities for students/faculty
	International research cooperation
	Joint degrees/projects
	International student recruitment
	International visiting scholars
	International conferences and seminars
	Internationalized curricula
	Published papers in international journals
	International/intercultural extracurricular activities
	Interaction of international and domestic students
Service	Infrastructure investment and construction
	Orientation programs
	Language support
	Consultancy
	Libraries and computing services
	Pastoral and tutorial arrangements
	Support of families
	Student security and welfare provision

interact with and influence each other and highlight different aspects of internationalization strategies.

When it comes to internationalization initiatives, governance focuses on administrative systems, leadership and organization, financial budgets and monitoring and evaluation systems (e.g., AIEA, 1989; Brandenburg et al., 2009; David, 1992; Ellingboe, 1998; Papp, 2008; Soliman et al., 2018; Taylor, 2010). The managerial dimension plays an important role in establishing a receptive environment for promoting internationalization as well as in constructing a policy framework for developing international strategies. Governance is significant because the change of key personnel in a university, such as the vice-chancellor, as suggested by Soliman et al.'s (2018) study, could result in incoherent policies and strategies for internationalization. It is often argued that the more HEIs view internationalization from a holistic perspective, the more likely it is that administrative processes will be put in place to support internationalization activities (Brandenburg et al., 2009).

The importance of administrative staff, and therefore the importance of the personal qualities of these university members, to the overall success of internationalization has tended to be neglected up until now (Brandenburg et al., 2009). Papp (2008) argues that all levels and areas of administration, but especially academic affairs, student affairs, and the President's office, must be visibly and vocally committed to internationalization. Financial resources, equipment, and activities also play a role in internationalization at the institutional level. A significant level of internationalization cannot realistically be achieved if the HEI lacks the necessary investment (Brandenburg et al., 2009). Resources, incentives, and rewards could be provided for students, faculty, and professional staff to promote internationalization. Teaching, travel, and other experiences abroad need to be funded for faculty and staff so that they can infuse their expanded perspectives into their classrooms and other interactions with students. For students, scholarships and other incentives could be provided so that they can take advantage of academic courses, internships, and projects available outside their home country (Papp, 2008).

The academic category involves teaching, learning, and research, which are the core functions of a university. Components of the academic category promote academic mobility and research collaborations (AIEA, 1989; Ellingboe, 1998; Huang, Raimo, & Humfrey, 2016; Kedziora, Klamut, Karri, & Kraslawski, 2017; Knight, 2008; Liu, 2012; Stockley & de Wit, 2011; Svensson, 1994; Taylor, 2010; Weck & Denman, 1997). Academic mobility has risen in prominence as a critical aspect of universities' internationalization. The near-universal enthusiasm for academic mobility is 'nested in long-standing assumptions about the internationalized character of universities, the freewheeling transferability of intellectual capacity and the contribution of knowledge transfer to national innovation and competitiveness' (Marginson & van der Wende, 2007, p. 62). Over the past three decades, the number of students enrolled in universities outside their country of citizenship has risen dramatically, from 0.8 million worldwide in 1975 to 4.6 million in 2015 (OECD, 2017), a more than fivefold increase. The United States is the top OECD destination country for mobile tertiary students. Of the three million international students in OECD areas, nearly one-third are enrolled in US programs. After the United States, the UK draws over 14% of international students, Australia 9.8%, and Canada 5.7%. International students in these countries mainly come from Asia, accounting for 87% of international students in Australia, 76% in the United States, and 54% in the UK. The EU is another key area of inward mobility, with 1.52 million international students enrolled in European programs. The Russian Federation is also a major destination country with 226,000 students enrolled from abroad, of whom two-thirds come from neighboring countries with historical links with the former Soviet Union, such as Kazakhstan (26%), Ukraine (9%), and Belarus (8%) (OECD, 2017). Other regions, such as Africa, Latin America, and the Caribbean, are also seeing growing numbers of international students, reflecting the internationalization of universities in an increasing number of countries.

In the last fifteen years, there has been a remarkable increase in short-term movement across borders for academic purposes, varying by nation and academic field (Marginson & van der Wende, 2009). For example, under Europe's Erasmus Program, more than 46,000 staff from thirty-three European countries had spent time abroad by 2012. More than 4000 HEIs in thirty-three countries have participated in staff exchanges, and more are willing to join (Valiulis, 2013). Partly related to this increased academic mobility, international collaboration has grown considerably in academic research. This is reflected in the growth of internationally co-authored (or collaborative) scientific articles, the increased citation of foreign scientific articles, the rise of foreign funding for research and development (Vincent-Lancrin, 2009), the large number of participants in international conferences, and frequent international research visits (Trondal, 2010).

Another trend in terms of internationalizing universities' academic activities is the increasing use of common textbooks, course materials, syllabi, and English as a teaching language worldwide, which lead to more internationalized curricula (Altbach, 2006). The OECD defines internationalized curricula as 'curricula with an international orientation in content, aimed at preparing students for performing in an international and multicultural context, and designed for domestic as well as foreign students' (IDP, 1995). Curricula consist of ideas (content) and ways of engaging with ideas (progress), which could include activities that are outside the classroom or adjacent to the formal education process such as travel and engagement with other cultures, study of a foreign language, or living in another culture (Elkin, Devjee, & Farnsworth, 2005). There has been a growing focus on developing curricula with an international focus, leading to internationally recognized professional qualifications. This includes interdisciplinary approaches and instruction in a foreign language (Leask, 2001; Welch, 2002). Running English or bilingual programs is particularly trendy in non-English-speaking countries. A number of universities in Japan, for instance, are planning to introduce a new quarterly semester system to align their academic calendar with the rest of the world, thereby enabling the launch of new English language dual-degree programs (Science/AAAS Custom Publishing Office, 2015). Researchers argue that internationalized curricula develop graduates' intercultural competence as well as help them develop a sense of political responsibility, turning them into defenders of democratic principles in their society and true architects of social change (Gacel-Avila, 2005). Students who have been trained and educated and carried out research using a curriculum with international content that meets international quality standards are expected to then be able to work in international business environments and understand the needs, nature, and structure of players in the international arena (Yesufu, 2018).

The service category refers to both facilities that institutions provide and the services offered to help international students. This could include things like infrastructure construction, academic advice and guidance, language support, technical assistance, welfare provision, and accommodation (Arum & Van de Water, 1992; Knight, 2008; Marginson, 2011a; Science/AAAS Custom Publishing Office, 2015; Taylor, 2010; Zolfaghari, Sabran, & Zolfaghari, 2009). According to Taylor (2010), the wider university environment has a significant impact on students' satisfaction and academic achievement. As found in a number of studies, international students reported poorer life satisfaction, poorer perceived social support, greater dissatisfaction with their environmental circumstances, and higher levels of health-compromising behaviors, such as smoking and illicit drug use, in comparison with their domestic counterparts (e.g., see Krämer, Prüfer-Krämer, Stock, & Tshiananga, 2004; Skromanis et al., 2018). Universities, therefore, need to offer accessible support services to international students as part of their internationalization strategies to help students adapt to the new environment. Building enduring and meaningful connections between international students and the host culture has been shown to improve mental health and assist with the adjustment process (Hyun, Quinn, Madon, & Lustig, 2007). In order to improve the accessibility and effectiveness of support services, there has been a call for these programs to be more culturally specific and to be reinforced frequently throughout the academic year (Mori, 2000; Redfern, 2016). Internet-based delivery methods may also provide a solution to the lack of support (Stallman & Kavanagh, 2016).

Few studies have shed light on the close link between the components of institutional internationalization strategies. Since internationalization is expected to permeate the core functions of a university, the three categories and the components involved in each must be related to each other in order to make internationalization strategies an entity rather than dispersed initiatives. For example, Horta's (2009) study demonstrated that an internationally oriented teaching body positively correlates to the internationalization of the student body. Internationalized teaching styles also contribute to the successful internationalization of curricula, since internationalizing university curricula is a complex process that is as much about how and by whom a lecture is delivered as it is about the content being taught (Leask, 2001). The internationalization of faculty contributes considerably to the reputation of a university through work-related migration or participation in international conferences and publications (Brandenburg et al., 2009). And an internationalized curriculum relies on learning processes as well—therefore, students' international experiences are also expected to induce curricula change (van Damme, 2001).

The sustainability of strategies developed to internationalize the academic functions of a university relies heavily on governance. If a sustainable organizational policy and structure does not underpin program activities, they may vanish when supporters leave the institution, resources become scarcer, or new priorities emerge. Strategies that embed an international focus into the administrative system are important for ensuring that academic internationalization becomes central to the mission of the university. Otherwise, internationalization could be marginalized or treated as a passing fad (Knight & de Wit, 1995).

HEIs' strategies are the key to the success of internationalization. Universities have become more selective in their strategies, often concentrating their efforts on a limited number of high-profile initiatives. There might not be a 'one-size-fits-all' strategy for universities; in fact, there are no uniform criteria for a good strategy, given universities' diverse cultural contexts. Strategies should correspond with each university's individual objectives and targets, taking their strengths, weaknesses, history, characteristics, and resources into account. The international, regional, and national environment may also influence institutional strategies. Strategies can often be intertwined and can be implemented in whatever way works best for each HEI.

Approaches to Implementing Internationalization Strategies

There are a number of ways to describe the process of university internationalization (e.g., see Ayoubi & Massoud, 2007; de Wit, 2002; Rubzki, 1998; van der Wende, 1996). As a leading scholar in the field, Jane Knight (1994) proposed a six-phase model of the process of institutional internationalization:

- **Awareness** of need, purpose, and benefits of internationalization for students, staff, faculty, and society,
- **Commitment** by senior administration, Board of Governors, faculty, staff, and students,

- **Planning**: Identify needs and resources, purposes and objectives, priorities and strategies,
- **Operationalize**: Develop academic activities and services, taking into account organizational factors and the university's guiding principles,
- **Review**: Assess and enhance the quality, impact, and progress of initiatives, and
- **Reinforcement**: Develop incentives, recognition, and rewards for faculty, staff, and student participation (Knight, 1994, p. 12).

Unlike most models, this process is seen as continuous rather than linear. HEIs would move through the six phases at their own pace, with two-way flows taking place between different steps.

Universities may be at different stages in the process of internationalization and implement their internationalization strategies in different ways. Over two decades ago, David (1992, p. 187) developed a two-dimensional model to describe the approaches by which HEIs can implement internationalization:

- Some universities will take aboard international elements in a sporadic, irregular, often knee-jerk way, with many loose ends in terms of procedure structure. Others will develop precise, explicit procedures from ad hoc to the highly systematic. There is thus a spectrum from the ad hoc to the highly systematic.
- For some universities, internationalization is a relatively marginal activity—an interesting and stimulating addendum to a predominantly regional or national focus. For others, internationalization is highly central to their work and permeates every aspect of institutional life. There is thus another spectrum from marginality to centrality.

The way in which HEIs implement internationalization is not fixed and may change over time. Often, institutions use different approaches at the same time or are in a transition period from one approach to another. The differentiation of HEIs means that institutions vary in missions, priorities, and strategies. As a result, there can be significant differences in their paths toward internationalization.

Summary

This chapter explained the basic concepts related to university internationalization and provided an initial framework to conceptualize the phenomenon in the dramatically changing global context. It also covered the major driving forces that shape HEIs' governance and performance. As a strategy to respond to the changing global landscape, internationalization has been a priority for many contemporary universities. Due to the substantial national and institutional investment in internationalization, it is necessary to monitor and assess university performance to ensure that the internationalization strategies being instituted are contributing to the quality of education and research.

This chapter also showed that there are generic components of institutional internationalization strategies. These components indicate the structural and philosophical similarities between institutions and allow meaningful comparisons to be made between universities when it comes to internationalization. They also suggest that it would be possible to develop an instrument to measure and compare university internationalization performance across institutional and national boundaries.

Finally, the chapter demonstrated that an international dimension strengthens many areas of a university while also illustrating how much controversy and ambiguity still surround the definition of university internationalization. A clear construct of the phenomenon has yet to be established, which has affected the efforts made to develop instruments for measuring university internationalization performance. The difficulties of measuring internationalization will be considered in the next chapter.

References

AIEA. (1989). *Guidelines for international education at U.S. colleges and universities: Final draft*. Association of International Education Administration.

Aigner, J. S., Nelson, P., & Stimpfl, J. R. (1992). *Internationalizing the university: Making it work*. Springfield: CBIS Federal.

Alden, J., & Lin, G. (2004). *Benchmarking the characteristics of a world-class university: Developing an international strategy at university level*. London: Leadership Foundation for Higher Education.

Altbach, P. G. (2004). *The costs and benefits of world-class universities*. Retrieved from http://www.aaup.org/publications/Academe/2004/04jf/04jfaltb.htm.

Altbach, P. G. (2006). Globalization and the university: Realities in an unequal world. In J. J. F. Forest & P. G. Altbach (Eds.), *International handbook of higher education* (pp. 121–139). Dordrecht: Springer.

Altbach, P. G., & de Wit, H. (2015). Internationalization and global tension: Lessons from history. *Journal of Studies in International Education, 19*(1), 4–10.

Altbach, P. G., & Knight, J. (2007). The internationalization of higher education: Motivations and realities. *Journal of Studies in International Education, 11*(3–4), 290–305.

Altbach, P. G., Reisberg, L., & Rumbley, L. E. (2009). *Trends in global higher education: Tracking an academic revolution*. A Report Prepared for the UNESCO 2009 World Conference on Higher Education. Paris: UNESCO.

Altbach, P. G., & Selvaratnam, V. (1989). *From dependence to autonomy: The development of Asian universities*. Dordrecht and Boston: Kluwer Academic.

Amirbek, A., & Ydyrys, K. (2014). Education as a soft power instrument of foreign policy. *Procedia—Social and Behavioral Sciences, 143*(14), 501–503.

Arimoto, A. (2011). Japan's internationalization of higher education: A response to the pressures of globalization. In D. W. Chapman, W. K. Cummings, & G. A. Postiglione (Eds.), *Crossing borders in East Asian higher education* (pp. 195–210). CERC Studies in Comparative Education, Vol. 27. Dordrecht: Springer.

Arkoudis, S., Baik, C., Marginson, S., & Cassidy, E. (2012). *Internationalising the student experience in Australian tertiary education: Developing criteria and indicators*. Melbourne: Centre for the Study of Higher Education.

Arum, S., & Van de Water, J. (1992). The need for a definition of international education in U.S. universities. In C. B. Klasek, B. J. Garavalia, K. J. Kellerman, & B. B. Marx (Eds.), *Bridges to the future: Strategies for internationalizing higher education* (pp. 191–203). Carbondale, IL: Association of International Education Administrators.

Aucoin, P. (1990). Administrative reform in public management: Paradigms, principles, paradoxes and pendulums. *Governance, 3*(2), 115–137.

Australian Government. (2015). *Draft National Strategy for International Education*. Retrieved 23 August 2015, from https://internationaleducation.gov.au/International-network/Australia/InternationalStrategy/Documents/Draft%20National%20Strategy%20for%20International%20Education.pdf.

Ayoubi, R. M., & Massoud, H. K. (2007). The strategy of internationalization in universities: A quantitative evaluation of the intent and implementation in UK universities. *International Journal of Educational Management, 21*(4), 329–349.

Bartell, M. (2003). Internationalization of universities: A university culture-based framework. *Higher Education, 45*(1), 43–70.

Bauman, Z. (2002). *Society under siege*. Cambridge: Polity Press.

Beck, U. (1999). *What is globalization?* Cambridge: Polity Press.

Beerkens, E. (2002). International inter-organisational arrangements in higher education: towards a typology. *Tertiary Education and Management, 8*(4), 297–314.

Beerkens, E. (2004). *Global opportunities and institutional Embeddedness: Higher education consortia in Europe and Southeast Asia*. University of Twente. Retrieved from http://doc.utwente.nl/50803/1/thesis_Beerkens.pdf.

Beigel, F. (2013). The internationalization and institutionalization of research and higher education in Latin America: The emergence of peripheral centers. In F. Beigel (Ed.), *The politics of academic autonomy in Latin America* (pp. 31–45). Farnham: Ashgate.

Blackmore, J. (2000). Globalization: A useful concept for feminists rethinking theory and strategies in education? In N. C. Burbules & C. A. Torres (Eds.), *Globalization and education: Critical perspectives* (pp. 224–261). New York: Routledge.

Blackton, C. (1951). The Colombo Plan. *Far Eastern Survey, 20*(3), 27–31.

Block, P. (1995). *Policy and policy implementation in internationalization of higher education*. Amsterdam: European Association for International Education (EAIE).

Bottery, M. (2005). The individualization of consumption: A Trojan horse in the destruction of the public sector? *Educational Management Administration and Leadership, 33*(3), 267–288.

Boulton, G., & Lucas, C. (2008). *What are universities for?* Retrieved from http://www.leru.org/index.php/public/publications/publications-2002-2009/.

Brandenburg, U., & de Wit, H. (2011). The end of internationalization. In H. de Wit (Ed.), *Trends, issues and challenges in internationalization of higher education* (pp. 27–28). Amsterdam: Centre for Applied Research on Economics and Management Hogeschool van Amsterdam.

Brandenburg, U., Ermel, H., Federkeil, G., Fuchs, S., Groos, M., & Menn, A. (2009). How to measure the internationality and internationalization of higher education institutions: Indicators and key figures. In H. de Wit (Ed.), *Measuring success in the internationalization of higher education* (EAIE

Occasional Paper No. 22, pp. 65–76). Amsterdam: European Association for International Education.

Cai, Y., & Kivistö, J. (2013). Tuition fees for international students in Finland. *Journal of Studies in International Education, 17*(1), 55–78.

Cantwell, B. (2015). Are international students cash cows? Examining the relationship between new international undergraduate enrollments and institutional revenue at public colleges and universities in the US. *Journal of International Students, 5*(4), 512–525.

Cantwell, B., & Maldonado-Maldonado, A. (2009). Four stories: Confronting contemporary ideas about globalisation and internationalization in higher education. *Globalisation, Societies and Education, 7*(3), 289–306.

Castells, M. (1996). *The rise of networked society*. Oxford: Blackwell.

Chan, D. K. K. (2008). Revisiting post-colonial education development: Reflections on some critical issues. In M. Marson (Ed.), *Comparative Education Bulletin: Special Issue: Education and development in post-colonial societies* (Vol. 11, pp. 21–36). Hong Kong: Comparative Education Society of Hong Kong.

Chankseliani, M. (2018). Four rationales of higher education internationalization: Perspectives of U.K. universities on attracting students from former Soviet countries. *Journal of Studies in International Education, 22*(1), 53–70.

Ching, G. S., & Chin, J. M.-C. (2012). Managing higher education institution internationalization: Contemporary efforts of a university in Taiwan. *International Journal of Research Studies in Management, 1*(1), 3–17.

Coelen, R. J. (2009). Ranking and the measurement of success in internationalization: Are they related? In H. de Wit (Ed.), *Measuring success in the internationalization of higher education* (EAIE Occasional Paper No. 22, pp. 39–47). Amsterdam: European Association for International Education.

Currie, J. (2014). Global trends and universities: Rankings, international students and MOOCs. *HERDSA News, 36*(3), 1.

David, J. L. (1992). Developing a strategy for internationalization in universities: Towards a conceptual framework. In C. B. Klasek, B. J. Garavalia, K. J. Kellerman, & B. B. Marx (Eds.), *Bridges to the future: Strategies for internationalizing higher education* (pp. 177–190). Carbondale, IL: Association of International Education Administrators.

de Wit, H. (1995, Fall). Education and globalization in Europe: Current trends and future developments. *Frontiers: The Interdisciplinary Journal of Study Abroad, 1*, 28–53.

de Wit, H. (1997). Strategies for internationalization of higher education in Asia Pacific countries: A comparative introduction. In J. Knight & H. de

Wit (Eds.), *Internationalization of higher education in Asia Pacific countries* (pp. 21–45). Amsterdam: European Association for International Education, in cooperation with IDP Education Australia.
de Wit, H. (1998). *Rationales for internationalization of higher education.* Retrieved 5 April 2012, from http://www.ipv.pt/millenium/wit11.htm.
de Wit, H. (2000). Changing rationales for the internationalization of higher education. In L. C. Barrows (Ed.), *Internationalization of higher education: An institutional perspective. Papers on higher education* (pp. 9–20). Burcharest, Romania: The Administrative Officer (CEPES/UNESCO).
de Wit, H. (2002). *Internationalization of higher education in the United States of America and Europe: A historical, comparative, and conceptual analysis.* Westport, CT: Greenwood Press.
de Wit, H. (2011a). Globalisation and internationalization of higher education. *RUSC Revista de Universidady Sociedad del Conocimiento, 8*(2), 241–248.
de Wit, H. (2011b). Law of the stimulative arrears? In H. de Wit (Ed.), *Trends, issues and challenges in internationalization of higher education* (pp. 7–23). Amsterdam: Centre for Applied Research on Economics and Management Hogeschool van Amsterdam.
de Wit, H. (2015, Spring). Is the international university the future for higher education? *International Higher Education, 80*, 7.
Deem, R., Mok, K. H., & Lucas, L. (2008). Transforming higher education in whose image? Exploring the concept of the "world-class university in Europe and Asia". *Higher Education Policy, 21*(1), 83–97.
Dewey, P., & Duff, S. (2009). Reason before passion: Faculty views on internationalization in higher education. *Higher Education, 58*(4), 491–504.
Dunn, A. H., & Faison, M. Z.-J. (2015). The shuttering of educational studies: Neoliberalism, the political spectacle, and social injustice at a "world class" university. *Educational Foundations, 28*(1), 9–30.
Ebuchi, K. (1989). Foreign students and internationalization of the university: A view from the Japanese perspective. In *Proceedings of OECD/Japan seminar in higher education and the flow of foreign students* (pp. 45–56). Hiroshima: Hiroshima University.
Elkin, G., Devjee, F., & Farnsworth, J. (2005). Visualising the "internationalisation" of universities. *International Journal of Educational Management, 19*(4), 318–329. https://doi.org/10.1108/09513540510599644.
Ellingboe, B. J. (1998). Divisional strategies to internationalize a campus portrait: Results, resistance, and recommendations from a case study at a U.S. university. In J. A. Mestenhauser & B. J. Ellingboe (Eds.), *Reforming the higher education curriculum: Internationalizing the campus* (pp. 198–228). Phoenix, AZ: American Council on Education and Oryx Press.

Enders, J., & Fulton, O. (2002). Blurring boundaries and blistering institutions. In J. Enders & O. Fulton (Eds.), *Higher education in a globalizing world: International trends and mutual observations; A Festschrift in honour of Ulrich Teichler* (pp. 1–14). London: Kluwer Academic.

European Commission. (2013). *Communication from the Commission to the European Parliament, the Council, the European Economic and Social Committee and the Committee of the Regions*. Retrieved from http://ww.w.xploit-eu.com/pdfs/Europe%202020%20Flagship%20Initiative%20INNOVATION.pdf.

Foreign Affairs, Trade and Development Canada. (2014). *Global markets action plan: The blueprint for creating jobs and opportunities for Canadian through trade*. Retrieved 23 August 2015, from http://international.gc.ca/global-markets-marches-mondiaux/assets/pdfs/plan-eng.pdf.

Foskett, N. (2010). Global markets, national challenges, local strategies: The strategic challenge of internationalization. In F. Maringe & N. Foskett (Eds.), *Globalisation and internationalization in higher education: Theoretical, strategic and management perspectives* (pp. 35–50). London: Continuum.

Gacel-Avila, J. (2005). The internationalization of higher education: A paradigm for global citizenry. *Journal of Studies in International Education, 9*(2), 121–136.

Georghiou, L., & Larédo, P. (2015). *Dimensions of internationalization—Universities at home and abroad: A position paper*. Retrieved from https://hal-upec-upem.archives-ouvertes.fr/hal-01275905/document.

Giddens, A. (1990). *The consequences of modernity*. Stanford: Stanford University Press.

Giroux, H. (2007). *The university in chains: Confronting the military-industrial-academic complex*. Boulder, CO: Paradigm.

Graham, E., Faiyaz, D., & John, F. (2005). Visualising the "internationalization" of universities. *International Journal of Educational Management, 19*(4), 318–329. https://doi.org/10.1108/09513540510599644.

Harari, M. (1992). The internationalization of curriculum. In C. B. Klasek, B. J. Garavalia, K. J. Kellerman, & B. B. Marx (Eds.), *Bridges to the future: Strategies for internationalizing higher education* (pp. 52–79). Carbondale, IL: Association of International Education Administrators.

Harris, S. (2008). Internationalising the university. *Educational Philosophy and Theory, 40*(20), 346–357.

Harris, S. (2009). Translation, internationalization and the university. *London Review of Education, 7*(3), 223–233.

Hazelkorn, E. (2013). World-class universities or world-class systems? Rankings and higher education policy choices. In P. T. M. Marope, P. J.

Wells, & E. Hazelkorn (Eds.), *Rankings and accountability in higher education: Uses and misuses* (pp. 71–94). Paris: UNESCO.

Hazelkorn, E. (2016). *Global rankings and the geopolitics of higher education: Understanding the influence and impact of rankings on higher education, policy and society*. Florence: Taylor & Francis.

Healey, N. M. (2008). Is higher education in really 'internationalising'? *Higher Education, 55*(3), 333–355. https://doi.org/10.1007/s10734-007-9058-4.

Healey, N. M. (2017). Beyond 'export education': Aspiring to put students at the heart of a university's internationalization strategy. *Perspectives: Policy and Practice in Higher Education, 21*(4), 119–128. https://doi.org/10.1080/13603108.2017.1286399.

Hertig, H. P. (2016). *Universities, rankings and the dynamics of global higher education: Perspectives from Asia, Europe and North America*. London: Palgrave Macmillan.

Horta, H. (2009). Global and national prominent universities: Internationalization, competitiveness and the role of the State. *Higher Education, 58*(3), 387–405.

Hoyler, M., & Jöns, H. (2013). Global geographies of higher education: The perspective of world university rankings. *Journal of Physical, Human, and Regional Geosciences, 46*(May), 45–59.

Hser, M. P. (2005). Campus internationalization: A study of American universities' internationalization efforts. *International Education, 35*(1), 35–48.

Huang, F. (2007). Internationalization of higher education in the era of globalisation: What have been its Implications in China and Japan? *Higher Education Management and Policy, 19*(1), 47–61.

Huang, I. Y., Raimo, V., & Humfrey, C. (2016). Power and control: Managing agents for international student recruitment in higher education. *Studies in Higher Education, 41*(8), 1333–1354.

Huisman, J., & Currie, J. (2004). Accountability in higher education: Bridge over troubled water? *Higher Education, 48*(4), 529–551.

Hyun, J., Quinn, B., Madon, T., & Lustig, S. (2007). Mental health need, awareness, and use of counseling services among international graduate students. *Journal of American College Health, 56*(2), 109–118.

IDP Education Australia. (1995). *Global student mobility 2025: Forecasts of the global demand for international higher education*. Canberra: IDP.

Jiang, X.-P. (2008). Towards the internationalization of higher education from a critical perspective. *Journal of Further and Higher Education, 32*(4), 347–358.

Johnston, J., & Edelstein, R. (1993). *Beyond borders: Profiles in international education*. Washington, DC: Association of American Colleges and American Assembly of Collegiate.

Jowi, J. O. (2012). African universities in the global knowledge economy: The good and ugly of internationalization. *Journal of Marketing for Higher Education, 22*(1), 153–165.

Kahane, D. (2009). Learning about obligation, compassion, and global justice: The place of contemplative pedagogy. *New Directions for Teaching and Learning, 2009*(118), 49–60.

Kameoka, Y. (1996, October–November). The internationalization. *The OECD Observer, 202*, 34–36.

Kearns, P., & Schofield, K. (1997). *Learning across frontiers: Report on the internationalization of staff development in vocational education and training*. Melbourne: Australian National Training Authority.

Kedziora, D., Klamut, E., Karri, T., & Kraslawski, A. (2017). Higher education offshoring as an innovative response to global learning challenges. *International Journal of Management, Knowledge and Learning, 6*(2), 239–260.

Kerr, C. (1994). *Higher education cannot escape history: Issues for the twenty-first century*. Albany: State University of New York Press.

Kim, T. (2006). Building a business: A comparative note on the changing identities of the British university. In J. Sprogøe & T. Winther-Jensen (Eds.), *Identity, education, and citizenship: Multiple interrelations B2—Identity, education, and citizenship: Multiple interrelations* (pp. 197–224). Berlin: Peter Lang.

Kim, T. (2009). Transnational academic mobility, internationalization and interculturality in higher education. *Intercultural Education, 20*(5), 395–405.

Kim, E. Y., & Choi, S. (2011). Korea's internationalization of higher education: Process, challenge and strategy. In D. W. Chapman, W. K. Cummings, & G. A. Postiglione (Eds.), *Crossing borders in East Asian higher education* (pp. 211–229). Hong Kong: Comparative Education Research Centre, University of Hong Kong.

Kinser, K., & Green, M. F. (2009). *The power of partnerships: A transatlantic dialogue*. Washington, DC: American Council on Education.

Knight, J. (1994). *Internationalization: Elements and checkpoints* (CBIE Research No. 7). Ottawa: CBIE.

Knight, J. (1997). Internationalization of higher education: A conceptual framework. In J. Knight & H. de Wit (Eds.), *Internationalization of higher education in Asia Pacific countries* (pp. 5–19). Amsterdam: EAIE.

Knight, J. (2004). Internationalization remodeled: Definition, approaches, and rationales. *Journal of Studies in International Education, 8*(1), 5–31.

Knight, J. (2008). *Higher education in turmoil: The changing world of internationalization.* Rotterdam: Sense Publishers.

Knight, J., & de Wit, H. (1995). Strategies for internationalization of higher education: Historical and conceptual perspectives. In J. Knight & H. de Wit (Eds.), *Strategies for internationalization of higher education: A comparative study of Australia, Canada, Europe, and the USA* (pp. 5–32). Amsterdam: European Association for International Education.

Krämer, A., Prüfer-Krämer, L., Stock, C., & Tshiananga, J. T. (2004). Differences in health determinants between international and domestic students at a German university. *Journal of American College Health, 53*(3), 127–132.

Kreber, C. (2009). Different perspectives on internationalization in higher education. *New Directions for Teaching and Learning, 2009*(118), 1–14.

Kuroda, K., Yuki, T., & Kang, K. (2010). *Cross-border higher education for regional integration: Analysis of the JICA-RI survey on leading universities in East Asia* (JICA-RI Working Paper No. 26). Tokyo: JICA Research Institute.

Le Phan, H. (2013). Issues surrounding English, the internationalization of higher education and national cultural identity in Asia: A focus on Japan. *Critical Studies in Education, 54*(2), 160–175.

Leask, B. (2001). Bridging the gap: Internationalizing university curricula. *Journal of Studies in International Education, 5*(2), 100–115.

Leitner, K. H., Elena, S., Fazlagic, J., Kalemis, K., Marinaitis, Z., Secundo, G., ... Zaksa, K. (2014). *A strategic approach for intellectual capital management in European universities: Guidelines for implementation.* Bucharest: UEFISCDI Blueprint Series.

Lenn, M. P. (1999). The new technologies and borderless higher education: The quality imperative. *Higher Education in Europe, 23*(2), 241–251.

Lewkowicz, M. A., Young, L. D., Budrytė, D., & Boykin, S. A. (2018). Bringing the study of American government to life in a diverse classroom: Internationalization and individualization. In *Curriculum Internationalization and the Future of Education* (pp. 1–17). IGI Global. https://doi.org/10.4018/978-1-5225-2791-6.ch001.

Liu, J. (2012). On the internationalization of higher education institutions in China. *Higher Education Studies, 2*(1), 60–64.

Lotz-Sisitka, H., Wals, A. E. J., Kronlid, D., & McGarry, D. (2015). Transformative, transgressive social learning: Rethinking higher education pedagogy in times of systemic global dysfunction. *Current Opinion in Environmental Sustainability, 16*(October), 73–80. https://doi.org/10.1016/j.cosust.2015.07.018.

Lumby, J., & Foskett, N. (2016). Internationalization and culture in higher education. *Educational Management Administration and Leadership, 44*(1), 95–111. https://doi.org/10.1177/1741143214549978.

Marginson, S. (2011a). Imagining the global. In R. King, S. Marginson, & R. Naidoo (Eds.), *Handbook on globalization and higher education* (pp. 10–39). Cheltenham: Edward Elgar.

Marginson, S. (2011b). Strategizing and ordering the global. In R. King, S. Marginson, & R. Naidoo (Eds.), *Handbook on globalization and higher education* (pp. 394–414). Cheltenham: Edward Elgar.

Marginson, S. (2016). High participation systems of higher education. *Higher Education, 87*(2), 243–271. https://doi.org/10.1353/jhe.2016.0007.

Marginson, S., Murphy, P., & Peters, M. (2010). *Global creation: Space, mobility and synchrony in the age of the knowledge economy*. New York: Peter Lang.

Marginson, S., & Rhoades, G. (2002). Beyond national states, markets, and systems of higher education: A glonacal agency heuristic. *Higher Education, 43*(3), 281–309.

Marginson, S., & van der Wende, M. (2007). *Globalisation and higher education* (OECD Education Working Papers No. 8). OECD Publishing. http://dx.doi.org/10.1787/173831738240.

Marginson, S., & van der Wende, M. (2009). The new global landscape of nations and institutions. *OECD research and innovation* (pp. 17–62). Paris and Washington, DC: Organisation for Economic Co-operation and Development.

Maringe, F. (2010). The meanings of globalization and internationalization in higher education: Findings from a world survey. In F. Maringe & N. Foskett (Eds.), *Globalisation and internationalization in higher education: Theoretical, strategic and management perspectives* (pp. 17–34). London: Continuum.

Maringe, F., & Foskett, N. (2010). Introduction: Globalization and universities. In F. Maringe & N. Foskett (Eds.), *Globalisation and internationalization in higher education: Theoretical, strategic and management perspectives* (pp. 1–13). London: Continuum.

Marope, M., & Wells, P. (2013). University rankings: The many sides of the debate. In P. T. M. Marope, P. J. Wells, & E. Hazelkorn (Eds.), *Rankings and accountability in higher education uses and misuses* (pp. 7–19). Paris: UNESCO.

McBurnie, G. (2000). Pursuing internationalization as a means to advance the academic mission of the university: An Australian case study. *Higher Education in Europe, 25*(1), 63–73.

Meiras, S. (2004). International education in Australian universities: Understandings, dimensions and problems. *Journal of Higher Education Policy and Management, 26*(3), 371–380.

Michavila, F., & Martinez, J. M. (2018). Excellence of universities versus autonomy. *Funding and Accountability. European Review, 26*(1), 48–56. https://doi.org/10.1017/S1062798717000539.

Middlehurst, R. (2000). *The business of borderless education.* London: Committee of Vice Principles and Chancellors.

Ministry of Education, Culture, Sports, Science and Technology, Japan. (2010). *Outline of the student exchange system: Study in Japan and abroad.* Retrieved 23 August 2015, from www.mext.go.jp/component/english/__icsFiles/afieldfile/2011/12/14/1303740_1.pdf.

Ministry of Higher Education Malaysia. (2011). *Internationalization policy 2011.* Retrieved 23 August 2015, from http://www.academia.edu/2257039/Internationalization_policy_for_higher_education_Malaysia_2011.

Mohrman, K. (2005, Spring). World-class universities and Chinese higher education reform. *International Higher Education, 39,* 22–23.

Mok, K. H. (2007). Questing for internationalization of universities in Asia: Critical reflections. *Journal of Studies in International Education, 11*(3–4), 433–454.

Mok, K. H., & Yu, K. M. (2013). *Internationalization of higher education in East Asia: Trends of student mobility and impact on education governance.* Hoboken: Taylor & Francis.

Moller, K. (2000). The international challenge for vocational education and training. In J. Sogaard & N. Wollschlager (Eds.), *Internationalising vocational education and training in Europe: Prelude to an overdue debate: A discussion paper* (pp. 57–70). Thessaloniki: CEDEFOP European Centre for the Development of Vocational Training.

Mori, S. (2000). Addressing the mental health concerns of international students. *Journal of Counseling and Development, 78*(2), 137–144. https://doi.org/10.1002/j.1556-6676.2000.tb02571.x.

Morphew, C. C., & Swanson, C. (2011). On the efficacy of raising your university's ranking. In J. C. Shin, R. K. Toutkoushian, & U. Teichler (Eds.), *University rankings: Theoretical basis, methodology and impacts on global higher education* (pp. 185–199). Dordrecht: Springer.

Naidoo, R., & Jamieson, I. (2005). Knowledge in the marketplace: The global commodification of teaching and learning in higher education. In P. Ninnes & M. Hellsten (Eds.), *Internationalizing higher education: Critical explorations of pedagogy and policy* (pp. 37–51). Hong Kong: Comparative Education Research Centre.

Ng, S. W. (2012). Rethinking the mission of internationalization of higher education in the Asia-Pacific region. *Compare: A Journal of Comparative and International Education, 42*(3), 439–459.

Nye, J. (2015). China and soft power. *South African Journal of International Affairs, 19*(2), 151–155.

Oakman, D. (2010). *Facing Asia: A history of the Colombo Plan*. Canberra: ANU Press.

OECD. (1997). *In search of results: Performance management practices in ten OECD countries*. Paris: Public Management Committee, OECD.

OECD. (2017). *Education at a glance 2017: OECD indicators*. Paris: OECD. http://dx.doi.org/10.1787/eag-2017-en.

Palmer, J. D., Roberts, A., Cho, Y. H., & Ching, G. S. (2011). *The internationalization of East Asian higher education: Globalization's impact*. Basingstoke: Palgrave Macmillan.

Papp, D. S. (2008). Strategic perspectives on internationalizing a university. *Presidency, 11*(3), 22.

Ramírez, Y., & Tejada, Á. (2018). Corporate governance of universities: Improving transparency and accountability. *International Journal of Disclosure and Governance, 15*(1), 29–39. https://doi.org/10.1057/s41310-018-0034-2.

Rauhvargers, A. (2011). *Global university rankings and their impact*. Brussels: European University Association. Retrieved 3 March 2013, from http://www.eua.be/pubs/Global_University_Rankings_and_Their_Impact.pdf.

Redfern, K. (2016). An empirical investigation of the incidence of negative psychological symptoms among Chinese international students at an Australian university. *Australian Journal of Psychology, 68*(4), 281–289. https://doi.org/10.1111/ajpy.12106.

Rizvi, F. (2007). Rethinking educational aims in an era of globalization. In P. D. Hershock, M. Mason, & J. N. Hawkins (Eds.), *Changing education: Leadership, innovation and development in a globalizing Asia Pacific* (pp. 63–91). Hong Kong: Comparative Education Research Centre.

Rubzki, R. E. J. (1998). *The strategic management of internationalization: Towards a model of theory and practice* (PhD dissertation). University of Newcastle upon Tyne.

Sadlak, J. (2001). Globalization in higher education. *International Educator, 10*(4), 3–5.

Salmi, J. (2009). *The challenge of establishing world-class universities*. Washington, DC: The World Bank.

Schoorinan, D. (1999). The pedagogical implications of diverse conceptualizations of internationalization: A U.S. based case study. *Journal of Studies in International Education, 3*(2), 19–46.

Science/AAAS Custom Publishing Office. (2015). *Internationalization of university education in Japan*. Washington, DC: The American Association for the Advancement of Science.

Scott, P. (1998). Massification, internationalization and globalization. In P. Scott (Ed.), *The globalization of higher education* (pp. 108–129). Buckingham: The Society for Research into Higher Education/Open University Press.

Scott, P. (2000). Globalisation and higher education: Challenges for the 21st century. *Journal of Studies in International Education, 4*(1), 3–10.

Scott, P. (2005). Universities and the knowledge economy. *Minerva: A Review of Science, Learning and Policy, 43*(3), 297–309.

Shin, J. C., & Toutkoushian, R. K. (2011). The past, present, and future of university rankings. In J. C. Shin, R. K. Toutkoushian, & U. Teichler (Eds.), *University rankings: Theoretical basis, methodology and impacts on global higher education* (pp. 1–18). Dordrecht: Springer.

Sidhu, G., & Kaur, S. (2011). Enhancing global competence in higher education: Malaysia's strategic initiatives. In S. Marginson, S. Kaur, & E. Sawir (Eds.), *Higher education in the Asia-Pacific: Higher education dynamics* (Vol. 36, pp. 219–236). Dordrecht: Springer.

Skromanis, S., Cooling, N., Rodgers, B., Purton, T., Fan, F., Bridgman, H., … Mond, J. (2018). Health and well-being of international university students, and comparison with domestic students, in Tasmania, Australia. *International Journal of Environmental Research and Public Health, 15*(6), 1147–1160.

Soderqvist, M. (2002). *Internationalization and its management at higher education institutions: Applying conceptual, content and discourse analysis*. Helsinki: Helsinki School of Economics.

Soliman, S., Anchor, J., & Taylor, D. (2018). The international strategies of universities: Deliberate or emergent? *Studies in Higher Education*. https://doi.org/10.1080/03075079.2018.1445985.

Soria, K. M., & Troisi, J. (2014). Internationalization at home alternatives to study abroad: Implications for students' development of global, international, and intercultural competencies. *Journal of Studies in International Education, 18*(3), 261–280. https://doi.org/10.1177/1028315313496572.

Sowter, B. (2013). Issues of transparency and applicability in global university rankings. In P. T. M. Marope, P. J. Wells, & E. Hazelkorn (Eds.), *Rankings and accountability in higher education: Uses and misuses* (pp. 55–68). Paris: UNESCO.

Stallman, H. M., & Kavanagh, D. J. (2016). Development of an internet intervention to promote wellbeing in college students. *Australian Psychologist, 53*(1), 60–67. https://doi.org/10.1111/ap.12246.

Steiner, D. (2000). 'The show is not the show/but they that go': The Janus-Face of the internationalized university at the turn of the century. In L. C. Barrows (Ed.), *Internationalization of higher education: An institutional perspective. Papers on higher education* (pp. 63–74). Bucharest, Romania: The Administrative Officer (CEPES/UNESCO).

Stier, J. (2004). Taking a critical stance toward internationalization ideologies in higher education: Idealism, instrumentalism and educationalism. *Globalisation, Societies and Education, 2*(1), 83–97.

Stier, J., & Borjesson, M. (2010). The internationalised university as discourse: Institutional self-presentations, rhetoric and benchmarking in a global market. *International Studies in Sociology of Education, 20*(4), 335–353.

Stockley, D., & de Wit, H. (2011). The increasing relevance of institutional networks. In H. de Wit (Ed.), *Trends, issues and challenges in internationalization of higher education* (pp. 45–58). Amsterdam: Centre for Applied Research on Economics and Management Hogeschool van Amsterdam.

Sułkowski, Ł. (2016). Accountability of university: Transition of public higher education. *Entrepreneurial Business and Economics Review, 4*(1), 9–21. https://doi.org/10.15678/EBER.2016.040102.

Svensson, L. G. (1994). Formation of professional values towards Europe: The role of professional education and organization. *Higher Education Policy, 7*(3), 27–33.

Take, H., & Shoraku, A. (2018). Universities' expectations for study-abroad programs fostering internationalization: Educational policies. *Journal of Studies in International Education, 22*(1), 37–52.

Tarling, N. (2012). Making a difference: Overseas student fees in Britain and the development of a market in international education. *Britain and the World, 5*(2), 259–286.

Taylor, J. (2010). The response of government and universities to globalization. In F. Maringe & N. Foskett (Eds.), *Globalisation and internationalization in higher education: Theoretical, strategic and management perspectives* (pp. 83–96). London: Continuum.

Teichler, U. (2004). The changing debate on internationalization of higher education. *Higher Education, 48*(1), 5–26.

Teichler, U. (2017). Internationalization trends in higher education and changing role of international student mobility. *Journal of international Mobility, 5*(1), 177–216.

Tilak, J. B. G. (2016). Global rankings, world-class universities and dilemma in higher education policy in India. *Higher Education for the Future, 3*(2), 126–143.

Trondal, J. (2010). Two worlds of change: On the internationalization of universities. *Globalisation, Societies and Education, 8*(3), 351–368.

Turner, Y., & Robson, S. (2008). *Internationalizing the university: An introduction for university teachers and managers.* London: Continuum.

Valiulis, A. V. (2013). Students and academic staff international mobility—A supplementary tool for better learning. *World Transactions on Engineering and Technology Education, 11*(3), 204–208.

van Damme, D. (2001). Quality issues in the internationalization of higher education. *Higher Education, 41*(4), 415–441.

van der Wende, M. (1996). *Internationalising the curriculum in Dutch higher education: An international comparative perspective* (PhD dissertation). Utrecht University.

van der Wende, M. (1997). Missing links: The relationship between national policies for internationalization and those for higher education in general. In T. Kalvemark & M. Van der Wende (Eds.), *National policies for the internationalization of higher education in Europe* (pp. 10–41). Stockholm: National Agency for Higher Education.

van der Wende, M. (2001). Internationalization policies: About new trends and contrasting paradigms. *Higher Education Policy, 14*(3), 249–259.

van der Wende, M. (2007). Internationalization of higher education in the OECD countries: Challenges and opportunities for the coming decade. *Journal of Studies in International Education, 11*(3/4), 274–289.

van der Wende, M., Beerkens, E., & Teichler, U. (1999). Internationalization as a cause for innovation in higher education. In B. Jongbloed, P. Maassen, & G. Neave (Eds.), *From the eye of the storm: Higher education's changing institution* (pp. 65–93). Dordrecht: Kluwer.

Van Ginkel, H. (1997). Networking and strategic alliances: Dynamic patterns of organization and cooperation. *CRE Action, 109,* 91–105.

Verger, A., & Hermo, J. P. (2010). The governance of higher education regionalisation: Comparative analysis of the Bologna Process and MERCOSUR-Educativo. *Globalisation, Societies and Education, 8*(1), 105–120.

Vincent-Lancrin, S. (2009). What is changing in academic research? Trends and prospects. In OECD Research & Innovation (Ed.), *Higher Education to 2030, Volume 2. Globalisation* (pp. 145–178). Paris and Washington, DC: Organisation for Economic Co-operation and Development.

Wan, X.-L., & Geo-JaJa, M. A. (2013). Internationalization of higher education in Africa: Characteristics and determinants. *World Studies in Education, 14*(1), 79–101.

Waters, M. (1995). *Globalization*. Cambridge: Polity Press.
Weck, A., & Denman, B. (1997). Internationalization of higher education: Retrospect and prospect. *Forum of Education, 52*(1), 14–29.
Welch, A. (2002). Going global? Internationalizing Australian universities in a time of global crisis. *Comparative Education Review, 46*(4), 433–471.
Wescott, C. (2005, August 27–28). *Promoting knowledge exchanges through diasporas*. G-20 Workshop on Demographic Challenges and Migration, Sydney.
West, C. (2013). To charge or not to charge? That is Tuition. *International Educator, 22*(4), 34–43.
Windham, D. M. (1996). Overview and main conclusion of the seminar. In OECD (Ed.), *Internationalization of higher education* (pp. 7–29). Paris and Washington, DC: Organisation for Economic Co-operation and Development.
Yang, R. (2002). University internationalization: Its meanings, rationales and implications. *Intercultural Education, 13*(1), 81–95.
Yang, R. (2004). Openness and reform as dynamics for development: A case study of internationalization at South China University of Technology. *Higher Education, 47*(4), 473–500.
Yesufu, L. O. (2018). Motives and measures of higher education internationalization: A case study of a Canadian university. *International Journal of Higher Education, 7*(2), 155–168.
Yudkevich, M., Altbach, P. G., & Rumbley, L. E. (2015). Global university rankings: The "Olympic Games" of higher education? *Prospects, 45*(4), 411–419. https://doi.org/10.1007/s11125-015-9365-y.
Zolfaghari, A., Sabran, M. S., & Zolfaghari, A. (2009). Internationalization of higher education: Challenges, strategies, policies and programs. *US-China Education Review, 6*(5), 1–9.

3

Measuring University Internationalization

Now we turn to the complex business of measuring university internationalization. As discussed in the previous chapter, the increased requirements for accountability of universities has pushed more and more universities in different countries to adopt the new public management (NPM) model. Consequently, performance measurement is widely used in universities that adopted the NPM model in major Western countries, such as the UK (Johnes & Taylor, 1990; Yorke, 1991), the United States (Burke & Freeman, 1997; McLendon, Hearn, & Deaton, 2006), Germany (Orr, Jaeger, & Schwarzenberger, 2007), Australia (Freeman, 2014). As a way to quantify, either quantitatively or qualitatively, the input, output, or level of activity of an even or process, performance measurement plays a central role in performance management, which often in attempt to improve the effectiveness and efficiency of public sectors and promote innovation (Forrester, 2011; Radnor & Barnes, 2007). Studies show that performance measurement in universities has been most frequently used for managing financial resources, research productivity, and teaching quality, but least for managing community service or other third missions of universities (e.g., see Jarmo & Pentti, 2003; Kallio & Kallio, 2014; Kallio, Kallio, & Grossi, 2017;

Zhivan, 2017). Internationalization, as a third mission of universities, has taken on greater importance in the past three decades and a number of efforts have been made to capture the performance of universities in this aspect. This chapter provides a review of the variety of available instruments for measuring university internationalization, which helps identify the weaknesses of current instruments and further highlight the need for a new tool to be developed in this project.

Available Instruments for Measuring University Internationalization

Overview of Previous Studies

The first international endeavor made to assist institutions in assessing their internationalization performance was the International Quality Review Program (IQRP) developed by the Institutional Management in Higher Education, OECD, together with the Academic Cooperation Association. The IQRP was a self-assessment tool to help institutions review their goals, assess the appropriateness of their strategies, and include internationalization as a key part of their overall quality assurance system (Knight & de Wit, 1999). There are two main components of the tool: a self-assessment report and an external review by an international panel. Following this endeavor, there was a considerable growth in the number of studies and projects that attempted to develop appropriate indicators of internationalization in the decade thereafter. Not surprisingly, the first sets of indicators that were developed came from countries where internationalization had gained more importance because of increasing flow of foreign students. In 2001, the American Council on Education (ACE) simplified the review process of the IQRP and further developed it into a five-point-scale measurement to classify research universities in the United States within two groups: highly active and less active in internationalization (Green, 2005). Later, Horn, Hendel, and Fry (2007) designed a new instrument which included 19 indicators for research universities in America. The new measure allows designers to generate an overall score of internationalization for each university, and the score is used to determine the position of a given institution in the ranking system. In 2012, the Committee on Institutional Cooperation (CIC) launched a benchmark project for comparing the performance of 9 American universities in the field of international learning mobility. In the project, data for 21 indicators were collected to benchmark the participant universities' performance in promoting students' international learning (Potts, Ramirez, & Huckel, 2013).

In the UK, Ayoubi and Massoud (2007) identified three variables to examine the achievement of British universities in internationalization. The score of the three variables was consolidated into a single international factor for each institution and compared with the international strategy intent factor of the institution to judge whether a particular university is an internationalization-speaker or an internationalization-achiever. Also, a set of 66 tentative indicators was proposed by Krause, Coates, and James (2005) to monitor and measure the internationalization of HEIs in Australia.

Indicator sets have also been developed in European countries. In 2006, the Center for Higher Education Development (CHE) in Germany developed an instrument that included 186 key figures and indicators for HEIs to assess their performance in internationalization (Brandenburg & Federkeil, 2007). In the Netherlands, in 2007, a tool was designed by the Netherlands Organization for International Cooperation in Higher Education (Nuffic) to help universities map internationalization. Constituents of the Mapping Internationalization tool (MINT) include the goals of internationalization, international activities, facilities, quality assurance, and key figures (van Gaalen, 2009). Later in 2010, another set of indicators was established by German Academic Exchange Service (DAAD) to enable institutions to evaluate the level of internationalization and to compare themselves with peers (DAAD, 2010).

Most recently, more cross-border instruments have been established in the European region. For example, the IMPI project resulted in a set of transferable indicators, which captured 22 components of 9 dimensions of university internationalization. This indicator set aimed to meet the needs of different types of institutions in Europe for monitoring and assessing their internationalization performance. HEIs can select the relevant indicators from the set to accommodate their own needs (Beerkens et al., 2010). Another example is the EMQT, which incorporates both qualitative and quantitative approaches in helping HEIs practice internal and external assessment in terms of the quality of their student mobility (Managing Committee of the EMQT Project, 2011). Additionally, European Science Foundation (ESF) sponsored a project on developing internationalization indicators for research institutions in Europe, in which 9 indicators were selected for research performing organization to evaluate their internationalization (van den Besselaar, Inzelt, Reale, de Turckheim, & Vercesi, 2012). In accrediting HEIs according to the level of their internationalization, the IMS 2020 project, funded by European Commission, produced more than 100 indicators for labeling medical schools in Europe (Gajowniczek & Schlabs, 2013).

In addition, there has also been increasing interest in measuring university internationalization in Asian countries. In Japan, Osaka University set up a study to develop evaluation criteria for internationalization of Japanese HEIs. As a result, an 'a la carte menu' of indicators was established for both self-review and benchmarking purposes (Furushiro, 2006). Also, Paige (2005) arrived at a list of more than 80 indicators for assessing whether certain realities of internationalization are present in Japanese universities. In Taiwan, efforts were made by a couple of researchers to identify suitable indicators to capture the performance of universities in being internationalized. For example, as early as in 2007, Hsieh developed an indicator system that consists of eight major areas: international enrollment, domestic students' international awareness, research achievements, academic exchange, international cooperation, course content, administrative support, and faculty background. These areas are captured by 61 indicators. Cheng (2008) developed a set of indicators and a weighting system for internal and third-party assessment of internationalization at Taiwan's universities of technology. In 2009, Chen studied five universities and came up with 74 indicators of internationalization grouped into six dimensions: teachers, students, research, curriculum, international visibility, and administration and campus. Chin and Ching (2009) built up three lists of indicators based on practitioner, expert, and student perspectives, respectively. The issue of measuring university internationalization also drew the attention of Chinese scholars. A set of 18 indicators was generated for ranking HEIs in Mainland Chinese in terms of internationalization (Chen, Zeng, Wen, Weng, & Yu, 2009). The cross-border approach is also appreciated in Asian countries. In 2016, UNESCO's Asia and Pacific Regional Bureau for Education in Bangkok, Thailand, hosted a meeting of high-level education officials to discuss drawing up a range of indicators on higher education internationalization in the ten member states of the Association of Southeast Asian Nations (ASEAN) plus Australia, China, India, Japan, New Zealand, and South Korea—a group referred to as ASEAN+6 (Sharma, 2016).

Other than the studies and projects mentioned above, other instruments have also been developed to help assess university internationalization. For example, the Netherlands Flemish Accrediting Association (NVAO) has established a certificate for institutional internationalization, containing six standards for evaluating degree programs, with potential ratings in each category of unsatisfactory, satisfactory, good, or excellent (NVAO, 2011). Additionally, the CeQuInt project conducted by European Consortium for Accreditation in higher education developed an assessment framework that can be used to evaluate the internationalization of a program or an institution and which, if completed successfully, can lead to the award of a European Certificate for Internationalization (Aerden & Weber, 2013). As the focus of the project is the indicators of internationalization and indicators were not included in those tools, they are not discussed in detail in this review.

Similarities and Differences in Existing Instruments

In this section, the various available tools will be closely examined to identify similarities and differences in a number of aspects, including the context of the tool applied to; target audience; the purposes of the tool (self-assessment, comparison/benchmarking, ranking, classification or accreditation); the unit of measurement (program, department or institution); the approach used to developing the instrument; the participant involved in developing the instrument (e.g., experts or stakeholders); and the method of data collection (institutional surveys, peer reviews or external database). A summary of all these distinctive features of each existing instrument is provided in Appendix B.

National Context and Target Audience

Instruments for measuring university internationalization have been developed to accommodate a variety of audiences and different contexts. Most of the available tools are constructed to serve a particular national context, such as the project launched by Osaka University in Japan and the indicator set established by Chen et al. (2009) that focuses on the Chinese context. Other projects aim to serve a broader context, usually at regional or even international level. For example, the IMPI project tends to provide an instrument that could be applied to the European region first and then globally. Other examples include the EMQT, IMS 2020, and the project sponsored by ESF to develop indicators for research institutions in Europe. It is interesting to note that the first attempt made to measure university internationalization, the IQRP, intends to be international in application, which aims at serving HEIs in both developed and developing countries. It may indicate that the measurement of internationalization itself was born with a cross-border purpose.

Some of the available measures are designed to serve a particular type of HEIs. For example, the five-point-scale measurement designed by ACE and the indicator set established in Horn et al.'s (2007) study target at research universities. The IMS 2020 is tailored for medical schools exclusively. Other projects attempt to develop measurements that have the potential to accommodate a wide range of users including large and small, comprehensive and specialized, private and public institutions, such as the IQRP, MINT, and the EMQT.

Purposes

Measurement tools are generally used for three purposes: (1) self-evaluation, examining the strength and weakness of an institution in a particular area; (2) comparisons (benchmarking), setting an organizational identity or profiling, showing both internal and external stakeholders the strengths and ambitions of an organization in general or in a specific field; and (3) classification/ranking, knowing where an organization stands in a group. Additionally, they might be used to provide information for the wider public or for experts and academics involved in a certain domain (Shavelson, 1991).

In many cases, the purpose of assessment tools is to help institutions analyze their own situations (self-evaluation). Self-evaluation is internal assessment, aimed at measuring the institutional performance in relation to its own objectives and targets. As such, self-evaluation does not serve a public purpose nor say anything about the institution's relative performance. The internal value of self-assessment is that it enables an institution to identify weaknesses and areas for possible improvements. The assessment tool developed in the IQRP and the indicator set established by van den Besselaar et al. (2012) intend to only serve a self-evaluation purpose. Sometimes, however, an internal self-evaluation can have an external component such as peer review process or panel visit. In this case, implicit comparison with other institutions might be made.

If the institution explicitly wants to know where it stands vis-à-vis competitors, measures can be developed for benchmarking, which enable comparisons to be made between institutions or between an institution and the average of a peer group (Beerkens et al., 2010). Comparison is one of the ultimate purposes to develop measurements (Dickson & Lim, 1991; Gaither, 1994; Jarratt, 1985; Ogawa & Collom, 1998; Selden, 1985; Sizer, Spee, & Bormans, 1992). Different from self-evaluation, the targets and standards used in comparison are external and relative. Comparisons can be made against an absolute standard or reference point (Oakes, 1986). In the case of comparing institutional internationalization performance, there are no inherent, absolute standards or reference points to judge the 'goodness,' or there may be no standard on which everyone could agree. For example, HEIs intend to increase the number of international students in order to internationalize the campus life and students' experience. However, it is not clear how many international students are required to achieve the goal. In this circumstance, reference to peers' performance or to past performance may be the only reasonable way to make comparisons. Comparing across time or locations does not tell whether conditions are bad or good; it only shows whether things are better or worse (Oakes, 1986).

Comparison with like institutions could just be the first step. The ultimate purpose is to identify the good practice or weaknesses of an institution and then initiate efforts to improve policy development, management, and administration. Learning from good practice could probably bring the institution on a par with the leaders in the field. For example, in the CIC benchmark project, data were collected from 9 universities in the United States in relation to their performance of promoting student mobility, in order to make comparisons between the institutions and to set examples of good practice.

Both self-evaluation and comparison have an internal function, usually aiming at improvement. Other indicator sets have been specifically designed with the intention of ranking, classifying, or accrediting institutions. For these purposes, standards and criteria are set outside of the institution, often by external parties. Another important difference with benchmarking is that university rankings are not primarily intended to be used as management tools for quality improvement, but rather aim to provide the public with information on the relative performance of institutions (Beerkens et al., 2010). The empirical study conducted by Ayoubi and Massoud (2007) served the purpose of classification. In their study, 117 British universities were classified into four clusters: international losers, international speakers, international winners, and international actors, according to the extent a given university's international strategic intent declaration matched with its real international achievements. In Horn et al.'s (2007) study, data of 19 indicators were collected to rank internationalization performance of 77 top universities in the United States.

Attempts made to develop measures for university internationalization may merely serve the purpose of research, and therewith, the focus may be academics and experts. The objective here is more to start a discussion. Examples are the indicator sets developed by Chin and Ching (2009), which investigated different stakeholder groups' perception of indicators that should be taken into account when assessing HEIs' internationalization performance in Taiwan, and the indicator set established in Krause et al.'s (2005) study for measuring internationalization of HEIs in Australia.

Measurements could also be designed for multi-purposes. Many available tools for assessing university internationalization fall into this category, such as the MINT, and the instrument developed in the projects conducted by Paige (2005) and by DAAD (2010). All of them aim to serve a combination of self-evaluation and benchmarking purposes. Additionally, the IMS 2020 aims at developing an 'International Medical School' label, providing standards and guidelines that will allow medical schools to compare their internationalization statuses and identify top international medical schools. The 'International Medical School' label enables the tool to perform an accreditation function.

Unit of Measurement

Instruments also have been designed for measuring different units. One could assess the institution as a whole, focusing on the central-level strategies and activities, such as the tools developed in IQRP, by Paige (2005) and by Ayoubi and Massoud (2007). Others might aim at a decentralized measurement such as at the faculty, school, and departmental levels or even take a program as the unit of analysis. For example, the IMS 2020 was designed to provide school or departmental measurement of internationalization. Some instruments can provide multi-level assessment like the IMPI. The indicators suggested in the project can be used for any unit, including program, department, school, and the entire institution. Since internationalization does not develop evenly nor possess the same features across different parts of an institution, central-level measurements may mask the differences between disciplines or units.

Approaches to Developing Instruments

One of the major issues with current instruments for measuring university internationalization is the approach adopted in different projects to develop the measures. The majority of studies may document the participants engaged in developing the instrument in the methodology section, but fail to clarify the approach in which the concept of university internationalization is constructed and the metrics or rubrics are generated. The approach adopted in most previous projects is neither explicitly stated nor adequately justified. An inappropriate approach may jeopardize the validity of the final instrument since it is closely related to how the phenomenon being measured is conceptualized.

As developing measurements for university internationalization is a relatively new practice, lessons can be borrowed from the two main approaches used to design educational indicators, which have been a priority on the policy agenda since the mid-1980s. Considerable theoretical work has been done to explore reliable ways to develop educational indicators. The two alternative approaches that dominate in the literature are the 'model approach' and the 'framework approach.' Most indicator schemes use some sort of input/output model. The same approach has been adopted for education as many scholars contend that one must first adopt a model of the educational system in order to develop measurements (Cooley, 1992; McEwen, 1993; Nuttall, 1994; Shavelson, McDonnell, & Oakes, 1989). A model enables educators to identify the key elements of education that they want to measure and specifies the key areas of interest. Moreover, models include the theoretical relationships between the components. These components are operationalized into measurable entities, and causal relationships between measured components inferred linearly, meaning that different components are defined as input, process, or output (Bottani, 1996; Nuttall, 1994). To this day, the RAND Corporation's inputs–process–outputs model (see Oakes, 1986; Shavelson, McDonnell, Oakes, & Carey, 1987) is the most widely cited in the literature. Other models borrow heavily from RAND's model and make their own modifications (e.g., McEwen, 1993; Porter, 1991; Scheerens, 1992).

Some academics are skeptical of these 'models' given their mechanistic and academic approach, and the potential that they are externally imposed upon institutions (Bramley, 1995; Bryk & Hermanson, 1993).

Criticisms of the model approach eventually led to the 'framework approach' as a more flexible and dynamic alternative for devising assessment tools (see Cuttance, 1994; Gray & Wilcox, 1994). A framework is generally understood as a structure for organizing domains of interests. By constructing or adopting a framework, instrument designers are still able to identify the key dimensions of interest without committing themselves to any mechanistic model. Frameworks do not usually imply causal relations between different components (Ogawa & Collom, 1998; Wyatt, 1994).

Although the 'framework approach' shares many of the characteristics with the 'model approach,' it is still distinguishable from the 'model approach.' The 'model approach' is more academic and emphasizes on the causal relationship of different components. It may convey misleading political implications, encouraging a production function orientation and the external manipulation of the process as if the components represented in the model are disconnected causal links. The 'framework approach,' however, is featured with more flexibility, dynamics, and freedom in developing measures (Bottani, Delfau, Hutmacher, & Desmond, 1991). It suggests more prudent political implications. If university internationalization process is more like an organic system, then any policy action may result in much more complex and pervasive consequences, which means if an action has certain intended effects, it will often produce a wide range of other effects throughout the process. The frameworks chosen for constructing assessment tools may vary, but they must represent the phenomenon of interest and identify its most important components.

Among the existing instruments for university internationalization, only Brandenburg and Federkeil's (2007) study adopted the 'input-output model approach.' In their project, factors contributing to the creation of findings (such as staff structure, curricular, and resources) were subsumed under input indicators, whereas output indicators measured findings at the end of academic processes (e.g., graduates or research finds). In all other projects and studies, although the researcher did not indicate explicitly the approach they adopted to develop the instrument, indeed, they employed the 'framework approach,' identifying the key dimensions of internationalization that they intended to measure and then developed indicators accordingly. The reason for abandoning the 'model approach' could be twofold. Firstly, internationalization is such a complex phenomenon that it may be unreasonable to assume in practice that variables related to university internationalization are clearly defined. For example, the ability to distinguish between different elements of internationalization and how they might be categorized as inputs or outputs may be more opaque than clear (Beerkens et al., 2010). Some output factors (e.g., the number of international students) can directly be turned into input factors (e.g., for an international classroom). Secondly, internationalization is not the goal in itself; it is a means to other ends (de Wit, 2011; Green, 2012; Krause et al., 2005). From this perspective, the whole process of internationalization could be seen as an input or process factor that influences the ultimate outcomes of higher education.

Among the instruments developed through the 'framework approach,' some of them were derived from an existing framework of internationalization. For example, in Horn et al.'s (2007) study, five key domains of international education were derived based on Mestenhauser's (2002) framework.[1] More commonly (see, e.g., the IQRP, IMPI, EMQT, MINT, and IMS 2020), no explicit framework was employed or established, and instruments were designed based on consultants/experts, the researcher or other stakeholders' knowledge and judgment of the phenomenon, identifying the domains of internationalization that the tool intended to measure. The domains figured out in different projects varied from one to the other.

---

[1] Mestenhauser (2002) uses a system perspective to portray several key learning domains of international education and 'perspectives' through which the domains can be examined. The learning domains are composed of international studies and relations; area studies; foreign languages; international dimensions of academic disciplines; educational exchanges; development contracts and interuniversity agreements; and organizations, administration, policy, governance, and financing. By combining these learning domains and variables relevant to research universities, Horn et al. (2007) result with five rubrics: student characteristics, scholar characteristics, the international research orientation, curriculum content, and organizational support.

Participants Involved in Developing Measurements

Different parties can be involved in the process of developing measurements for internationalization. Instruments can be constructed based on consultants/experts or the researcher's knowledge and judgment. The expert-based method is also known as the Delphi method, which has been widely employed in previous studies such as the IQRP, DAAD's (2010) project, Krause et al. (2005), Green (2005), and Horn et al.'s (2007) studies as well.

In some recent projects, different stakeholder groups also have been engaged in the process of instrument development. In measuring internationalization, institutions are probably the most obvious stakeholders to engage in such a consultation. The capacity of a measurement to drive improvement is determined by whether people see them as providing relevant and reasonable information on targeted phenomenon. This work is suggested to begin with a range of stakeholders' reviews. For example, in the IMPI project, representatives from six meta-level institutions were involved from the initial stage of the project. Similarly, representatives from member organizations were actively engaged in the IMS 2020 project. Within an institution, various stakeholder groups can be involved in the enquiry such as university policymakers, academics, administrators, and students. Chin and Ching (2009) proposed their indicator sets by interviewing 22 internationalization officers, 3 scholars in related fields, and 35 international students from different HEIs in Taiwan.

Methods to Collect Data

A final distinctive element of the available instruments is the manner in which data have been collected. Not all the available tools have been put into practice. Data were only collected in some studies for the purpose of piloting the instrument. Basically, there are two levels of data resource: publicly accessible data and institutional data. Since measuring university internationalization performance remains a relatively new practice, the external accessibility of data is limited. Normally, data are collected through institutional surveys. In Green (2005), Chen et al. (2009), and DAAD's (2010) studies as well as in the MINT, IMPI, EMQT, and CIC benchmarking projects, data were collected in this manner.

The main concern of these institutional self-reported data is the lack of objectivity, particularly in the case where politically sensitive data are requested or when clear normative values are attached to the measurement, institutions might be inclined to 'massage' their data (Beerkens et al., 2010). To deal with this, external components such as peer review or panel visits are sometimes used as a complimentary. For example, in the IQRP, a peer review team was established, consisting of three or four members, to visit the evaluated institution and develop a peer review report for it. The report provided by the team gave comments on the quality of the institutional self-assessment report and suggested possible improvement initiatives (Knight & de Wit, 1999).

Another way to increase the objectivity of data is to limit the measurement to criteria that can be checked externally (e.g., quantitative indicators) as opposed to data that is intrinsically subjective or at least very hard to make objective (e.g., qualitative standards or guidelines) and collect the data through publicly accessible channels such as databases or (inter)-national statistical offices. Horn et al. (2007) developed their indicator set by only taking the publicly accessible indicators into account and collected all the data through different public databases and institutions' Web sites. Also, Ayoubi and Massoud (2007) adopted only three variables as the proxies of international achievements of 117 British universities, of which the data were also publicly accessible. They collected the data from Higher Education Statistics Agency in the UK.

Relying on external, objective sources to provide data may increase the validity or trustworthiness of the final measurement; however, it has its own limitations. Without available comprehensive statistics in relation to internationalization, data that can be gained from public channels remain limited. Even within institutions, data on internationalization are not regularly recorded. If the instrument only depends on external resources, it is very likely to make a partial rather than an all-round measurement. In order to make a comprehensive and in-depth assessment, information that is only accessible to the institutions themselves is required.

Indicators as Preferred Measurements

Among the various tools available, it could be noticed that although they are varying in nature (some are quantitative measurements and others are a mixture of quantitative and qualitative measurements), quantitative indicators are included in almost every single instrument. The instruments designed by Ayoubi and Massoud (2007), Horn et al. (2007), and Chen et al. (2009) consist of quantitative indicators exclusively. Other instruments, such as IMPI, IMS 2020, and CIC International Mobility Benchmark, are also composed of indicators and complemented by qualitative metrics.

Why indicators are favored by scholars to be employed for measuring university internationalization performance? As a straightforward, intelligible, self-explanatory, and relatively objective tool, indicators have served analytical and evaluative purposes in the education field for a long time.[2] The overriding purpose of indicators is to characterize the nature of a system through its components, to illustrate how they are related and how they change over time (Shavelson, 1991). They are increasingly used by policymakers for decision-making (Dickson & Lim, 1991; Gaither, 1994; Oakes, 1986; van den Besselaar et al., 2012).[3] Unlike statistics, which aim at measuring facts, indicators refer to conceptual models coming from research. They embed normative

---

[2]Since the mid-1980s, educational indicators have been a priority on education and policy agenda. Considerable theoretical work and empirical studies have been done in efforts to develop reliable and useful educational indicators at state, national, and international levels (Ogawa & Collom, 1998; Tuijnman & Bottani, 1994; Wyatt, 1994). International interest in educational indicators has been driven by the concerns on expanding the enrollment capacity of education system while simultaneously improving the quality of education. Policymakers realized that these goals set high demands on policy analysis and, accordingly, that the comparative knowledge base in education was in need of improvement (Tuijnman & Bottani, 1994). In this circumstance, various educational indicators were developed to serve measurement and evaluation purposes.

[3]The policy-relevant purposes that indicators serve imply that the selection of a set of indicators should base on an understanding of which components of the system are critical to its health and which features signal important changes in its condition (Dickson & Lim, 1991; Gaither, 1994; Oakes, 1986).

choices. In this sense, they are proxies of the phenomena they represent (Barre, 2001). The use of indicators ultimately involves comparisons—against oneself, a norm, or others (Dickson & Lim, 1991; Gaither, 1994; Selden, 1985; Sizer et al., 1992).[4] With the reliable, strategic, and comparable information provided by indicators, boards and administrators can understand more fully about the condition of their institution, from then, to formulate improved policies and strategies for more distinctive competitive position (Taylor, Meyerson, & Massy, 1993). Due to the versatile feature of indicators, in seeking to measure university internationalization, they have the potential to serve as valid and convenient tools to provide information needed.

Dimensions and Indicators of University Internationalization

As discussed in the previous chapter, no consensus has been achieved on the key components of university internationalization. The lack of a clear conceptual framework has led to the variation in the dimensions and components identified and captured by the range of existing instruments. Designers of various measures have to make their own decisions on the domains of internationalization that could be assessed by their instruments. Some instruments were designed to measure a particular dimension of internationalization rather than providing a holistic assessment. A simple example is the CIC benchmarking project, in which only student mobility is captured. The indicator project conducted by van den Besselaar et al. (2012) serves another example. In this project, the internationalization of research is the only domain assessed by the proposed indicator set. Additionally, the EMQT focuses exclusively on the mobility of students and staff.

---

[4]It is interesting to notice that even in the initial phase of educational indicators development, efforts (e.g., OECD, 1992) were made to establish a cross-national system for comparisons.

More often, instrument designers aim to offer a comprehensive assessment of university internationalization. The dimensions and components identified in different projects vary significantly. In this study, the term 'dimension' is distinguished from 'component.' A dimension is used to describe an aspect of university internationalization, which is an aggregated concept. A dimension may consist of several components, which center on the dimension and mirror different facets of the dimension. In some studies, indicators or qualitative guidelines were developed to capture diverse dimensions, and these dimensions were not further divided into smaller units, or components. For example, in Chin and Ching's (2009) work, 12 dimensions of university internationalization were identified. Similarly, in Horn et al.'s (2007) study, an indicator set was established to capture five broad aspects of university internationalization. In other projects, dimensions were identified and further divided into several components. The indicator set presented by Krause et al. (2005) captured 17 components of internationalization, which were clustered into five dimensions. Indicators were designed to measure 10 dimensions, which consist of 40 components in Paige's (2005) work. Also, in the IMPI project, 9 dimensions were pointed out, involving 22 components of university internationalization.

As determining the dimensions and components to be included in an instrument is a crucial step in developing measurements, in this section current instruments are closely cross-checked for two purposes. Firstly, the cross-check helps identify the key dimensions and components that could be measured by indicators. Secondly, by cross-checking the indicators that have been developed in previous studies, a list of available indicators is generated.

Key Dimensions and Components

The quantitative nature of indicators determines that not all components of university internationalization can be measured by indicators. Indicators are more likely to capture those components that can easily be quantified. By cross-checking the current instruments, elements that can be captured by indicators were identified. Specifically, 18 measurable components have been acknowledged in most instruments as indicative of an institution's internationalization performance. These components can be grouped to reflect five dimensions of university internationalization, as shown in Table 3.1. Either the component or the dimension was termed and grouped in different ways in the previous studies. The terminology and typology used in this study suggest one way to define and cluster the elements.

Elements in relation to university governance have been recognized as crucial factors affecting institutional internationalization performance and built into measurements in the majorities of previous studies. Only in the projects that aimed to design an instrument for assessing a particular aspect of internationalization, such as the EMQT and CIC benchmarking projects, were governance-related components excluded. The significance of the governance dimension in university international strategies was explained in the previous chapter. This dimension involves five components. The first is the human resource (personnel) allocated for internationalization initiatives within an institution like the establishment of an international office and the assignment of a rector or vice-chancellor for international affairs. Financial investment in internationalization activities is another commonly mentioned component. In some studies (e.g., Horn et al., 2007), the established infrastructure to facilitate internationalization such as the available reference in international collections and the accommodation for overseas students were regarded as part of university governance. In other studies (e.g., Krause et al., 2005), the scope of the governance dimension was even extended to include cooperative agreements, partnerships, and networks with other HEIs. And finally, the international presence of a university is another component that is included in the governance dimension (e.g., DAAD, 2010).

As discussed in Chapter 2, the best-known strategy for internationalization is internationalizing the student body and promoting student mobility. It is not surprising that students, as one of the key dimensions of internationalization, have been included in almost all available instruments and a wide range of indicators has been developed to measure it. Basic elements that constitute this dimension include international students on campus, which could be further divided into

Table 3.1 Dimensions and components measured by indicators

Dimension	Component	Study/project
Governance	Human resources for international activities	IQRP, Paige (2005), Green (2005), Krause et al. (2005), Osaka University Project, Ayoubi and Massoud (2007), Brandenburg and Federkeil (2007), Horn et al. (2007), Chin and Ching (2009), Chen et al. (2009), MINT Project, IMPI Project, IMS 2020 Project
	Financial support for international initiatives	
	Infrastructures and facilities	
	Network and partnerships	
	Institutional international presence	
Student	International students	IQRP, Paige (2005), Green (2005), Krause et al. (2005), Ayoubi and Massoud (2007), Brandenburg and Federkeil (2007), Horn et al. (2007), Chin and Ching (2009), Chen et al. (2009), MINT Project, DAAD Project, IMPI Project, EMQT Project, IMS 2020 Project, CIC Benchmarking Project
	Mobility of students	
	Overseas opportunities for graduates	
Staff	International profile of faculty	IQRP, Paige (2005), Green (2005), Krause et al. (2005), Osaka University Project, Brandenburg and Federkeil (2007), Horn et al. (2007), Chin and Ching (2009), Chen et al. (2009), MINT Project, DAAD Project, IMPI Project, EMQT Project, IMS 2020 Project
	International perspective of faculty	
Curriculum	Courses with an international component	IQRP, Paige (2005), Green (2005), Krause et al. (2005), Osaka University Project, Brandenburg and Federkeil (2007), Horn et al. (2007), Chin and Ching (2009), Chen et al. (2009), MINT Project, DAAD Project, IMPI Project, IMS 2020 Project
	Requirements for international studies	
	Students' participation in international studies	
	Joint degree programs	
Research	Internationally cooperative research programs	IQRP, Green (2005), Krause et al. (2005), Osaka University Project, Brandenburg and Federkeil (2007), Horn et al. (2007), Chin and Ching (2009), Chen et al. (2009), MINT Project, DAAD Project, IMPI Project, van den Besselaar et al. (2012), IMS 2020 Project
	Internationally focused research centers	
	International research students	
	Internationally acknowledged research achievements	

full-time fee-paying and short-term exchange international students, learning mobility of students, and overseas opportunities for graduates.

Components related to the internationalization of faculty are also widely included in existing measures. Exceptions include van den Besselaar et al.'s (2012) study, in which indicators were developed for the research aspect of internationalization exclusively, and the CIC benchmarking project that designed the instrument for measuring student learning mobility alone. Here, the term 'faculty' refers to academic (teaching and researching) staff in an institution. The administrative staff are not taken into account. The international characteristics of an institution's faculty can be reflected in two facets. One is the international profile of the faculty team, which is usually measured by the percentage of international faculty and the number of international visiting scholars. The other is the international perspective of faculty members. In fact, this dimension is closely related to the next curriculum dimension as international perspectives of teaching staff determine to what extent teaching practices can be internationalized.

International perspective is a less tangible concept, and Sanderson (2011) suggests several criteria that embody it. According to him, if a teacher possesses an international perspective, he/she is supposed to:

- Incorporate internationalized content into subject material,
- Have a critical appreciation of one's own culture and its assumptions,
- Have some knowledge of other countries and cultures, but a preference for being open to and appreciating other worldviews,
- Use universal teaching strategies to enhance the learning experiences of all students,
- Understand the way one's academic discipline and its related profession are structured in a range of countries,
- Understand the internal labor market in relation to one's academic discipline.

Even with the criteria, it remains challenging to directly measure to what extent a lecturer has some knowledge of other countries and cultures or has a preference for being open to and appreciating other worldviews. To solve the problem, indicators related to the international experience of an academic staff are used as proxies for the international perspective of academic staff since lecturers who have studied and lived overseas are arguably more likely to have developed an international attitude.

Like the student dimension, elements in relation to 'international curricula' have been found in the majority of available measurements except the ones that were constructed for single dimension assessment. Although definitions of internationalized curricula are neither universal nor uncontested, operational definitions have been developed, including interdisciplinary approaches with an area or regional base, explicitly comparative curricula, subjects with an international focus, courses leading to internationally recognized professional qualifications, and curricula that were broadened by an international component (Leask, 2001; Welch, 2002). van der Wende (1996, p. 187) outlines nine elements that contribute to the internationalization of curriculum:

- An international subject,
- An international comparative approach,
- Content prepares students for defined international professions,
- Foreign languages or linguistics which explicitly address cross-culture communication issues and provide training in intercultural skills,
- Interdisciplinary programs such as regional and area studies, covering more than one country,
- Internationally recognized professional qualifications,
- Joint or double degree,
- Compulsory parts offered at institution(s) abroad, taught by local lectures,
- Content especially designed for foreign students.

In the existing assessment tools, indicators have been developed to measure four elements of the curriculum dimension: courses with an international component, requirements for international studies, students' participation in international studies, and joint degree programs.

The last generic dimension that can be identified from the current instruments is research. Compared with the other four dimensions, not all measurement designers include research as a separate dimension in their instruments. In some studies such as the DAAD (2010) project, the international character of research is measured by international/external funding. Others (e.g., Paige, 2005) do not involve any research-related elements in their measurement scheme. One possible explanation for the deliberate omission of the research dimension is the argument that any research-intensive university is by definition strongly internationalized in its research activities. In this case, there seems little point in trying to develop specific indicators for measuring internationalization of research, since the usual research performance indicators probably serve as suitable proxies for internationalization of research (Krause et al., 2005). For the tools that include the research dimension, four components are included in the dimension: internationally cooperative research programs, internationally focused research centers, international research students, and internationally acknowledged research achievements.

The above five dimensions cover most of the components identified in the previous chapter as crucial constituents of university internationalization strategies. However, some important elements are excluded, such as student security and welfare provision, pastoral and tutorial arrangements, and consultancy. This does not mean those omitted components are of no importance to the internationalization performance of HEIs or they should not be taken into account when building measurements for university internationalization. The only reason for the exclusion of those elements is that they are difficult to quantify, and thus, indicators can provide little meaningful information. Some of them were included in some of the existing instruments, measured by qualitative evaluation standards (e.g., yes/no questions). Only in MINT and IMPI were there indicators that measured service-related components, such as 'the number of student and staff use different types of services provided in the unit.'

The dimensions and components that can be captured by indicators suggest that university internationalization is not an intangible concept without measurable elements. Most components of the phenomenon have the potential to be quantified and measured by indicators. The preconditions to establish a set of indicators in this study have been met.

Available Indicators

The term 'indicator' was not used consistently in all existing studies on measuring university internationalization and tended to be misused to include all kinds of descriptive information. Across different educational settings, various definitions of indicators have been proposed by different scholars (e.g., Dickson & Lim, 1991; Lashway, 2001; Oakes, 1986; Ogawa & Collom, 1998; Selden, 1985; Shavelson, 1991) and have resulted in a consensus on the quantitative nature of indicators. Qualitative information, such as perceptions collected through surveying and demonstrative data like specific examples that represent standards, are more likely to be regarded as complementary to indicators (Jongbloed & Westerheijden, 1994).

By examining all the available indicators developed in previous research, about 200 of them align with the definition of indicator used in this study, presenting quantitative values of university internationalization performance. These indicators are not mutually exclusive. Many of them convey similar meanings with slightly different choices of words. By combining the similar indicators to avoid repetition, around 150 indicators remained. The 150 indicators can be categorized into two groups: one is a key figure, which presents a value without any reference to other values (e.g., the number of international students), while the other describes such a key figure in relation to some other figures (e.g., the proportion of international students in relation to the total number of students on the campus), which may eliminate the effect of variation in size. The latter type of indicators has better capacity in serving a comparison purpose because they are immune to the impact of the size of a particular institution.

The available indicators are also presented at different levels of aggregation. For example, the international profile of the student body of a given institution can be measured by the indicator of 'percentage of international students on campus' as an entity or by split indicators like 'percentage of international undergraduates and postgraduates' separately. Split indicators may help portray a more in-depth and all-round picture of the situation. However, they may bring the risk of making an indicator set over complicated and minimize the transferability of the indicator across different contexts. Indeed, as the study proceeds, more indicators have emerged in other studies, and the number increased to more than 500. However, a close examination of these new indicators shows that they have not changed the approach adopted in the present study since most of the new indicators are oversplit. For example, the IMPI project finished with 35 indicators that were suggested to measure the financial support component. The component was divided into more than ten sub-units and for each sub-unit, more than three indicators could be used to assess the performance.

Indicators are favored by practitioners and researchers as a means of measurement because of their simplicity and operability. An immediate challenge in developing an indicator set is to balance simplicity and comprehensiveness. One cannot achieve both goals; compromise is inevitable (Stecher & Koretz, 1996). In the literature, simplicity is often advocated, even if it seems less attractive technically (Ewell & Jones, 1994). Numerous authors have argued that an extensive indicator set would be unmanageable (James, 2003; Shavelson et al., 1989), too complex (Blank, 1993), and lacking utility (Porter, 1991). Moreover, equipment, funding, time, and human resources are required for collecting, analyzing, and reporting data; therefore, a comprehensive set of indicators would be very costly to develop and maintain (Oakes, 1986; Pollard, 1989).

Another problem with oversplit indicators is transferability. If the indicator is designed to measure a very specific internationalization program or initiative, it could be highly sensitive to the context and may not be applicable to various contexts. For example, in order to assess student mobility, indicators of 'the proportion of students who undertake an internship abroad' and 'the proportion of students who participate in international summer schools' could be employed. However, given the diverse exchange programs developed in different HEIs, these indicators may not be applicable in every university and then cannot be used for benchmarking. A more aggregated indicator like 'the proportion of students who have international academic experiences' would be better in terms of transferability. Indeed, indicators are expected to capture significant parts of the phenomenon being measured but not necessarily all or even most parts of it (Gray, 1990). Given the above considerations, oversplit indicators were excluded in this project.

Since most of the current instruments are generally national or regional in scope, some indicators are not suitable for international comparison. For example, 'the number of Peace Corps volunteers' was adopted as an indicator to measure the student dimension in Horn et al.'s (2007) study. However, in any context other than the United States, this indicator would be irrelevant and invalid. On a practical level, it would be desirable that indicators are generic enough to enable meaningful comparison across institutions, disciplines, and programs. Striking a balance between the alternative demands of being generic and sensitive challenges the development of any indicator set (Krause et al., 2005).

Filtering the oversplit indicators and indicators that can be only applied to a particular context, 98 indicators remained as the indicator pool for developing the indicator set in this study (see Table 3.2).

Limitations of Indicators

Indicators only can provide a snapshot of what is happening about internationalization and cannot substitute for a comprehensive in-depth assessment of all aspects of the performance (Porter, 1988; Shavelson, 1991). They cannot meet all data needs, portray the phenomenon perfectly, or show cause-and-effect relationships (Pollard, 1989). They do not tell everything about the situation. Instead, indicators can provide a 'at a glance' indication of the current conditions (Oakes, 1986). The information gained from indicators suggests that precision of measurement is often unattainable. Therefore, indicators should be modestly regarded as signals or guides rather than absolute measures (Bottani et al., 1991; Sizer et al., 1992). Given the nature and characteristics of indicators, not all aspects valued in internationalization can be easily quantified and measured by indicators. Qualitative measures are necessary for some of the vital components that defy quantification. Indicators are less capable of replacing a fuller assessment that looks at internationalization as part of an in-depth self-evaluation and audit of the organizational process.

Table 3.2 A short list of available indicators for university internationalization

Dimension	Component	Indicator
Governance	Human resources for internationalization initiatives	Number of institutional-level administrative staff for international activities
		Percentage of department that have administrative staff for international activities
		Percentage of international administrative staff
		Number of languages that actual command by the administrative staff
		Proportion of employees with international experience (minimum 3 months) relative to the total number of international-related administrative staff
		Number of training programs for administrative staff in response to internationalization
		Number of training programs for administrative staff of partner institutions abroad in the past academic year
		Percentage of administrative staff who have taken part in international administration exchange programs
		Percentage of administrative staff who have taken in internationally oriented further training programs
	Financial support for internationalization initiatives	Percentage of total budget available (excluding personnel costs) for internationalization
		Funds per student available to support international student exchange (HEIs' internal funding)
		Funds per graduate student to support international research experiences
		Percentage of the HEIs' own funds for international visiting lecturers/professors in relation to the total budget for academic
		Amount of the HEIs' own funds for international projects with international cooperation partners per annum
		Percentage of budget available for international projects per annum
		Percentage of the total amount of scholarships for international doctoral candidates
		Number of available scholarships from university funds for international postdoctoral researchers
	Infrastructures and facilities	Percentage of books in international collection
		Percentage of journals in international collection

Dimension	Component	Indicator
	Institutional cooperation	Number of institutional-level memberships in international organizations and consortia
		Number of partnerships in which at least one mobility has taken place
		Number of programs offered through consortium
		Number of formal inter-institutional agreements
		Percentage of the partnerships in each region of the world (EU, Europe outside EU, Africa, Asia, North America, South America, Pacific, total)
		Total sum of scholarship for stay abroad (externally procured funding)
	International presence	Number of overseas offices
		Number of participations in fairs abroad
		Number of available languages of university's Web site
		Number of committee activities in international professional associations
Student	International students	Percentage of international students on campus
		Percentage of international undergraduate students on campus
		Percentage of international graduate students on campus
		Number of incoming international exchange students
		Number of international students attend joint or double/multiple degree programs
		Percentage of foreign students from different regions (e.g., EU, Europe outside EU, Africa, Asia, North America, South America, Pacific)
	Mobility of students	Number of programs organized abroad
		Number of programs for undergraduate international research experience
		Percentage of student participation in study abroad and student exchange
		Ratio of the outgoing students to incoming students
		Number of incoming international exchange students in relation to the number of partnership agreements
		Number of outgoing exchange students in relation to the number of partnership agreements

(continued)

Table 3.2 (continued)

Dimension	Component	Indicator
	Overseas opportunities for graduates	Percentage of graduates of foreign nationality
		Percentage of graduates with joint or double/multiple degrees
	Interaction of international and domestic students	N/A
Faculty	International profile of the faculty team	Percentage of international faculty members
		Number of international visiting staff for academic purposes per year
		Total number of days of stay of all international visiting staff for academic purposes per year
	International perspective and experience of faculty	Percentage of faculty who holds overseas degrees
		Percentage of faculty with highest academic qualification awarded by an institution abroad
		Percentage of faculty proficient in a language other than the primary language of teaching/research
		Percentage of faculty who have held a visiting lectureship abroad
		Percentage of faculty undertaking international staff exchanges or sabbaticals
		Percentage of faculty who has at least one-year overseas experience
		Number of faculty with international experience in the past academic year
		Percentage of faculty participating in international research projects
		Number of training programs for faculty members in response to internationalization
		Percentage of faculty who have spent at least 1 semester abroad in the past academic year
		Number of faculty taking intercultural training in the past academic year
		Number of faculty taking English language training in the past academic year

Dimension	Component	Indicator
Curriculum	Courses with an international component	Number of courses offering foreign language studies
		Number of foreign language teaching hours per week
		Number of course partnerships set up with institutions in other countries
		Percentage of programs available through online learning modes
		Percentage of programs available for offshore delivery
		Percentage of courses in which teaching and assessment occur in languages other than the home country
		Percentage of courses taught wholly or partly in English
		Number of Bachelor programs offered in a foreign language
		Number of Master programs offered in a foreign language
		Number of PhD programs offered in a foreign language
		Percentage of courses that use foreign textbooks
		Percentage of courses with a mandatory period abroad
		Number of courses offered for countries/cultures/societies studies
	Requirements for international studies	Credits required for foreign language studies
	Students' participation in international studies	Number of domestic students registered in courses taught in foreign languages
		Number of students registered in courses of online learning modes
		Number of foreign students registered in courses taught in a foreign language
	Joint/double degree programs	Number of programs in which it is possible to obtain a degree in language other than the home country
		Number of international professional qualification offered
		Number of double or joint programs
		Percentage of students who attend joint or double/multiple degree program
	Internationally accredited courses	N/A

(continued)

Table 3.2 (continued)

Dimension	Component	Indicator
Research	Internationally cooperative research programs	Percentage of research projects involving international partnership and collaboration
		Percentage of research projects wholly funded by sources outside of host nation
		Percentage of research projects funded by international agencies (e.g., the World Bank)
		Amount of research funds from other countries
		Number of double doctoral degree
	Internationally focused research centers	Percentage of research centers focused on international research
	International research students	Percentage of international doctoral candidates
		Percentage of international postdoctoral researchers
		Percentage of doctoral candidates in double doctoral degree study programs
		Percentage of international doctoral candidates
		Percentage of international postdoctoral researchers
		Percentage of doctoral candidates in double doctoral degree study programs
	Internationally acknowledged research achievements	Number of international conferences organized by the HEI per year
		Number of presentation in international conferences per faculty member per year
		Number of participation (students/faculty/administrative staff) in international conferences (with qualified contribution) per year
		Number of publication cited in SCI, EI, ISTP per year
		Number of publications in international journals per faculty per year
		Percentage of academic publications (peer-review) published in English or another foreign language (non-English-speaking countries only)
		Number of faculty/students involved in articles published internationally in the past academic year
		Number of co-editorships in international journals
		Number of highly cited author (HiCi) according to Thomson 11
		Percentage of patents filed outside the country

Further, raw numbers rarely speak for themselves and cannot constitute an accountability system, but require careful interpretation. They merely provide information about the situation. No matter how sophisticated the data collected, they may not substitute for informed human judgment (Lashway, 2001; Oakes, 1986). Although indicators are desirable measures for policymakers, practitioners, and researchers to use for generating policy-relevant information, these limitations are suggested to be bear in mind when using indicators to measure university internationalization performance.

Summary

Valuable lessons can be learnt from previous endeavors to design measurements for university internationalization. The process of indicator development in this project is aided significantly by previous studies from where 98 indicators were identified to serve as the indicator pool. More importantly, the limitations of the existing instruments highlight the places that need particular attention in designing the indicator set in this project. Firstly, due to the lack of a clear construct for university internationalization, those available tools framed the phenomenon in their own ways, mostly from a Western perspective. Even for the instruments designed to accommodate HEIs in the Asian region (e.g., Chen et al., 2009; Chin & Ching, 2009), the way that internationalization was understood and conceptualized remained highly Western centered. By no means can be it assumed that the phenomenon takes place in exactly the same manner in those Asian counties nor can it be assumed that policymakers, practitioners and researchers from those countries interpret university internationalization in similar ways as their counterparts do in the Western countries. Therefore, in order to develop an indicator set that can be applied to various national and regional contexts, voices from different parts of the world need to be taken into account.

Secondly, current measurements were mostly developed by researchers without engaging university practitioners in the process. Only some of the recent projects such as MINT, IMPI, and EMQT incorporated practitioners in their instrument design. Since the ultimate audience of the indicator set developed in this study will be individual universities, practitioners' perceptions need to be highly valued. Their involvement will maximize the utility and acceptance of the instrument.

Thirdly, in some of the existing instruments, evidence suggests a 'mushrooming effect' (Beerkens et al., 2010), meaning the continuous growth in the number of indicators. Mushrooming leads to a very complex indicator system that might be unusable. Very extensive data might take so long to collect and analyze that the information would lose its timeliness. Mushrooming may also cause the devaluation of indicators. Rarely are indicators self-defined; therefore, a large number of indicators may require extensive explanation and a guide attached to the indicators and data collection procedure. As a result, the maneuverability of the whole set and the use of the indicators are much likely to be reduced (James, 2003; Oakes, 1986; Ogawa & Collom, 1998). The indicator set developed in this project is expected to involve an appropriate number of indicators, to make it feasible in terms of time, cost, and expertise required to collect the relevant information.

By reviewing the key issues in relation to university internationalization and its measurement, it is clear that in order to develop a new set of indicators, there are two major tasks. First is to establish a solid construct of the phenomenon, which outlines the generic key components that are involved in university internationalization practices in different countries. Second, appropriate indicators need to be selected to measure the components included in the construct.

References

Aerden, A., & Weber, M. (2013). *Frameworks for the assessment of quality in internationalisation* (Occasional Paper). Certificate for Quality in Internationalisation: European Consortium for Accreditation in Higher Education (ECA).

Ayoubi, R. M., & Massoud, H. K. (2007). The strategy of internationalization in universities: A quantitative evaluation of the intent and implementation in UK universities. *International Journal of Educational Management, 21*(4), 329–349.

Barre, R. (2001). Sense and nonsense of S&T productivity indicators. *Science and Public Policy, 28*(4), 259–266.

Beerkens, E., Brandenburg, U., Evers, N., van Gaalen, A., Leichsenring, H., & Zimmermann, V. (2010). *Indicator projects on internationalisation: Approaches, methods and findings* (A report in the context of the European project 'indicators for mapping & profiling internationalisation' (IMPI)). Gütersloh: CHE Consult GmbH.

Blank, R. K. (1993). Developing a system of education indicators: Selecting, implementing, and reporting indicators. *Educational Evaluation and Policy Analysis, 15*(1), 65–80.

Bottani, N. (1996). OECD international education indicators. *International Journal of Educational Research, 25*(3), 279–288.

Bottani, N., Delfau, I., Hutmacher, W., & Desmond, N. (1991). Lessons gained from the OECD/CERI international educational indicators project. In J. Hewton (Ed.), *Performance indicators in education: What can they tell us?* (pp. 35–42). Brisbane: Australian Conference of Directors-General of Education.

Bramley, G. (1995). *School performance indicators and school effectiveness: The conceptions and the critiques* (Working Papers in Education). Wolverhampton, UK: University of Wolverhampton.

Brandenburg, U., & Federkeil, G. (2007). *How to measure internationality and internationalisation of higher education institutions! Indicators and key figures*. Gütersloh: Centre for Higher Education Development.

Bryk, A. S., & Hermanson, K. L. (1993). Educational indicator systems: Observations on their structure, interpretation, and use. *Review of Research in Education, 19*(1), 451–484.

Burke, J. C., & Freeman, T. M. (1997). Performance indicators at SUNY and in New York: Where have we been? Where are we going? *Assessment Update, 9*(1), 3–15.

Chen, C.-G., Zeng, M.-C., Wen, D.-M., Weng, L.-X., & Yu, Z. (2009). The establishment of indicator system for the evaluation of internationalisation of research universities in China. *Peking University Education Review, 7*(4), 116–135 (in Chinese).

Cheng, J.-K. (2008). *Internationalization indicators for universities of technology* (Unpublished PhD thesis). http://ndltd.ncl.edu.tw/cgibin/gs32/gsweb.cgi?o=dnclcdr&s=id=%22097NTNU5037005%22.&searchmode=basic.

Chin, J. M.-C., & Ching, G. S. (2009). Trends and indicators of Taiwan's higher education internationalization. *Asia-Pacific Education Researcher, 18*(2), 185–203.

Cooley, W. W. (1992). *Educational indicators for Pennsylvania: Pennsylvania educational policy studies*. Pittsburgh, PA: Learning Research Development Center.

Cuttance, P. (1994). Monitoring educational quality through performance indicators for school practice. *School Effectiveness & School Improvement, 5*(2), 101–126.

DAAD. (2010). *Internationality at German universities: Concepts and collecting profile data*. German: German Academic Exchange Service (DAAD).

de Wit, H. (2011). Law of the stimulative arrears? In H. de Wit (Ed.), *Trends, issues and challenges in internationalisation of higher education* (pp. 7–23). Amsterdam: Centre for Applied Research on Economics and Management Hogeschool van Amsterdam.

Dickson, G. S., & Lim, S. (1991). *The development and use of indicators of performance in educational leadership*. Paper presented at the International Congress for School Effectiveness and Improvement, Cardiff, Wales.

Ewell, P. T., & Jones, D. P. (1994). Pointing the way: Indicators as policy tools in higher education. In S. Rupert (Ed.), *Charting higher education accountability: A sourcebook on state-level performance indicators* (pp. 6–16). Denver, CO: Education Commission of the States.

Forrester, G. (2011). Performance management in education: Milestone or millstone? *Management in Education, 25*(1), 5–9. https://doi.org/10.1177/0892020610383902.

Freeman, B. (2014). Benchmarking Australian and New Zealand university meta-policy in an increasingly regulated tertiary environment. *Journal of Higher Education Policy and Management, 36*(1), 74–87. https://doi.org/10.1080/1360080X.2013.861050.

Furushiro, N. (2006). *Developing evaluation criteria to assess the internationalization of universities* (Final Report Grant-in-Aid for Scientific Research). Osaka: Osaka University.

Gaither, G. (1994). *Measuring up: The promises and pitfalls of performance indicators in higher education* (ASHE-ERIC Higher Education Report No. 5). Washington, DC: George Washington University.

Gajowniczek, J., & Schlabs, T. (2013). *International medical school label methodology*. Retrieved 20 May 2014, from http://www.ims-2020.eu/downloads/FC_IMS_label_methodology.pdf.

Gray, J. (1990). The quality of schooling: Frameworks for judgement. *British Journal of Educational Studies, 38*(3), 204–223.

Gray, J., & Wilcox, B. (1994). Performance indicators: Flourish or perish. In K. A. Riley & D. Nuttall (Eds.), *Measuring quality: Education indicators-United Kingdom and international perspectives* (pp. 69–86). Bristol, PA: Falmer Press.

Green, M. F. (2005). *Measuring internationalization at research universities.* Washington, DC: American Council on Education.

Green, M. F. (2012). *Measuring and assessing internationalization.* Retrieved 21 June 2014, from http://www.nafsa.org/uploadedFiles/NAFSA_Home/Resource_Library_Assets/Publications_Library/MeasuringandAssessingInternationalization.pdf.

Horn, A. S., Hendel, D. D., & Fry, G. W. (2007). Ranking the international dimension of top research universities in the United States. *Journal of Studies in International Education, 11*(3–4), 330–358.

James, R. (2003). Suggestions relative to the selection of strategic system-level indicators to review the development of higher education. In A. Yonezawa & F. Kaiser (Eds.), *System-level and strategic indicators for monitoring higher education in the twenty-first century* (pp. 219–232). Bucharest: UNESCO-CEPES.

Jarmo, V., & Pentti, M. (2003). The impact of culture on the use of performance measurement information in the university setting. *Management Decision, 41*(8), 751–759. https://doi.org/10.1108/00251740310496260.

Jarratt, R. (1985). *Report of the steering committee for efficiency studies in universities.* London: Committee of Vice-Chancellors and Principles.

Johnes, J., & Taylor, J. (1990). *Performance indicators in higher education: UK universities.* Buckingham and Bristol, PA: Society for Research into Higher Education and Open University Press.

Jongbloed, B. W. A., & Westerheijden, D. F. (1994). Performance indicators and quality assessment in European higher education. *New Directions for Institutional Research, 1994*(82), 37–51.

Kallio, K.-M., & Kallio, T. J. (2014). Management-by-results and performance measurement in universities—Implications for work motivation. *Studies in Higher Education, 39*(4), 574–589. https://doi.org/10.1080/03075079.2012.709497.

Kallio, K.-M., Kallio, T. J., & Grossi, G. (2017). Performance measurement in universities: Ambiguities in the use of quality versus quantity in performance indicators. *Public Money & Management, 37*(4), 293–300. https://doi.org/10.1080/09540962.2017.1295735.

Knight, J., & de Wit, H. (1999). *Quality and internationalisation in higher education/Programme on institutional management in higher education.* Paris: Organisation for Economic Co-operation and Development.

Krause, K.-L., Coates, H., & James, R. (2005). Monitoring the internationalisation of higher education: Are there useful quantitative performance indicators? In M. Tight (Ed.), *International relations* (International perspectives on higher education research, Vol. 3, pp. 233–253). Bingley: Emerald.

Lashway, L. (2001). *Educational indicators: ERIC digest.* Eugene, OR: Eric Clearinghouse on Educational Management.

Leask, B. (2001). Bridging the gap: Internationalizing university curricula. *Journal of Studies in International Education, 5*(2), 100–115.

Managing Committee of the EMQT Project. (2011). *The outcomes of the EMQT project.* Retrieved 20 May 2014, from http://www.emqt.org/images/stories/Outcomes_of_the_EMQT_Project_Presentation.pdf.

McEwen, N. (1993). *Lessons from the educational quality indicators initiative.* Ottawa, ON: Canadian Educational Researchers' Association.

McLendon, M. K., Hearn, J. C., & Deaton, R. (2006). Called to account: Analyzing the origins and spread of state performance-accountability policies for higher education. *Educational Evaluation and Policy Analysis, 28*(1), 1–24. https://doi.org/10.3102/01623737028001001.

Mestenhauser, J. A. (2002). In search of a comprehensive approach to international and global education: A systems perspective. In W. Grünzweig & N. Rinehart (Eds.), *Rockin' in red square: Critical approaches to international education in the age of cyberculture* (pp. 165–213). Münster, Germany: Lit Verlag.

Nuttall, D. (1994). Choosing indicators. In OECD (Ed.), *Making education count: Developing and using international indicators* (pp. 79–97). Paris and Washington, DC: OECD Publications and Information Centre.

NVAO. (2011). *Frameworks for the assessment of internationalisation.* Retrieved 18 June 2014, from http://www.nvao.net/page/downloads/Beoordelingskader_BKK_Internationalisation_14-11-2011.pdf.

Oakes, J. (1986). *Educational indicators: A guide for policymakers.* CPRE Occasional Paper Series. Washington, DC: Center for Policy Research in Education.

OECD. (1992). *The OECD international education indicators: A framework for analysis.* Paris and Washington, DC: OECD Publications and Information Centre.

Ogawa, R., & Collom, E. (1998). *Educational indicators: What are they? How can schools and school districts use them?* Riverside: University of California, California Educational Research Cooperative.

Orr, D., Jaeger, M., & Schwarzenberger, A. (2007). Performance-based funding as an instrument of competition in German higher education. *Journal*

of Higher Education Policy and Management, 29(1), 3–23. http://www.tandfonline.com/loi/cjhe20.
Paige, R. M. (2005). Internationalization of higher education: Performance assessment and indicators. 名古屋高等教育研究, *5*(8), 99–122.
Pollard, J. S. (1989). *Developing useful educational indicator systems: Insights on educational policy and practice* (Number 15). Austin, TX: Southwest Educational Development Lab.
Porter, A. (1988). Indicators: Objective data or political tool? *Phi Delta Kappan, 69*(7), 503–508.
Porter, A. (1991). Creating a system of school process indicators. *Educational Evaluation and Policy Analysis, 13*(1), 13–29.
Potts, D., Ramirez, K., & Huckel, D. (2013). *CIC international learning mobility benchmark* (Public Report 2012). Retrieved from https://uma-broad.umn.edu/assets/files/PDFs/educators/cicInternationalMobility.pdf.
Radnor, Z. J., & Barnes, D. (2007). Historical analysis of performance measurement and management in operations management. *International Journal of Productivity and Performance Management, 56*(5–6), 384–396. https://doi.org/10.1108/17410400710757105.
Sanderson, G. (2011). Internationalisation and teaching in higher education. *Higher Education Research & Development, 30*(5), 661–676.
Scheerens, J. (1992). Process indicators of school functioning. In OECD (Ed.), *The OECD international education indicator: A framework for analysis* (pp. 53–76). Paris and Washington, DC: OECD Publications and Information Centre.
Selden, R. W. (1985). *Educational indicators: What do we need to know that we don't know now?* Washington, DC: National Center for Education Statistics.
Sharma, Y. (2016, November 25). The push for Asian higher education internationalisation indicators. *University World News.* Retrieved from http://www.universityworldnews.com/article.php?story=20161123124836365.
Shavelson, R. J. (1991). *What are educational indicators and indicator systems?* Washington, DC: Eric Clearinghouse on Tests, Measurement Evaluation.
Shavelson, R. J., McDonnell, L. M., & Oakes, J. (1989). *Indicators for monitoring mathematics and science education: A sourcebook.* Santa Monica, CA: RAND.
Shavelson, R. J., McDonnell, L. M., Oakes, J., & Carey, N. (1987). *Indicator systems for monitoring mathematics and science education.* Santa Monica, CA: RAND.
Sizer, J., Spee, A., & Bormans, R. (1992). The role of performance indicators in higher education. *Higher Education, 24*(2), 133–155.

Stecher, B. M., & Koretz, D. (1996). *Issues in building an indicator system for mathematics and science education*. Santa Monica, CA: RAND.

Taylor, B. E., Meyerson, J. W., & Massy, W. F. (1993). *Strategic indicators for higher education: improving performance*. Princeton, NJ: Peterson's.

Tuijnman, A., & Bottani, N. (1994). International education indicators: framework—Development and interpretation. In OECD (Ed.), *Making education count: Developing and using international indicators* (pp. 21–34). Paris and Washington, DC: OECD Publications and Information Centre.

van den Besselaar, P., Inzelt, A., Reale, E., de Turckheim, E., & Vercesi, V. (2012). *Indicators of internationalisation for research institutions: A new approach*. Retrieved from http://archives.esf.org/fileadmin/Public_documents/Publications/mof_indicators2.pdf.

van der Wende, M. (1996). *Internationalising the curriculum in Dutch higher education: An international comparative perspective* (PhD dissertation). Utrecht University, Utrecht, Netherlands.

van Gaalen, A. (2009). Developing a tool for mapping internationalisation: A case study. In H. de Wit (Ed.), *Measuring success in the internationalisation of higher education* (EAIE Occasional Paper No. 22, pp. 77–91). Amsterdam: European Association for International Education.

Welch, A. (2002). Going global? Internationalizing Australian universities in a time of global crisis. *Comparative Education Review, 46*(4), 433.

Wyatt, T. (1994). Education indicators: A review of the literature. In OECD (Ed.), *Making education count: Developing and using international indicators* (pp. 99–121). Paris and Washington, DC: OECD Publications and Information Centre.

Yorke, M. (1991). Performance indicators: Towards a synoptic framework. *Higher Education, 21*(2), 235–248.

Zhivan, A. (2017). The use of performance measurement in universities. *International Journal of Public Sector Management, 30*(2), 102–117. https://doi.org/10.1108/IJPSM-05-2016-0089.

4

China

Since the first modern HEI was founded in China in 1895, foreign elements have never been absent from China's higher education system (Welch & Cai, 2011; Yang, Liu, Dong, & Xu, 2011; Yang, Xia, & Yang, 2009; Yang, 2010). Indeed, one of the challenges that has been faced by Chinese scholars and educational practitioners over more than a century is the smooth and equal integration of Chinese education traditions and the Western educational philosophies and methods. As early as the late Qing period, Chinese scholars began to study Western models of universities and started to establish academic contacts. But at that time, the purpose of learning Western knowledge and technology—including models of higher education—was to assist China in gaining the strength of Western powers; in other words, they desired to 'Learn the techniques of the Barbarians in order to control the Barbarians' (Yang, 2002, p. 30). This attitude toward Western models of higher education reflected the desire to preserve Chinese values, even if it was now necessary to learn science and technology from the West. The conflict was rife between traditional Confucianism and Western knowledge and eventually ended with a compromise between the two sides at the end of the nineteenth century, which is known as '*Zhongxue Weiti;*

Xixue Weiyong (Chinese knowledge for norms, Western knowledge for use)' (Welch & Cai, 2011; Zhang, 2010).

When it comes to the Republican Era (1911–1949), a number of modern HEIs were established by the Chinese returnees from other countries. Institutional models were largely Japanese at the time, although the latter was strongly influenced by German models. The US influences came to be more important in the 1920s, including via the visit of John Dewey and Paul Monroe (Liao, Tan, & Zhu, 2008; Welch & Cai, 2011; Yang et al., 2011). The predominant influence after the new China was founded in 1949 came from the Soviet Union. Higher education in China was reorganized under technical principles, with the aim of underpinning industrialization. Curricula were imported from the Soviets with the support of hundreds of experts in this transition (Welch & Cai, 2011; Yang et al., 2009). After almost 20 years of China's higher education being isolated from any foreign influences between 1958 and 1976, China reopened its door to the outside world, and higher education in China embarked on internationalization in a modern approach (Huang, 2007; Yang, 2002).

University Internationalization as a National Priority

Internationalization is regarded as a practical means of lifting China's modern higher education and research toward international standards and continuously enhancing quality (Huang, 2003; Liu, 2007; Wang, 2008; Yang, 2002). Against this context, the emphasis on the internationalization of China's higher education is mainly a result of increasingly fierce global competition. The Chinese government recognizes the importance of an educated workforce for economic growth, innovation, and national competitiveness, and it has made significant efforts to promote the internationalization of domestic HEIs (Bi & Huang, 2010; Wang, 2008). This is consistent with many other international cases, where the most prevalent driver for internationalization is economic competitiveness.

HEIs in China have been approaching internationalization through a variety of strategies that exhibit shifting priorities in different periods. In the first decade that China embraced internationalization (the late 1970s to late 1980s), the internationalization of higher education was fundamentally characterized by the growth in the number of state-funded students and faculty members sent abroad for further studies or research. Initially, almost all were sent with public funding and were selected from the leading universities. Since 1981, when the Chinese government issued a document permitting students to go abroad at their own expense, the number of Chinese students studying overseas has risen dramatically, reaching 608,400 in 2017, 89% of whom were private students.[1] From 1985 until now, China remains the country with the largest number of students studying abroad. Since the majority of those who choose to study abroad since 1990 have been self-funded, going abroad for further study is now more a matter of individual choice rather than a national strategy for internationalizing higher education.

Since the 1990s, particular attention has been paid to promoting the development of transnational education programs in China (Gide, Wu, & Wang, 2010; Hou, Montgomery, & McDwell, 2011; Huang, 2007; Tan, 2009). Two important and fundamental policies were issued to encourage the importation of foreign higher education services and joint programs as an important complementary component of Chinese higher education and as a practical way to meet the challenges of worldwide competition. One was the *Contemporary Regulation on Operation of Higher Education Institutions in Cooperation with Foreign Partners*, published by the former State Commission of Education in 1995; the other was the *Notice of Strengthening Degree-Granting Management in Activities Concerning Operation of Institutions in Cooperation with Foreign Partners*, which was created by the Degree-Granting Commission of the State Council in 1997 (Gide et al., 2010).

---

[1] Data source: Ministry of Education of the People's Republic of China (2017). In 2017, the number of students studying abroad and returning to China increased simultaneously. Available at http://www.moe.edu.cn/jyb_xwfb/gzdt_gzdt/s5987/201803/t20180329_331771.html.

Unlike the case in Singapore, the involvement of foreign partner institutions in China has been largely developed by individual institutions, rather than targeted and invited by the government. By 2012, the total number of transnational education programs had reached 1780 (Ministry of Education, P.R.C., 2013a). With the rapidly expanded scale of transnational education programs, the Chinese government has shown more concern about assuring the quality of these programs. The State Council enacted the *Regulations on Chinese-Foreign Cooperation in Running Schools* in 2003, and in the next year the Ministry of Education issued the *Implementation Measures for Regulations on Chinese-Foreign Cooperation in Running Schools* to standardize this kind of transnational cooperation and to encourage the development of partnerships with high-quality foreign educational bodies to provide high-quality education services (Tan, 2009).

In more recent years, increasing emphasis has been placed on two aspects of China's higher education internationalization. On the one hand, in order to address the problem of brain drain, the Chinese government has initiated a series of incentive measures, such as offering competitive salaries, providing assistance with housing, and helping with schooling for children, to reduce the outflow of Chinese scholars and students overseas. In 2012, the returnees from overseas reached 272,900, a 46.57% increase compared with the number in 2011 (Ministry of Education, P.R.C., 2013b). Among those returnees, many were very well-qualified professional experts with advanced knowledge that is urgently needed. On the other hand, in order to achieve a more balanced two-way flow of students to boost cross-cultural exchanges, the Chinese government has been making great efforts to increase international enrolments. Flagship programs and initiatives at the national level have been launched to build world-class universities in China, including the 'Double first-class construction' project[2] and the One

---

[2] In 2017, the Chinese government introduced a project to establish world-class universities and world-class disciplines by the end of 2050. The full list of the sponsored universities and disciplines was published in September 2017, which includes 42 first-class universities (36 Class A schools and 6 Class B schools) and 465 first-class disciplines (spread among 140 schools including the first-class universities).

Belt, One Road initiative.[3] Having these internationally renowned universities, China aims to gradually reposition itself as a destination for international students to pursue tertiary education and as an exporter of educational service in the globalized education landscape (Wang, 2008; Welch & Cai, 2011; Yang et al., 2011). In 2017, there were 489,200 inbound international students from 204 nations studying in China, in comparison with the number of 71,673 in 2010.[4]

With the enhanced research capacity, collaborative research between Chinese and international scholars has also been experiencing notable growth. In 2017, more than 22% of China's indexed documents involved international collaboration, increased by 4.4% in comparison with the figure from 1996. Although considerable efforts have been made to encourage internationally collaborative research, there remains a gap between China and other major Western countries such as the United States (35.40%) and the UK (54.58%) in terms of publishing with authors from other countries.[5]

Internationalization and the Aspiration for World-Class Universities

As discussed in Chapter 2, the blossom of global ranking industry has created the aspiration for 'world-class universities' (WCUs) in different countries. China is no exception. Given that the five universities

---

[3]The One Belt, One Road initiative was proposed by the Chinese government in 2013 with the aim to enhance regional connectivity and embrace a brighter future. In 2016, the Ministry of China, P.R.C. launched the Promoting the One Belt, One Road initiative—Educational Action. The Action intends to strengthen educational communication and collaboration among countries included in the initiative, and to further develop China as a leading educational provider.

[4]Data source: Ministry of Education of the People's Republic of China (2017). In 2017, the number of students studying abroad and returning to China increased simultaneously. Available at http://www.moe.edu.cn/jyb_xwfb/gzdt_gzdt/s5987/201803/t20180329_331771.html.

[5]Data source: *Scimago Journal* & Country Rank. Available at https://www.scimagojr.com/countryrank.php.

in China involved in this project are all C9 League[6] members, it is not surprising that building WCUs is a key driver of the discourse of university internationalization. Almost all the interviewed university leaders emphasized the importance of internationalization as a means to serve the university's goal of becoming a WCU. Being a WCU requires international standards to be applied to the university's management, teaching, and research. For example, according to one of the interviewed Assistant Presidents, the research outputs of a university should be evaluated by its publications and citations in internationally prevalent citation indexes such as the Science Citation Index (SCI). In teaching, Massive Open Online Course (MOOC) provides a platform for HEIs across the world to display their courses. Teachers can compare their own lectures to other similar lectures offered by top universities in the world to learn different approaches and adjust their teaching strategies (Deputy Director of International Offices, T University).

Meaning of University Internationalization

The relationship of being internationalized and becoming a WCU also shapes university leaders' understanding of what internationalization means. Most frequently, internationalization is perceived as adopting international conventions in higher education management and practice, as illustrated by one of the interviewed leaders,

> Personally, I believe internationalization is more of an idea. We should use the state-of-the-art and proven effective approaches that are universally accepted in our higher education practice. In this respect, I do not think it is necessary to emphasize Chinese characteristics. What are Chinese characteristics? It could be a large dye tank, and everything can

---

[6]In 2009, Peking University, Tsinghua University, Fudan University, Shanghai Jiao Tong University, Nanjing University, University of Science and Technology of China, Zhejiang University, Xi'an Jiao Tong University, and Harbin Institute of Technology formalized an elite group to foster better students, sharing their resources. This group is called the C9 League, as known as China's Ivy League.

be put in. We are not currently running our universities in accordance with internationally prevalent trends or methods or concepts. To be internationalized largely means to change the mind. But this is not an easy task, as it may involve an ideological shift. Universities in mainland China are neither independent nor autonomous. In this case, there are lots of challenges facing universities in China. We have the willingness to change, but it takes time. Under this circumstance, our internationalization is to create an open and inclusive environment to embrace the most advanced concepts and approaches for us to use. (Deputy Director of International Office, F University)

This view is endorsed by the interviewee from T University, as he commented,

I think internationalization means internationalizing management. When our goal is to become a WCU, international rather than the Chinese standards should be referred to. Both our philosophy and approach should be global. One of our current tasks is to introduce internationally accepted management models to our university and school leaders, incorporating these into our operation. (Deputy Director of International Office, T University)

A professor from P University further argued that internationalization means to respect the nature of scholarship, which is essentially public good that does not distinguish between national boundaries. Only by developing knowledge and fostering talents on a common platform of the world could knowledge be accumulated for mankind and social progress be made. China enters the world's big family, exchanging with other countries and learning from each other's strengths. It is the mission of universities in China to promote communication between China and other countries and to achieve an integration of East and West in scholarship (Professor Y, delegated by the Director of International Office, P University). It is also highlighted by the interviewed university leaders that internationalization needs to serve the mission and outlook of a university. As the PVC of Z University gave an example,

For our university, internationalization serves our vision of building a WCU and cultivating future leaders with international perspectives. Being a WCU requires the university to be internationalized, which is reflected in its operation, curriculum design, campus culture, and student service and support. Future leaders should have a vision of the world and inter-cultural competence, which could be developed via international experiences on campus and overseas. (PVC, Z University)

Leadership and Structural Support for Internationalization

Being internationalized always requires substantial commitment of resources. Leadership and structural support for internationalization are the prerequisites for its sustainability and centrality at a particular university. In this regard, universities involved in this project are more or less the same. It is common for universities in China to have a position of PVC (international), who is supposed to perform as the representative of the universities in international affairs. The role of the PVC (international) is normally only vaguely defined and operated symbolically and administratively. The PVCs in Chinese universities are appointed because of their academic achievements, rather than their expertise in international affairs.

With respect to the planning and implementation of international strategies, the International Office (IO) of a university is usually the central functional department. Compared to the PVC (international), the director of the IO is the one who is actually involved with international activities across the campus, from planning to implementation. Along with the extended scope of internationalization, different departments and offices of the universities are involved with international activities. For example, the management of international students could be included in the portfolio of Dean's Office or Institute for International Students. Similarly, the Human Resources Department is responsible for the management of international faculty, and the Department of Science and Technology needs to look after international collaboration in research. It is not always smooth or easy for the IO to coordinate with other functional departments on international activities, as one of the directors raised the issue:

> The majority of staff working in my office can speak fluent English or even more languages, which allows them to communicate with overseas institutions. However, the English proficiency of administrative staff in other departments is barely average. Thus, they may feel less capable of engaging with international activities. (Deputy Director of International Office, F University)

It is also noteworthy that the IO in some universities has been experiencing transformation in its functions, from carrying out international activities alone, to guiding and helping other offices or schools develop their own internationalization plans. The role of IO has started to be reconfigured from that of 'organizer' to 'facilitator.' It now encourages everyone in the university to be involved in internationalization and provides advice and support to individual departments.

Two of the interviewees pointed out that in their universities, an International Communication Committee had been established, which was intended to provide consultation with regard to internationalization. The committee consists of department and school leaders, as well as academic staff who are proactive in international activities. However, both of the interviewees emphasized that, because the committee members are usually very busy, the committee does not function in the way that it is expected to; as a consequence, the IO remains the central sector for both decision-making and execution (Deputy Director of International Office, F University, and Deputy Director of International Office, T University).

At the school level, depending on the volume of international activities, there may be either an independent office or a specialist responsible for international affairs. For example, according to the Deputy Director of IO from T University, the School of Economics and Management is highly internationalized; therefore, they have a school-level IO with five staff members. This is not common for other schools of the university.

According to the interviewees, universities in China are facing more structural obstacles in pursuing internationalization in comparison with their counterparts in Western countries. The current management system of universities in China resembles that of the former Soviet Union, which is featured with high centralization and limited institutional autonomy. The Chancellors and Presidents of universities are appointed by the Ministry of Education. Functional departments and offices of universities are both executive and decision-making bodies. In the case that schools or faculties would like to launch any programs or take initiatives, they first have to go through the functional departments for deliberations. If universities intend to adopt the prevalent modern management model, they would require independence and freedom to express their own will and put it in into practice, which has not yet been achieved in China. The central government still applies strict control over universities, not only in terms of funding. Degrees in China are not owned by individual universities but by the nation. In this case, it is much more difficult to run double degree programs collaboratively with overseas HEIs. Even the establishment of a major is difficult for universities in China, as it has to be approved by the national governance body. Hiring professors could be challenging as well since the state sets wage standards for academic staff at universities (Deputy Director of International Office, F University, and Deputy Director of International Office, T University).

Dimensions of University Internationalization

Though different typologies were used by interviewees to describe the key dimensions of internationalization, common components could be identified from the interviews, including students, faculty, disciplines, research, management, and engagement. In terms of students, all interviewed leaders agreed with the importance of having an internationalized student body and providing students with international experiences. Another key dimension highlighted by all interviewees is the internationalization of faculty. Academic staff are required to have the ability to incorporate internationally prevalent concepts and approaches in their teaching and research. The employment of international scholars is also indispensable. They are expected to contribute to the internationalization of teaching, which hardly takes place naturally or automatically. As the Deputy Director of International Office from F University argued,

> We have recruited many international teachers; however, they did not contribute to the internationalization in a desirable way. The main reason is that they have problems with adapting themselves to our system and performance evaluation mechanism. How to maximize the value of international faculties and provide them with a favourable environment to play to their strengths is an urgent challenge facing with universities.

An internationalized staff body serves as the prerequisite for the internationalization of disciplines, which includes the curriculum, teaching approaches, and materials. According to some interviewees, programs that are instructed in English cannot be omitted from internationalized discipline building. In addition to students, staff, and disciplines, the internationalization of research makes another key dimension, as it, to some extent, reflects the research capability of a university in the international platform. The next most commonly reported dimension is management, which is used in its broadest sense. The internationalization of management is regarded as the safeguard to ensure internationalization can be embedded in the core functions of universities. Not only the management and administrative team but also facilities on campus need to be internationalized. For example, the information system of a university needs to be bilingual or even multilingual, and administrative staff are required to be bilingual as well in order to provide service to international students and staff. Engagement is the last dimension of university internationalization cited by the majority of interviewees. It includes the international image of a university, which is reflected in the fact that flagship universities in China attempt to play a proactive role in different international associations. International engagement of a university also means active contribution to the research on international issues, such as environmental protection and eliminating conflicts.

It is emphasized by the interviewed university leaders repeatedly that internationalization needs to be approached in a holistic manner. Universities at different stages of internationalization may prioritize a particular dimension, subject to the available recourses and individual institutional conditions and goals. There is no single dimension that outweighs others. These dimensions complement each other. For example, without the internationalization of research, internationalized teaching could be hardly implemented. With no internationalized teaching, students may not gain international experiences in the classroom (Professor Y, P University). The current focus of most universities involved in this project was the student and faculty dimensions. As the Deputy Director of International Office of F University put it, 'international exchange of students should always be prioritized, as the difference between universities and research institutes is that there are students at universities. Student development is the core function and responsibility of a university.' Other interviewees highlighted the importance of faculty, arguing that they are the core assets of the university. University internationalization should start with the core. The internationalization of faculty will lead to the internationalization of research and change student learning experiences even without international exchanges. Therefore, the internationalization of academic staff is a more fundamental and essential part of university internationalization, which is assumed to promote the openness of a university and international collaborations in other aspects.

A Changing Role in International Collaborations

In order to understand the current practice of internationalization taking place in universities in China, the interviewees were asked to elaborate on one of their institutional flagship programs. Through these programs, the trend and features of internationalization development in Chinese universities could be observed. It could be summarized as that with the rise of China's international status and the improvement of institutional capacity and reputation, universities in China are now pursuing equal, mutual, and reciprocal collaborations with partners overseas. As Professor Y from P University illustrated,

> The internationalization in the top universities in China has proceeded into a substantive stage, which is distinctive from that of a decade age when we were followers in international collaborations, and overseas HEIs were dominating the process. The gap between top universities in China and in major Western countries is narrowing. Our scholars' research capability and intercultural competence have improved significantly, which enables them to participate in in-depth academic communications with overseas leading scholars. The academic achievements of our researchers, the English proficiency, and international perspective of our faculty and students all make the head of state and senior scholars such as Noble Prize winners more willing to visit and give presentations at our university. Communication is always a two-way process and requires input from all participants.

This view is echoed by the example given by another interviewee:

> The transformation from superficial to in-depth substantive communication depends on the enhancement of researchers' capabilities. The research capacity of a university determines its role and status in the global higher education landscape. Our partnerships with Harvard, MIT, and Princeton are the best evidence of our research capacity. We send our freshmen to these elite universities for exchange. There are supervisors at the hosting universities who will guide the students' work at laboratories. Students from these universities will also come to our place for a six-week exchange and study with our professors. These programs have been successfully operated for three years. In addition, our research achievements enable us to work with overseas partners, playing an active role in major international discourses. A few years ago, we established a low carbon

research alliance jointly with Cambridge and MIT. (Deputy Director of International Office, T University)

The changing role in international collaborations also reflects in the selection of partners. The increased competitiveness of Chinese universities among peers creates the conditions for choosing high-quality partners to collaborate with. The scope of collaborations is also extended to include partners in those regions where were neglected before such as Russia, Middle East and Southeast Asia (Assistant President, N University).

Another signal that indicates the internationalization of universities in China has entered a new phase is the institutionalization of international collaborations. One of the participant universities established a joint college with Imperial College. The Chinese university invested in a building on the campus of Imperial College, and the joint college is operated by both universities. This institutional approach is not common in China so far. The joint college offers degree programs, research, and technology transfer, which reflects the core functions of universities: talent cultivation, research, and service. The establishment of the joint college is a milestone for international development of the university, as it shows the shift in internationalization strategy from importing to exporting, to achieve an equal and reciprocal collaboration with HEIs overseas. The principles for developing international collaborations could be summarized as the three S's at the university: strategic, substantial, and sustainable (PVC international, Z University).

Evaluation of University Internationalization Performance

This project intended to develop measurements for university internationalization performance. The interviewees were also asked about the current monitoring or evaluation of internationalization at their institutions. Only one of the participating universities established a relatively independent measurement for its internationalization performance. As the PVC introduced, there are specific targets set for different international activities, including discipline building, faculty, exchange of students, the recruitment of international students, etc. The IO is requested to review and evaluate the overall international development at the institutional level annually. The evaluation is primarily quantitative, using indicators such as the number of international faculty, the number of faculty with overseas degrees, and the proportion of international students across disciplines. As internationalization comes to its maturity, the focus has shifted from students to research and technology transfer (PVC international, Z University).

Another common approach is to integrate the evaluation of internationalization performance into discipline or department performance evaluation. The Deputy Director of IO at F University gave an example:

> In our annual evaluation of schools' and departments' performance, internationalization takes up five percentage of the overall score. A range of indicators are used, including attendance of international conferences, outgoing and incoming students and staff, co-authored publications, joint courses, joint degree programs, etc. The IO sets its own targets for student exchange. For example, we are aiming at providing 20 to 30 percent of our students with international experiences. We do not have a target for incoming students because there are not adequate courses delivered in English to accommodate international students.

In most participating universities, there are comprehensive statistics about internationalization performance; however, these data have not yet been used to inform institutional policy-making. As the Assistant President from N University commented, 'we do not have strict assessment mechanisms; rather, it is more about sharing experiences between schools and departments. We believe that assessment is not always effective. Conversely, it may impede reform or improvement.' This perspective is endorsed by Professor Y from P University, as he put it that 'evaluation as a management tool has pros and cons. Freedom inheres in the history of our university, and we are not comfortable to be evaluated by externally imposed standards. There have already been evaluations taking internationalization performance into account like the publications in English journals or indexed by SSCI or SCI. Academic staff expressed their dissatisfaction with these evaluations, which makes our university cautious in the use of evaluations.' He further articulated his concerns with developing measurement for internationalization. Given that internationalization is embedded in the core functions of universities, it may not be easy to tease out internationalization performance from overall performance in teaching, research, and service. Evaluation of internationalization is more likely to capture the quantifiable performance such as the number of visiting scholars or exchange students. These activities are constrained by the available financial resources of a university or even the quotas of national programs. All these factors influence the internationalization of a university, which can hardly be reflected solely through numbers. Due to these features of internationalization, it could be challenging to develop measurements for it, particularly to capture the effects of exchange and communication rather than chasing the numbers.

Indicators for Measuring Internationalization Performance of Universities in China

As the key dimensions and components were identified from the interviews, the project proceeded to the next step to select appropriate indicators to capture the components of university internationalization. From the 98 available indicators identified in Chapter 3, 57 draft indicators were selected to measure the six dimensions suggested by all interviewees.[7] A questionnaire was distributed by the

---

[7] The draft indicator list was developed based on the interview findings of all 17 universities across the three countries. Therefore, participants from different universities were presented with the

interviewee of each university to the relevant staff who are involved with international activities in their institutions to ask for their judgment on the importance and feasibility of each indicator. There are 72 responses collected from the six universities in China, with 63 useable ones. The demographic information shows that there are between 7 and 14 participants from each university responding to the questionnaire. Nearly half of all respondents are between the ages of 30–39, and three-quarters are female. The vast majority were working at the IO of each university, with only a few of them from different schools. Nearly 70% of the respondents were intermediate professional staff, and their responsibilities covered a wide range of international activities, including international partnerships and collaboration, international student recruitment and service, student exchange, international staff recruitment and management, and international curriculum management.

Arbitrariness could hardly be fully avoided when making the decision on what indicators should be included in the final measurement. In this project, indicators that are agreed on by more than three-quarters of respondents from each country as 'Very Important' or 'Somewhat Important' are retained in the tailored set for a particular country. This decision is just one possible scenario. Thirty-seven out of the 57 draft indicators meet the criteria and are included in the final set for universities in China, as presented in Table 4.1.

The selected indicators were cross-checked for their feasibility. Three indicators were cited by less than 70% of respondents as feasible: R10: Number of co-editorships in international journals; R11: Number of highly cited authors (HiCi) according to Thomson Reuters; and G6: Funding for international visiting scholars. The weakness of feasibility for the three indicators may reduce the possibility for them to be used in practice.

---

same list of indicators. The analysis of responses was conducted by country first to generate the tailored indicator set for each country, and later a cross-country analysis was undertaken to generate the comparable indicator list for using across national boundaries. The results of cross-country data analysis were documented in Chapter 8. The questionnaire can be found in Appendix A.

Table 4.1 Final indicators for measuring university internationalization performance (China)

Dimension	Indicator	Percentage of respondents rating as 'Very Important' or 'Somewhat Important'
Research	R1: Percentage of research projects involving international partnership and collaboration	93.6
	R4: Number of research centers operated with international partners	92.1
	R7: Number of international conferences organized	90.5
	R9: Percentage of publications cited by SCI, EI, ISTP	88.9
	R3: Number of research centers focused on international study	80.9
	R11: Number of highly cited authors (HiCi) according to Thomson Reuters	77.8
	R10: Number of co-editorships in international journals	77.7
Student	S6: Percentage of domestic students who have international study experiences	96.9
	S1: Percentage of international students (for degree study) on campus in total	95.3
	S7: Number of incoming international students (incl. exchanges and short-term programs that are no more than an academic year)	95.2
	S3: Percentage of international Master (coursework) students on campus	91.5
	S4: Percentage of international higher degree research (HDR) students on campus	87.3
	S2: Percentage of international undergraduate students on campus	85.7

(continued)

Table 4.1 (continued)

Dimension	Indicator	Percentage of respondents rating as 'Very Important' or 'Somewhat Important'
Faculty	F1: Percentage of international (by nationality) faculty members (full-time equivalent FTE)	92.1
	F2: Number of international visiting scholars for academic purposes	90.5
	F3: Percentage of faculty (FTE) who were awarded their highest academic qualification by an institution abroad	90.5
	F4: Percentage of faculty (FTE) proficient in a language other than the primary language of teaching/research	90.5
	F5: Percentage of faculty (FTE) who have at least one year of overseas experience (excl. degree study)	85.7
	F6: Percentage of faculty (FTE) who hold a visiting lectureship abroad	76.2
Curriculum	C5: Number of subjects offered in a foreign language	95.2
	C2: Number of subjects involving a partner in other countries	88.9
	C8: Number of joint degree programs (Bachelor, Masters, and PhD) collaborated with overseas higher education institution	88.9
	C9: Number of students registered in subjects taught in a foreign language	81.0
	C7: Number of subjects involving foreign countries/cultures/societies	76.2
Engagement	E2: Number of overseas partners with whom at least one academic activity (mobility, program, research) has taken place	90.5

(continued)

Table 4.1 (continued)

Dimension	Indicator	Percentage of respondents rating as 'Very Important' or 'Somewhat Important'
	E1: Number of memberships in international organizations and consortia	85.7
	E3: Percentage of partnerships by region (Europe, Africa, Asia, North America, South America, Pacific)	81.0
	E4: Proportion of international (by nationality) alumni relative to the total number of alumni	79.3
Governance	G8: Funding for international research projects	93.6
	G7: Funding to support the international mobility of students	92.7
	G3: Percentage of administration staff proficient in more than one working language	92.1
	G4: Percentage of administration staff who have participated in international exchange programs	90.5
	G5: Percentage of total budget available (excluding personnel costs) for internationalization activities	88.9
	G11: Percentage of library collection in other languages	87.3
	G2: Percentage of administration staff with international experience (minimum 3 months)	85.7
	G9: Number of scholarships for international students (all degree levels)	85.7
	G6: Funding for international visiting scholars	77.8

Summary

The China cases vividly illustrate the ways in which a nation's economic and cultural features can shape the university's approach to internationalization. Along with the bloom of national economy in recent decades, momentous changes could be observed in the role played by universities in China in terms of international collaborations. The substantial national investment in higher education has improved each university's research capacity, placing a number of flagship universities in the top ranks. Such improvement has led to changes in the demand and expectations for international collaborations. Twenty years ago, international collaborations for universities could mean building extensive partnerships with HEIs overseas, sending Chinese students for exchange, or running joint programs. However, these are no longer the priorities for international engagement today. In-depth collaborations in research, institutionalized development, and incoming students are the current foci. Universities in China have become more selective in the partners they collaborate with and the activities they participate in. Moreover, they are striving for an equal position in international collaborations. If decades ago they were comfortable with a follower role in their international development due to the lack of confidence and capacity, today's Chinese universities, particularly the top ones, are confident enough to initiate and lead transnational agendas. The confidence comes from both the economy and the culture.

The role of the national government in developing international collaborations also is noteworthy. Compared to the Singapore and Australia cases, which will be discussed in the next two chapters, the Chinese government takes the centrism approach, investing heavily in higher education and creating favorable policy environment rather than direct intervention. The Singaporean government plays a more straightforward role in driving international collaborations in the higher education sector, while the Australian government is less prominent in the process. The role of the Chinese government resembles an 'invisible' hand, and such a hand, to some extent, creates a dilemma for universities in China to embrace internationalization fully. The central government, on the one hand, subsidizes universities generously, while on the other hand, it enacts strict regulations on them. The lack of independence and autonomy has been complained about by the interviewed university leaders repeatedly, which conflicts with the freedom of scholarship in nature. It is an urgent challenge for higher education policymakers and practitioners to determine how to achieve an internationalized operation of the university under the firm control of the national government. A couple of interviewees mentioned that more in-depth reforms are required in the management and administration of universities to provide a more flexible environment for both international scholars and students. This issue may yet reach its peak; however, with the growing number of international students and staffs on campus and the further extension of the scope of international collaborations, the conflicts would manifest themselves in a more prominent way.

References

Bi, J. J., & Huang, X. J. (2010). The challenges and strategies of internationalization of Chinese universities. *Reform and Development*, *1*, 11–16 (in Chinese).

Gide, E., Wu, M. X., & Wang, X. P. (2010). The influence of internationalisation of higher education: A Chinese study. *Procedia Social and Behavioral Sciences*, *2*(2), 5675–5681.

Hou, J. X., Montgomery, C., & McDwell, L. (2011). Transition in Chinese-British higher education articulation programmes: Closing the gap between East and West. In J. Ryan (Ed.), *China's higher education reform and internationalisation* (pp. 104–119). Abingdon, Oxon and New York: Routledge.

Huang, F. (2003). Policy and practice of the internationalization of higher education in China. *Journal of Studies in International Education*, *7*(3), 225–240.

Huang, F. (2007). Internationalisation of higher education in the era of globalisation: What have been its implications in China and Japan? *Higher Education Management and Policy*, *19*(1), 47–61.

Liao, J. Q., Tan, G. X., & Zhu, X. G. (2008). Internationalization and localization of China's higher education. *Journal of Higher Education Management*, *2*(2), 1–7 (in Chinese).

Liu, D. Y. (2007). The choices and strategies for internationalisation of higher education. *Journal of Higher Education Policy and Management, 28*(4), 6–10 (in Chinese).
Ministry of Education, P.R.C. (2013a). *China-foreign cooperative education programmes*. Retrieved 23 March 2012, from http://edu.people.com.cn/n/2013/0314/c1053-20789582.html.
Ministry of Education, P.R.C. (2013b). *Statistics of Chinese students studying overseas and the returnees*. Retrieved 23 March 2012, from http://news.xinhuanet.com/overseas/2013-03/07/c_124429518.html.
Tan, Z. (2009). Internationalization of higher education in China: Chinese-foreign cooperation in running schools and the introduction of high-quality foreign educational resources. *International Education Studies, 2*(3), 166–170.
Wang, Y. B. (2008). Internationalization in higher education in China: A practitioner's reflection. *Higher Education Policy, 21*(4), 505–517.
Welch, A., & Cai, H. X. (2011). The internationalisation of China's higher education system. In J. Ryan (Ed.), *China's higher education reform and internationalisation* (pp. 9–33). Abingdon, Oxon and New York: Routledge.
Yang, F. L., Liu, J. L., Dong, Y. Z., & Xu, R. (2011). Trend and policy study of internationalization of higher education in China. *Journal of Tianjin University (Social Science), 13*(3), 279–283 (in Chinese).
Yang, M., Xia, D. J., & Yang, Q. N. (2009). The political and cultural factors in the internationalization process of Chinese higher education: The import of foreign textbooks. *Journal of Jinzhong University, 5*, 77–81 (in Chinese).
Yang, R. (2002). *Third delight: The internationalization of higher education in China*. New York and London: Routledge.
Yang, R. (2010). Chinese ways of thinking in the transformation of China's higher education system. In J. Ryan (Ed.), *China's Higher Education Reform and Internationalisation* (pp. 34–47). Hoboken: Taylor & Francis.
Zhang, H. S. (2010). Higher education reforms and problems in China: Challenges from globalization. In F. Maringe & N. Foskett (Eds.), *Globalisation and internationalisation in higher education: Theoretical, strategic and management perspectives* (pp. 125–137). London: Continuum.

5

Singapore

Singapore has a long history of embracing global ideas and norms. Since its independence, Singapore has built a reputation of hybridization for taking Western economic models and technology, while concurrently eschewing western ideas in favor of 'eastern' or 'Asian' values (Sanderson, 2002). The foundations of Singapore's ability to internationalize its higher education system are the Western heritage and the multilingual ability of most Singaporean citizens. Singapore has four official languages, including Mandarin, English, Malay, and Tamil. In 1965, the Singaporean government designated English as Singapore's first language, establishing English as the language of business, of government, and as the language of instruction in all government mainstream schools. English is also the medium for communication and negotiations with their neighboring countries.

Given that Singapore is a small island nation with extremely limited natural resources, the development of human resources has been regarded as fundamental to the further success of the city-state. The Singaporean government has been aware that only an educated and skilled labor force will be able to respond to the opportunities made available by the developing world economy and provide Singapore with a competitive advantage over other countries in the region (Ling, 2009; Mok, 2008; Sanderson, 2002). 'The university sector plays a crucial role in producing graduate manpower to support the new economy that is more dynamic and more demanding of graduates' ability to adapt, innovate and add value' (Singaporean Ministry of Education, 2003, p. 6). Since the quality of population would determine whether the nation would 'sink or swim,' Singapore's education policies have been intertwined with the nation's economic priorities (Cheung, Yuen, Yuen, & Cheng, 2011; Sidhu, Ho, & Yeoh, 2011). Several local and international studies have investigated the nexus between Singapore's education, migration, manpower, and population policies (Daquila, 2010; Raffin, 2007; Sidhu & Matthews, 2005).

The rationales for internationalizing Singapore's higher education are threefold: first, to contribute to achieving the goals of its educational policy such as fostering the country's value system and graduate attributes, including national unity, intercultural awareness, interpersonal and communication skills, and global citizenship; second, to train its students—including international students—to meet its manpower requirements and contribute to its labor force and population; and third, to promote Singapore as an educational hub in the region and in the world (Daquila, 2013).

Building an 'Educational Hub'

In the era of a 'knowledge-based' economy, research capacity assumes a new and perhaps unparalleled significance in economic discourse. Against this context, Singapore aims to become the 'education hub' or 'a Mecca for diploma, degrees and higher education' (Chan & Ng, 2008; Duhamel, 2004; Mok, 2008, 2011). The assertion of the hub status, transforming education into trade and industry for income generation, is not only for economic purposes. More importantly, it is used as a policy tool for 'soft power' assertion to enhance Singapore's national competitiveness in the global marketplace (Mok, 2012). In order to achieve the goal, in 2002, the Singaporean government launched the 'Global Schoolhouse' (GS) initiative. The GS initiative has three constituent parts: finance an identified group of world-class universities to establish operations in Singapore; attract 150,000 international students by 2015 to study in Singapore institutions; and re-model all levels of Singaporean education to inculcate the attributes of risk-taking, creativity, and entrepreneurialism (Singaporean Ministry of Trade and Industry, 2007).

Since 2002, a few leading world universities have been strategically invited from abroad by the Singapore government to set up centers of excellence and research in the city-state. Singapore is today home to 16 leading foreign tertiary institutions, including Harvard Business School, Chicago Graduate School of Business, Massachusetts Institute of Technology, and Johns Hopkins School of Medicine (Mok, 2011). Attracting these prestigious HEIs is part of the government's plan to turn Singapore into an exporter of higher education (Ziguras, 2003). The Yale-NUS College serves as a good example of the joint operation between domestic institutions and leading overseas partners. Founded in 2011, Yale-NUS College draws on the resources and traditions of the two great universities to pursue excellence through innovative teaching and research, and it offers students a wide range of undergraduate programs. Drawing on active modes of learning associated with an American liberal arts education, the college intends to introduce the student to the diverse intellectual traditions and cultures of Asia and the world (Yale-NUS College, 2015).

There are six public universities in Singapore, with five local polytechnic institutions offering high-standard industry training. In addition to local universities and polytechnics, both undergraduate and postgraduate degrees are offered by foreign universities with campuses based in Singapore and the international HEIs. These universities are usually private and have a smaller number of students than the local public institutions. Efforts have also been made to help leading domestic public universities—particularly, the National University of Singapore (NUS) and Nanyang Technological University (NTU)—to achieve world-class standards (Daquila, 2013; Han, 1999; Mok, 2011; Sanderson, 2002). An international advisory panel was set up in 1997 to advise the NUS and NTU on their future direction. Also, greater autonomy has been granted to these two universities to further reform the governance.

In recent years, Singapore's government has adopted a more cautious outlook on education hub ambitions. The city-state has capped international enrollment since Prime Minister Lee Hsien Loong announced the move in his National Day Rally speech in 2011. The international student numbers peaked and have begun to fall off, remaining well below the target enrollment for 2015. From a recent year high of 90,000 foreign students in 2010, enrollment slipped to about 75,000 by 2014 (ICEF, 2016). Despite the decrease in the number of international students, it can hardly be denied that Singapore is a popular destination for study, particularly for students from ASEAN, China, and India. Unlike the patterns of international student mobility in the 1970s and 1980s, when most overseas students mainly chose their student destinations in Europe, the United States and the UK, now Singapore is accepted as an alternative for students (Chan & Ng, 2008; Mok, 2012), whereas once Singapore was mainly a source country that sent their students abroad for tertiary study. The 'educational hub' policy has resulted in the improvement of higher education quality and capacity, thereby changing the pattern of student flow.

Unlike the case in Australia, where most international students are fee-paying and seen as a main source of income, a considerable proportion of foreign students in Singapore is subsidized by the Singaporean government with the clearly stated aim of recruiting top talent to enhance the reputation for excellence of local institutions (Sanderson, 2002). Due to the lack of qualified workforce in Singapore, the subsidies are provided in order to attract a highly skilled labor force to work in Singapore after study and to make a long-term contribution to Singapore's economic prosperity.

In respect to international collaborations in research, in 2000, only 27% of Singapore's indexed documents were published by authors from more than one country. Since then, a remarkable growth in international collaborative publications has been observed. The number reached 63.82% in 2017, more than doubled in comparison with the number in 2000. Compared to Australia and China, Singapore had the largest proportion of indexed documents involving international collaboration.[1]

It is obvious that the Singaporean government has resorted to a fairly systemic, controlled and measured approach toward the internationalization of its HEIs (Chan & Ng, 2008; Marginson, 2011; Mok, 2011; Sidhu et al., 2011). The proactive role played by the state in internationalizing local universities can be plainly seen from its highly selective process of inviting overseas partners to set up branch campuses. The government intervenes in the market by deciding who the partners are and what programs can be launched to fulfill its nation-building agenda (Chan & Ng, 2008). The government is also actively involved in the regulatory affairs in relation to international education. The small population, a competent bureaucracy, and the combination of a strong state and a liberal market economy enable the government to steer higher education system evolution vigorously by drawing on both private and public resources.

Given the focus and energy that is presently being invested in getting Singapore's HEIs to achieve world-class standing and attracting prestigious Western universities to establish themselves on the island, there is every possibility that Singapore will become a significant competitor in terms of education services export like the UK, the United States, and Australia, and strengthen its position as a regional or even worldwide 'education hub' over the next decade.

Internationalization as a Must

Three university leaders (one President and two PVC international) of two public universities in Singapore participated in this project, contributing their understandings of internationalization. Given the nature of Singapore as a city-state, it is not surprising that all participants agreed that internationalization is a must for universities in Singapore. As one of them put it,

---

[1]Source of data: SCImago Journal & Country Rank

> It's critical because Singapore is such a small place that collaboration is almost by definition international collaboration. Any student movement is almost by definition out of the country. If one is in the U.S., you could move from east coast to west coast, etc. But in Singapore, it's so small. We're just really small, so in that sense, for the university to be competitive, it's not enough to be competitive among three or four other universities, it has to be international. So, everything that we do, we have to think of its international dimension.

Internationalization as a must for universities is not only determined by the geographic characteristics of Singapore but also by the nature of scholarship. As knowledge is international, and the business model of universities is knowledge, dissemination of knowledge through teaching and discovery of new knowledge through research, universities should be internationalized by nature. As the interviewed President argued,

> The future challenges facing the world are international. Capital is international. Everything is international. I don't see why universities should not be there. Because everything around it is international. We cannot be a Singaporean island in an international world, particularly not here in Singapore, which is a playground for international capital, international companies, multicultural. International activity in our university in the 21st century is not an add-on, it's an integrated part of the university, is the soul of the university, of the teaching, of the student population, of the faculty population and in governance and management.

In addition, internationalization is vital to the nation's economic prosperity and security as it brings international students, who are mainly highly subsided by the Singaporean government and treated as the future workforce for Singapore. They are required to work at least three years in Singapore after they graduate (PVC international, Y University). The role of international students in Singapore is also unique, distinguished from their counterparts in either China or Australia. Overseas students, especially seekers of particular degrees, from Chinese universities are substantially funded by the Chinese government, but they are not required to work in China after graduation. The subsidy provided by the government is to attract more international students, aiming at lifting China's reputation and the boost of two-way communication and exchange. Comparatively, most overseas students in Australia pay much higher tuition fees compared to their domestic peers, making education the third national exporting industry.

The strategic position of Singapore, geographically and culturally, as a meeting point for the West and East leads to the particular way in which its university leaders define internationalization of the university. According to the interviewed President, 'internationalization of the university is to create thousands of meeting places on the individual scheme or institution scheme. Meeting places, intellectual and cultural meeting places.' While as internationalization is natural and necessary to Singapore, it could result in the situation that internationalization is taken for granted, without strategic planning or clear guidelines. As one of the PVCs reflected, 'to be honest up to that point, we had engaged a lot of international activities, but we didn't have a strategy. We didn't have a road map. We didn't have a plan. We were doing a lot of things but where is the coherence?' By saying this, she stressed the importance of having explicit goals for international efforts in order to achieve desirable outcomes.

Constructing University Internationalization

One of the participating universities developed a robust framework of their international engagement, which the PVC articulated. The framework outlines four key dimensions of internationalization, including people, programs, benchmarks, and partnerships. Each of the four dimensions consists of several elements. The people dimension refers to students, faculty, staff, and alumni. All of these have an international dimension. Rather than merely having international presence in these groups, internationalization means sufficient diversity and the contributions of diversity to learning and research outcomes and the capabilities of faculties. The program dimension is further divided into education, research, and enterprise programs. Educational programs offered in this university intend to give students international experiences and exposure. International collaborations in research are expected to enhance the quality and impact of research output.

In respect to entrepreneurial activities, no matter if it is entrepreneurial education or industry spinoffs, if there is research that leads to industrial application, it has to have real impact internationally rather than just locally given that Singapore is a city-state. The partnership dimension refers to networks that the university is connected to. Again, mere participation in these networks is not adequate; it is also important to play an active and leadership role.

The last benchmark dimension deals with the ranking of the university in major league tables as well as the indicators used to evaluate its research and education quality (PVC international, N University). In respect to the priority across the dimensions, as the PVC suggested, they are certainly bent out differently. But this is partly by accident and history and less so by design where they spent more attention on something than others. By far, the most institutional attention was placed on education, and the engagement of international alumni is lagging far behind. It by no means that this dimension is less important than others but because the university does not have enough experience and spent insufficient time on it. At the individual level, international collaboration in research is given the highest priority by most faculty members in Singapore.

The President of the other university argued that people are the most important asset of the university and are the ingredients of all activities that take place on the campus. Therefore, the construct of internationalization should be centered on people, and the international profile of the university will be determined by the faculty, management team, and students. Almost 70% of faculties are foreigners, and international students make up 20% of the undergraduates, 65% of postgraduates, and almost 80% of PhDs. Having international representation in leadership is also important, which gives international perspectives in the university operation and development. For example, the Vice-President of the university is English, the associate Provost for graduate service is German, one Dean is Canadian, one is American, and one is Indian-American. In addition to the international profile of faculties, students, and leadership, international collaboration is another key dimension. As he elaborated,

As the biggest engineering university in the world, even it is very good, ranked top 50 in the world, we still cannot have enough expertise, not sufficient knowledge, not sufficient equipment, or sufficient very advanced instrumentations. So, in order to be at the forefront of knowledge, you have to collaborate. So, we have very close collaboration with Imperial College in London. We're even setting up a medical school together with Imperial College. We work very close with Technical University in Munich. We work with Cambridge in chemical engineering, Berkeley in energy, and so forth. And we even lead a network of engineering universities. So that's another dimension, the interactive part.

Culture is another dimension, which refers to the integration of people from different backgrounds on campus. The diversity of the student cohort provides the prerequisite for cultural integration. There are international students from 100 different countries living on campus, and they are well connected in the university. For example, as the PVC international introduced,

There is no international college at our university. Every residential college has quota for students from different countries. There is no national student group in the campus, and it's not encouraged. Every student is encouraged to be integrated into the Student Union. Here, students' life on campus is integrated because most students graduate from here will work in international teams, so they need the skills to work with people from different backgrounds. This is part of education, soft skill education.

The last dimension identified by the university leaders is joint degree programs. The university is running more than 50 joint programs with universities from Europe and the United States among which 15 are at the doctoral level. These programs provide nearly half of the enrolled students with opportunities to study overseas for exchange. An even more ambitious target has been set: to offer 70% of students the opportunity for overseas experience during their course. Efforts will be made to achieve 100%, if possible. As intercultural awareness and multicultural intelligence are highly valued in the university and regarded as key capabilities for graduates to perform successfully in the globalized working environment, overseas experiences are the best way to achieve these educational goals. Every year, the university accommodates over 1000 exchange students to visit the campus, in addition to the 20% of full-time overseas students.

Flagship Internationalization Strategies

When looking at the flagship internationalization strategies at different universities, it is possible for us to learn how internationalization evolves at universities. It also indicates the trends and directions of the development of internationalization. The lessons from the two Singaporean universities show that institutionalization and serving national development needs are the current features of university internationalization. As the interviewed President points out, the new phase of internationalization is that institutions across the borders. Scholars and students have always travelled across boundaries, and now it is for the university itself. This signals the institutionalization of international development for universities, and it is common for top universities to operate branch campuses overseas. The example given by the PVC international of the other participating university echoes this view. The jointly running medical school at the university has innovated the way that graduate medical education could be delivered. The pedagogical tools developed in Singapore have been imported back to Duke University in the United States. Other medical schools have also discussed adopting this new model. This collaboration has sparked new ideas and resulted in new methods of teaching, which is neither strictly Singapore nor Duke but something unique. It is the combination of ideas that could hopefully break new ground in medical education. Institutionalized collaborations are powerful in creating new models or approaches to foster talent in comparison with those at the individual level.

Another noteworthy feature of university internationalization in Singapore is its role in serving national development. Entrepreneurship seems very appealing to the Singaporean government, and universities have developed various strategies to promote it via international collaborations. The examples highlighted by the PVC international of N University perfectly demonstrate the priority placed on the development of students' entrepreneurial spirits via different research and educational activities. For many years Singapore was very good at producing technocrats and individuals becoming engineers, doctors, lawyers, public servants, and the like. However, there was an identified gap in Singapore indicating that the innovation and the creativity are not strong. There were a lot of graduates who acquired solid professional skills but did not have experience starting up new things, new ideas, or new business. To reverse the situation, the government set up a committee that is chaired by the Deputy Prime Minister. The Research, Innovation and Enterprise Committee attempts to respond to that need and to promote the development of a whole variety of expertise of students.

> One of our flagship initiatives in research collaboration is the CREATE, which stands for the Campus for Research Excellence and Technology Enterprise. It's situated on our university town which is a new imitative across the highway. It was brought in through government funding. A lot of overseas universities want to collaborate with Singapore universities: MIT, Cambridge, Berkeley…
>
> Another successful program is the university's overseas colleges, which offers students the opportunity to work with companies overseas for one year and take courses at the partner institutions in entrepreneurship or technopreneurship. The idea is to help develop entrepreneurs. Silicon Valley is very popular with our students, and they go there to work with data companies. Because data companies are normally very small, they learn everything about how to start a new. They do many different jobs, some of them are writing proposals to get funding for the start-up. Some of them are in marketing, some of them are in product design, many things. Many of them came back and then started their own companies. And some have been very successful. We give quite a lot of time, attention, and resources to this program, but it is actually in a small scale compared to our other programs. We are looking at only about 180 students a year in all seven places. The reason is that this program is quite costly given that start-ups cannot finance our students and we support them. Another consideration is that Singapore needs entrepreneurs but not a lot; what we need are only the successful ones. We also do not want everybody who goes to be entrepreneurs because we also need doctors, lawyers, etc.

In addition to these entrepreneurial focused programs, the Program for Leadership in University Management (PLUM) is another example that illustrates how university internationalization strategies respond to national development strategies. As Singapore's government is seeking a leading role in the educational agenda regionally and internationally, this PLUM runs high-level workshops and seminars with university leaders from different Asian universities. Through the PLUM, university leaders from different countries discuss the challenges encountered in university management and build leadership. In the recently completed one with Chinese universities, the theme was leadership in internationalized universities. A series of key questions in relation to university internationalization was extensively discussed by participants, including the meaning of internationalization, the recruitment of faculty, and innovative educational programs.

Evaluation of Internationalization Performance

Both universities implement some sort of measurement or evaluation of their internationalization performance; however, the university leaders noticed the insufficiency in this area and the challenges for measuring internationalization effectively. In one of the universities, indicators were used to monitor the change in the number of international students, faculty members, and research collaborations. In respect to their research impact, international indexes were used for evaluation. The President of one university pointed out that all these activities are easy to monitor, but the hard part is to measure the thinking, the international soul, and the international spirit. According to the PVC international of the other university, measurement of their internationalization performance in different areas is a weak point, and they are paying more attention to it. Existing measurements for international education programs included feedback collected from students about their learning experiences and outcomes. In terms of research, they use indicators to track research impact, and the data showed that international collaborations ended up with higher impact factors. Collaboration with certain places heightened the impact even more. This information consists of the basis for evidence-based decision-making. She also highlighted the difficulty in developing a valid measurement for end-product of internationalization. For example,

> In the student dimension, student diversity is one thing, but how well our students are mixing? Integrating with the locals? We haven't monitored. I know it is hard to monitor. We need to think harder about monitoring rather than just saying that we have hundreds and hundreds of representatives on campus. Is that good enough in itself? I think not. The true intercultural understanding comes from actual interaction and integration. So that is an example of areas where we are not thinking, and we need to pay some attention to monitor outcomes.

Indicators for Measuring Internationalization Performance of Universities in Singapore

In order to select the appropriate indicators for Singaporean universities to use to measure their internationalization performance, the questionnaire that lists 57 draft indicators was sent to the interviewed university leaders for distribution to relevant staff. There are 17 responses collected from the two universities, with 12 useable ones (four from one university and eight from the other). The demographic information shows that five respondents were aged between 30 and 39, followed by three between 21 and 29. Eight respondents are female, and two respondents have a nationality other than Singaporean. Most respondents worked at the International Office, and half of the respondents were at middle management positions. The same rules were applied to the responses to select the appropriate indicators.[2] Forty out of the 57 draft indicators meet the criteria and are included in the final set for universities in Singapore, as presented in Table 5.1.

---

[2] In this project, indicators that are agreed on by more than three-quarters of respondents from each country as 'Very Important' or 'Somewhat Important' are retained in the tailored set for a particular country.

Table 5.1 Final indicators for measuring university internationalization performance (Singapore)

Dimension	Indicator	Percentage of respondents rating as 'Very Important' or 'Somewhat Important'
Research	R1: Percentage of research projects involving international partnership and collaboration	100.0
	R4: Number of research centers operated with international partners	91.7
	R5: Percentage of international post-doctoral researchers	91.7
	R10: Number of co-editorships in international journals	91.7
	R2: Percentage of research projects wholly funded by sources outside of host nation	83.3
	R6: Proportion of total research income generated by research involving international collaboration	83.3
	R11: Number of highly cited authors (HiCi) according to Thomson Reuters	83.3
	R3: Number of research centers focused on international study	75.0
	R8: Number of presentations in international conferences (with qualified contribution) per faculty member	75.0
Student	S1: Percentage of international students (for degree study) on campus in total	100.0
	S2: Percentage of international undergraduate students on campus	100.0
	S3: Percentage of international Master (coursework) students on campus	100.0
	S4: Percentage of international higher degree research (HDR) students on campus	100.0
	S7: Number of incoming international students (incl. exchanges and short-term programs of no more than an academic year)	100.0
	S8: Ratio of the outgoing domestic students to the incoming international students (no more than an academic year)	100.0
	S6: Percentage of domestic students who have international study experiences	91.7
	S5: Percentage of international students by region	81.3

(continued)

Table 5.1 (continued)

Dimension	Indicator	Percentage of respondents rating as 'Very Important' or 'Somewhat Important'
Faculty	F1: Percentage of international (by nationality) faculty members (full-time equivalent FTE)	91.7
	F3: Percentage of faculty (FTE) who were awarded their highest academic qualification by an institution abroad	83.3
	F2: Number of international scholars visiting for academic purposes	75.0
	F5: Percentage of faculty (FTE) who have at least one-year overseas experience (excl. degree study)	75.0
	F7: Percentage of faculty (FTE) who had international experience for academic purposes in the past academic year	75.0
Curriculum	C8: Number of joint degree programs (Bachelor, Masters, and PhD) collaborated with overseas higher education institution	91.7
	C2: Number of subjects involving a partner in other countries	83.3
	C1: Number of subjects offering foreign language studies	75.0
	C6: Number of programs with a mandatory period abroad	75.0
	C7: Number of subjects on foreign countries/cultures/societies	75.0
	C11: Number of students who attend joint degree programs in collaboration with overseas higher education institutions	75.0
Engagement	E2: Number of overseas partners with whom at least one academic activity (mobility, program, research) has taken place	100.0
	E4: Proportion of international (by nationality) alumni relative to the total number of alumni	100.0
	E1: Number of memberships in international organizations and consortia	91.7
	E3: Percentage of partnerships by region (Europe, Africa, Asia, North America, South America, Pacific)	91.7

(continued)

Table 5.1 (continued)

Dimension	Indicator	Percentage of respondents rating as 'Very Important' or 'Somewhat Important'
Governance	G5: Percentage of total budget available (excluding personnel costs) for internationalization activities	100.0
	G8: Funding for international research projects	100.0
	G7: Funding to support the international mobility of students	91.7
	G9: Number of scholarships for international students (all degree levels)	91.7
	G12: Number of participations in fairs abroad	91.7
	G1: Percentage of international staff (by nationality) in institutional senior management team	83.3
	G10: Number of scholarships for international post-doctoral researchers	83.3
	G2: Percentage of administration staff with international experience (minimum 3 months)	75.0

The selected indicators were cross-checked for their feasibility. Seven indicators were cited as feasible by fewer than 70% of respondents, including:

1. F1: Percentage of international (by nationality) faculty members (full-time equivalent FTE),
2. F2: Number of international scholars visiting for academic purposes,
3. F3: Percentage of faculty (FTE) who were awarded their highest academic qualification by an institution abroad,
4. F5: Percentage of faculty (FTE) who have at least one-year overseas experience (excl. degree study),
5. F7: Percentage of faculty (FTE) who had international experience for academic purposes in the past academic year,
6. G7: Funding to support the international mobility of students,
7. G2: Percentage of administration staff with international experience (minimum 3 months).

The weakness of the three indicators in feasibility may reduce the possibility for them to be used in practice.

Summary

Singapore is a very special case for understanding university internationalization, and its involvement in this project provided a unique context to consider the different trajectories of internationalization evolution and the role the national government plays in the process. The uniqueness of Singapore is primarily attributed to its geographic location as an intersection and to the long history of migration from other Asian countries, particularly China, which brought it heritage of oriental culture and exposure to Western culture. In my own view, Singapore is one of the most internationalized countries in the world, in every aspect. Its economic, political, and social functions are all an integration of East and West, or more boldly stated, the hybrid of some of the best aspects of Eastern and Western culture. This internationalized characteristic has permeated into every area of life in Singapore. The university is not an exception. In this regard, Singapore is better blessed than many other countries in embracing globalization and internationalization because it has become a norm and a must for universities there to think and operate internationally.

The uniqueness of the Singapore case also manifests itself in the small size and strong economy of the country, whose lessons may not easily be applied to other large countries. The city-state nature determines that all universities in Singapore operate in a homogeneous environment, which means the policy-making and decision-making processes are more likely to be straightforward and effective. However, in larger countries, the environment in which a university nests could be more complex. Policy-making requires taking local, regional, and national contexts into account, and there are normally many agencies involved in decision-making. In addition, as one of the four Asian tigers, Singapore has been prosperous for many decades with a solid and robust economic and financial system. Unlikely in most Western countries where public funding for universities has continuously shrunk, the higher education sector of Singapore has been continually and substantially funded by the government. Such national supports allow Singaporean universities to be more selective in international student recruitment and international partnership development. The geographic and economic features of the nation provide the prerequisites for the government to intervene directly in university internationalization strategies and activities. However, as a trade-off for the effectiveness and powerful leadership, the sustainability of universities' international development highly depends on the national policies. The Singapore case best demonstrates the necessity to take different national contexts into account when investigating university internationalization behaviors. Otherwise, any conclusions drawn from a narrow national or regional perspective could be biased and misleading and may not reveal the true complexity and diversity of the phenomenon.

References

Chan, D., & Ng, P. T. (2008). Similar agendas, diverse strategies: The quest for a regional hub of higher education in Hong Kong and Singapore. *Higher Education Policy, 21*(4), 487–503.

Cheung, A. C. K., Yuen, T. W. W., Yuen, C. Y. M., & Cheng, Y. C. (2011). Strategies and policies for Hong Kong's higher education in Asian markets: Lessons from the United Kingdom, Australia, and Singapore. *International Journal of Educational Management, 25*(2), 144–163.

Daquila, T. C. (2010). International student mobility: A comparative study between Australia and Singapore. In S. Morshidi & S. Kaur (Eds.), *Contemporary issues in the global higher education marketplace: Prospects and challenges* (pp. 23–54). Malaysia: University Sains Malaysia & National Higher Education Institute.

Daquila, T. C. (2013). Internationalizing higher education in Singapore: Government policies and the NUS experience. *Journal of Studies in International Education, 17*(5), 626–647.

Duhamel, D. (2004, October). Can Singapore become the Boston of Asia? *Continued Education, 2004*, 39–40.

Han, C. (1999). Singapore: Review of education events in 1998. *Asia-Pacific Journal of Education, 19*(2), 103–113.

ICEF. (2016). *Singapore adopting a more cautious outlook on education hub ambitions*. Retrieved from http://monitor.icef.com/2016/04/singapore-adopting-a-more-cautious-outlook-on-education-hub-ambitions/.

Ling, J. (2009). An analysis on the university internationalization in Singapore. *Around Southeast Asia, 3*, 52–55 (in Chinese).

Marginson, S. (2011). The Confucian model of higher education in East Asia and Singapore. In S. Marginson, S. Kaur, & E. Sawir (Eds.), *Higher education in the Asia-Pacific: Strategic responses to globalization* (pp. 53–75). Dordrecht and London: Springer.

Mok, K. H. (2008). Singapore's global education hub ambitions: University governance change and transnational higher education. *International Journal of Educational Management, 22*(6), 527–546.

Mok, K. H. (2011). The quest for regional hub of education: Growing heterarchies, organizational hybridization, and new governance in Singapore and Malaysia. *Journal of Education Policy, 26*(1), 61–81.

Mok, K. H. (2012). The rise of transnational higher education in Asia: Student mobility and studying experiences in Singapore and Malaysia. *Higher Education Policy, 25*(2), 225–241.

Raffin, A. (2007). Education, globalisation and equality. In K. F. Lian & C. K. Tong (Eds.), *Social policy in post-industrial Singapore* (pp. 97–120). Leiden, The Netherlands: Brill.

Sanderson, G. (2002). International education developments in Singapore. *International Education Journal, 3*(2), 85–103.

Sidhu, R., Ho, K. C., & Yeoh, B. (2011). Emerging education hubs: The case of Singapore. *Higher Education, 61*(1), 23–40.

Sidhu, R., & Matthews, J. (2005). International education for what? Under what conditions? The Global Schoolhouse Project. *Social Alternatives, 24*(4), 6–12.

Singaporean Ministry of Education. (2003). *Preliminary finding of the committee to review the university sector and graduate manpower planning*. Singapore: Ministry of Education.

Singaporean Ministry of Trade and Industry. (2007). *Developing Singapore's education industry*. Retrieved from http://www.mti.gov.sg/ResearchRoom/Documents/app.mti.gov.sg/data/pages/507/doc/ERC_SVS_EDU_MainReport.pdf.

Yale-NUS College. (2015). *Vision and mission*. Retrieved 27 April 2015, from http://www.yale-nus.edu.sg/about/vision-and-mission/.

Ziguras, C. (2003). The impact of the GATS on transnational tertiary education: Comparing experiences of New Zealand, Australia, Singapore and Malaysia. *Australian Educational Researcher, 30*(3), 89–109.

6

Australia

Australia is a multicultural society. This multiculturalism helps create an environment conducive to the internationalization process in higher education (Back & Davis, 1995). Australia's prime international focus is the Asia-Pacific region, and this is expressed in its foreign policy, in its trade, and in its international education programs (Back & Davis, 1995; Harman, 2005). As the Asian Studies Council (1988) argues, Australia is 'a nation with a European cultural past located in the Asian region' (p. 85), and it is in the national interest to bring 'the reality of our education, employment and skills into alignment with the reality of our location in the Asian region' (p. 87). Over the past decades, Australian universities have made impressive developments in embracing internationalization. With government encouragement and financial support, HEIs have invested considerably in forging links with overseas institutions, expanding the study of Asian languages, and internationalizing curricula (Harman, 2005; Krause, Coates, James, 2005). By far, the most dramatic and important developments in internationalization have been reflected in commercial terms: the large volume of foreign enrollments and education service export (Harman, 2004; Marginson, 2011; Rizvi, 2004).

Australia's development as a higher education exporter has been prompted by important shifts in Commonwealth (Australian) Government policy since the mid-1980s with regard to international students, the funding of higher education, and economic reform (Back & Davis, 1995; de Wit & Adams, 2011; Harman, 2004). Until the mid-1980s, for almost a century Australia regarded the education of overseas students almost exclusively in terms of foreign aid to nearby developing countries and as a means of establishing good relations with current and potential trading partners (Back & Davis, 1995; Harman, 2005). Since the 1980s, with increased demand for high-quality education, especially from developing countries with expanding economics but an inability to provide sufficient student places, export education has developed surprisingly quickly. Most Australian universities began to formalize their international strategies and to bring them within the overall university strategic framework.

Education as an Industry

Australia today is the third most prevalent destination for foreign students. In 2016, Australia hosted 336,000 international students, just behind the United States and the UK (OECD, 2018). Considering the relative size of Australia's population, such high representation among the international student market is indicative of the ongoing importance of this sector to Australia. International education is the nation's third largest export after coal and iron. The value of international exports reached AUD$28.6 billion in 2017. University education added an estimated AUD$140 billion to the Australian economy in 2014, and universities directly employed 120,000 full-time equivalent staff (Universities Australia, 2018).

The OECD figures also indicate that foreign students accounted for nearly one-fifth of all student enrollments in Australian universities in 2016 (OECD, 2018). In 2013, the number of international students enrolled by the Australian higher education sector was 217,520. In terms of nation of origin, the vast majority of overseas students (87%) in Australia came from Asian countries (OECD, 2018). Australia is heavily dependent on international student tuition. This is because for two decades Australian universities have faced falling public investment and need the revenue from international student tuition to supplement their incomes (Marginson, 2012; Murray, Hall, Leask, Marginson, & Ziguras, 2011).

The majority of international students come to Australia undertake a first degree and master's degree by coursework programs. Compared with the United States and the UK, the doctoral programs in Australia are less attractive (Marginson, 2011; OECD, 2018). Nearly half of enrollments at the master's level in Australia are international students. More than one-third of enrollments at the doctoral level are international, while the figure is over 40% in both the UK and the United States (OECD, 2018). The factors that enable the rapid expansion in the number of international students in Australian higher education involve the low cost due to a depreciated Australian dollar, proximity, safety, cultural tolerance, and non-academic services (Marginson, 2011; Turpin, Iredale, & Crinnion, 2002). As the above figures suggest, at least from the perspective of international student recruitment and education services export, Australian higher education is highly internationalized.

In addition to the high volume of international student enrollment, Australian HEIs have developed extensive international links with universities in other parts of the world. Up to 2014, there were 8515 formal agreements set up between Australia HEIs and overseas universities, 7911 of which are currently active. Over 60% of current agreements include a component of academic or research collaboration, and more than half provide for student exchange. Over 70% of the agreements offer opportunities for staff exchange. Australian international university links are observed to be dominated by North-East Asia (27%) and North-West Europe (29%). Most recently, Latin America has been identified by Australian universities as a strategic priority for international engagement; there are 278 formal agreements in place between Australian and Latin American institutions, comprising just 4% of agreements but showing an increase of 38% in comparison with the number in 2012 (Universities Australia, 2014).

The extensive international links also facilitate the outbound mobility of Australian university students. According to the i-graduate survey of

Australian Universities International Directors' Forum (AUIDF) members, students who took part in some form of overseas study experience increased 19.5% to 38,144 students in 2015, compared to 2014. This figure outperformed its peers, as the corresponding figures in the United States show 15% of students study abroad, in the UK it is 5% of graduates, and in Canada it is as low as 2.3% of domestic students. Almost two-fifths of all overseas experiences were in the United States, China, UK, Indonesia, and Canada, with the United States proving the most popular, attracting 13% of all experiences. China and the UK each attracted 9%.

A huge part of Australia's success is the New Colombo Plan, relaunched in 2013, which provides mobility grants to students to study and work overseas. The number of undergraduates studying in the program's 'priority destinations' (China, Indonesia, Japan, Cambodia, and India) in the Indo-Pacific increased 32% in 2015. Both Australian official departments and individual institutions acknowledge the significant value of their students having some overseas study experiences (Australian Bureau of Statistics, 2011). The opportunity to be immersed in a different culture provides unique knowledge and cultural understanding, while simultaneously strengthening Australia's global network.

Strong and Clear Institutional Commitment

There were nine leading universities in Australia that generously supported this project. Of the nine universities, eight of them had designated a very senior individual, a Deputy Vice-Chancellor (DVC) or Pro Vice-Chancellor (PVC), to be responsible for a wide range of international activities. The administrative focus on international strategies demonstrates the magnitude of the international dimension in university leadership and governance. The senior role for internationalization is expected to strengthen institutional capacity for coordination and communication at the central level and to enable the implementation of a wide range of international activities in a more strategic and coherent manner. The following statement by a PVC who was appointed recently illustrates the responsibilities of the role:

Mine is a new position, and I'm the first PVC of International in this university. That position brings together a number of existing units within the university, which have been reconfigured. Hopefully, together they will be more powerful and work better. Since the current world is competitive and because it is more difficult to get funding, we are starting to launch more coordinated activities across the campus. My job is largely to provide leadership in these activities, but also to contribute to better coherence and coordination of those activities so that our university can really make more of its own excellence. (Interviewee 2, Australia)

In the eight universities, the responsibilities of the senior role for internationalization were defined clearly and stated specifically. Generally, the role is meant to perform three main functions. First, it is responsible for the development of university-wide international strategies and for championing the international agenda. Second, the senior position is provided with sufficient staff and resources to implement comprehensive international strategies. There are a number of units under the umbrella of the senior portfolio that cover several key areas of international activities such as international marketing and recruitment, student exchanges, international programs, university partnerships and networks, and high-profile international events. The leadership role is required to pay attention to, and to nurture, each of the pillars, ultimately tying them together. The administration system established for international activities demonstrated further that internationalization in these universities is not a 'paper commitment,' but is one that has been institutionalized. This institutionalization of international strategies ensures the sustainability of internationalization even when there are changes in leadership. Third, and most importantly, being accountable for university-wide international strategies is expected to exert influence throughout the institution.

In addition to the units under the portfolio of the senior role, there are many divisions in the university that contribute to internationalization. Therefore, the PVC/DVC is expected to make the commitment to internationalization explicit for the whole university community and to coordinate different departments within the institution to make sure the university is reaching the goals of its international targets. The nature of the leadership role shows that internationalization has permeated most aspects of the university, including administration, research, teaching and learning, and service.

A Mixed Motivation for Being Internationalized

Although Australia has achieved splendid outcomes in commercializing its education provision, and the international education sector contributes significantly to the national economy, the primary driver considered by university leaders for being internationalized remains academic excellence. Specifically, internationalization is conducive to the competitiveness of the core pillars of university operation, the position of the university in the national and global higher education landscape, and the aspiration to build world-class universities. Interviewees stressed that internationalization is expected to benefit all key areas of the university: research, teaching and learning, governance, and engagement, as illustrated by the statement below:

> Internationalization is a driver of organisational development. It is the driver for competitiveness and globalized higher education. So those institutions that are highly internationalized are probably going to have a highly internationalized research and teaching academic profile, as well as a student profile. And all of that means they (are) probably going to have higher rates of co-publications and more internationally collaborative research with international funding. (Interviewee 1, Australia)

With respect to building research capacity, universities need to recruit research-capable candidates from overseas. Also, international collaboration in research is more likely to generate publications with a higher level of citations. On the teaching and learning side, integrating the international dimension into the curricula and programs allows universities to produce graduates who are globally employable.

In addition to the enhancement of academic quality, international strategies have been recognized by university leaders as a means to gain a 'competitive edge' and worldwide reputation. Marginson and van der

Wende (2007) argue that a new globalized higher education landscape is emerging. Within this growing landscape, the distribution of capacities and resources among nations and institutions often determines their global position and potential, but the possibilities are more open in the global setting than the national one. The findings show that Australian university policymakers are aware of these possibilities and have made endeavors to develop their universities to become a global thought leader or a global center for learning. As one of the PVCs said,

> Fundamentally, the rationale for being internationalized comes down to the university's key targets for the next 10–20 years, which include improving the rankings. In order to achieve it, we need strong international engagement. Regarding the rankings, we do very well in the matrix but not in the reputational sort of things. And one of the responsibilities of PVC (International) will be to make sure that we do things (which) enhance our reputation internationally and improve rankings. (Interviewee 8, Australia)

The aim of positioning oneself in the world often intertwines with the aspiration to build world-class universities. Being internationalized has been perceived as a key component of a world-class university. To become a leading university in the world, it is deemed that institutions need develop a comprehensive range of strengths and to be deeply internationalized, preparing students for global careers and citizens. As one PVC argued:

> Internationalization is integrated into the central because we take the pleasure of being one of the world's top universities, in (the) top 100 of Times and QS and top 150 in ARWU. Rankings are just one way of understanding our success. But for what else, I am ambitious to be a peer of good standing among the best universities in the world. So, the rankings help us understand if that is what we are achieving. (Interviewee 5, Australia)

In addition to academic incentives, at the institutional level, internationalization matters in the contemporary context because money is crucial, particularly in the circumstance of financial reduction. Not surprisingly, the financial revenue generated by recruiting overseas students is another main force pushing the internationalization agenda of Australian universities as a popular destination for international students. In the words of the Vice-Chancellor of an Australian university, 'internationalization is important financially. We have a lot of international students, particularly undergraduates. That is a very important part of the financial success of the university' (Interviewee 3, Australia). The interviewees also said that another driving force for internationalization is to build up international values and cross-culture understandings, and to create democratic communities and citizenship on the campus. The history of a university may impact its attitude toward internationalization. One participant Australian university was the first university in Australia to recruit international students, starting in the 1950s. It also acted as a pioneer in setting up international exchanges. As the PVC said, 'being international is in our DNA, and we are always being international in our outlook. It comes natural to us to think internationally' (Interviewee 5, Australia).

Making Meaning of Internationalization

As the literature shows, there is no simple, unique, or widely accepted definition of university internationalization. The understanding of university internationalization is conditioned by the time, context, and lens. Unsurprisingly, when the interviewees were asked to make meaning of the phenomenon, almost every participant described it in a unique way. Given the diversity of the meanings interpreted by the interviewees, the three dominant ideologies argued by Stier (2004), which deal with the perceptions of university internationalization, are used to analyze the interviewees' understandings. The three ideologies are *idealism*, *instrumentalism*, and *educationalism*. University policymakers rarely adhere merely to one of these ideologies, but often vacillate among them.

The *idealist* perceives internationalization based on the normative assumption that 'it is good per se.' It is believed that through university international cooperation, higher education can contribute to the creation of a more democratic, fair, and equal world (Stier, 2004). Aligned with this perspective, one interviewee suggested that 'university internationalization means fitting the purposes of the external world, and that external world, whether in research or in teaching and learning or in communities, is a globalised one' (Interviewee 1, Australia). She further explained that internationalization means being interconnected. There is a large volume of mobility of people, ideas, and communication. Therefore, the opposite of being internationalized is being parochial, having a very small vision of the purpose and the society. This view is echoed by another interviewee:

> Internationalizing is about bringing the various organisations together to solve international problems. So being international is not about chasing students' numbers or money, not about thinking of people overseas and getting dollars from their pockets. It is about a respectful interaction with the rest of the world, to bring together the stakeholders to solve the problem. (Interviewee 7, Australia)

In the *instrumentalist* viewpoint, internationalizing higher education is assumed to meet demands of a capitalist, global, and multicultural world. The primary objective is to ensure a sufficiently large labor force, with adequate skills for competence-demanding jobs. This is consistent with the pragmatic and economic goals inherent in instrumentalism (Stier, 2004). Different from the *idealist* that focuses on the overall improvement of the society, the *instrumentalist* is prone to treating university education as a global commodity. Some interviewees tended to interpret internationalization from this perspective, arguing that the key to internationalizing the university is to produce graduates who are internationally competent and employable. Or more broadly, internationalization can be taken as a means to survive in the profound impacts brought by globalization, as one PVC stated:

> Globalization means what is happening in the world will affect you financially, politically, and whatever. It will affect you and is out of your control. And internationalization is the strategy that you have to manage

the influences of globalisation. It is about how to swim in the world. (Interviewee 4, Australia)

The focus of *educationalists* is the growth of professionalization and academy. They argue that being exposed to an unfamiliar academic setting with its unique culture and teaching approach, norms, and grading system will enrich the overall academic experiences of both students and teaching staff (Stier, 2004). The educationalism ideology aligns with the academic motives. And internationalization, from this perspective, means in most, if not all, areas of university's activities that an international dimension is presented and adding value (Interviewee 2, Australia).

Criticism of a single definition of university internationalization was observed during the interview. One PVC found fault with too much time spent on discussing the definition of internationalization and suggested that it might be time to stop worrying about what it means. 'We are just doing it' (Interviewee 2, Australia). The reason to avoid a single fixed definition of internationalization, as he explained, is that universities have developed at different rates, and they have to define what internationalization means for them. What internationalization means today is different from what it meant in the twentieth century, so the meaning changes over time. This argument is advocated by another interviewee:

> Internationalization is a very amorphous term. There are dozens of elements that contribute to internationalization. And universities will pursue different pieces of that puzzle at different times. That is sort of the reason to be sceptical about the validity of a single definition for internationalization. (Interviewee 6, Australia)

This criticism, to some extent, reveals the nature of university internationalization. That is, as a concept, university internationalization might be beyond definition. The meaning-making of university internationalization is possibly filtered by institutional, national, international, and cultural contexts.

Embedding the International Dimension into University Operation

No matter how fantastic the description of internationalization is in the university's policy or strategic statement, the real impacts have to be achieved by operationalizing the international dimension in the university's daily work. Therefore, the interviewees were asked to identify the key dimensions and components of their institutional internationalization practices. This is also a crucial step for building the measurement because it will develop the concept into measurable domains and offer a way to frame the indicators. Interviewees described the dimensions in a variety of ways. Some catalogued the dimensions in a highly aggregated manner. One said that internationalization might not be separated from the key strategic functions and missions of the university; therefore, there are three dimensions of it: research, teaching and learning, and engagement (Interviewee 6, Australia). Others presented the dimensions more specifically, regarding every component of their international strategies as a dimension. In this study, the term 'dimension' is distinguished from 'component.' A dimension is used to describe an area of university internationalization strategies, which is an aggregated concept. A dimension may consist of several components, which center on the dimension and mirror different facets of it.

The student dimension of the internationalization practice was highlighted by all interviewed university leaders. Specifically, this relates to having an internationalized student body on campus and encouraging domestic students to experience being overseas. According to the interviewees, international recruitment is a current strategic focus of almost all Australian universities. In order to attract more international students, particularly students from Asian countries, universities have developed various strategies to make their programs more appealing. As one of the interviewees exemplified, the university that she was working at is the first university to establish foundation programs for international students to get them better prepared for overseas study. Regarding the recruitment strategy, she further explained that the university has market share strategies for each Asian country, ranking them into three tiers. Once the international students arrive at the campus, school officials must make sure they experience the real life in the city. To achieve this, the university offers opportunities to volunteer in local community and internships for international students. The university also has invested in infrastructure of the campus, accommodations, catering, student clubs and societies, and career support to make sure that non-academic experience is also a good one (Interviewee 5, Australia).

In addition to having an internationalized student body, it is equally important to provide domestic students international experiences either via mobility programs or on campus. As one of the PVCs stated:

> Student experience is very important. They need to have international experience, meeting international students, and feeling comfortable within different cultures. You can do that by sending the student overseas, but certainly by making sure the student body has more than 100 countries' representatives on campus. The international and intercultural experiences that students engage with will encourage them to take care of people, be interested in global issues, and ultimately become global citizens. (Interviewee 8, Australia)

Australian universities have established a wide range of exchange programs, long-term or short-term opportunities, including year-long or semester exchange, summer schools, internships, and field trips.

Elements in relation to the faculty dimension were also mentioned by a significant majority of participants. In addition to students, the international profile of a university is determined by the faculty. Recruiting international academic staff or staff with overseas academic experience will contribute to an internationalized academic team. As a migration country, Australia enjoys the advantage of a diverse society. The proportion of foreign-born faculty members in Australian universities is considerably high. For example, in one of the participant university, more than half the academic staff were born outside Australia. This is not uncommon in other universities. Recruiting international faculties is a natural practice for world-class universities; as one of the university leaders put it, 'if you repute as elite university, people want to come work for you. So, you hire the best staff from everywhere in the world regardless of who they are, simply because they are the best' (Interviewee 3, Australia).

Additionally, endeavors toward internationalizing research were reported by all university leaders as key components of their international practices. These components include international joint research projects, internationally focused research centers, international researchers, and international research achievements. In the words of one interviewed PVC, 'universities work together across boundaries, generating scientific outcomes with greater impacts, which can actually make a difference' (Interviewee 7, Australia).

Other elements recognized by most interviewees include practices to provide an internationalized curriculum to students. In doing so, universities develop various programs such as joint degree programs and courses with an international component. As one interviewee explained, 'an internationalized curriculum means the curriculum exposes students to a variety of global perspectives on the issues that they are studying, which helps prepare students for global careers' (Interviewee 6, Australia). To embed the international dimension into the curriculum also means more flexibility for students. For example, in one of the participant universities, a reform of undergraduate curricula has been undertaken recently in order to offer more choices of units for students to choose. This allows their students to complete a course in Vietnamese or Chinese, and to travel to enroll in some programs in Asia as part of their degree. As traditionally, Australian universities attempted to squash all units in the four years with no space for students to do any units about things they actually like to do. Therefore, the university designed the undergraduate curriculum to free up the space for those students to do units and to do the things they are interested in. It turned out that all of their students chose to do things around language or international components when the freedom is given (Interviewee 9, Australia).

A strong leadership in university international development is observed as a key feature of Australian universities. The leadership dimension includes the international presence in senior management teams, resources invested in international activities, and an internationalized service system. Leadership in a university's international development will guarantee that international practices take place in a deliberately planned way rather than ad hoc. As a newly appointed PVC, one interviewee argued that his priority at the moment was to clarify the distribution of labor in the variation of internationalization and the distribution of efforts between the central offices and the schools and colleges to further develop the capacity and capability of the central office to support the schools.

> It is not entirely clear at the moment who does what. That is why I am trying to understand who does what and trying to make it easier. For instance, we aim to increase our international students from Latin American by 10 percent next year. That is fine. But who is going to do it? Is there activity that take place at schools? Is there activity that take place at central office? Is it collaboration? I do not think we have a ready-made template for activity. It's happening ad hoc. It is working, but in a competitive environment, it is quite difficult to have any sort of confidence in the outcomes if it is happening ad hoc. (Interviewee 2, Australia)

University leaders also require a stronger leadership role played by the Australian government. As one of them put it, 'while we have more work to do at the government level. When I went to Beijing, I met the Ambassador of Australia, I went to the India Higher Commission, so I think in addition to student engagement, institutional engagement, there is also engagement at the governmental level. At our government and foreign governmental level' (Interviewee 1, Australia).

A number of elements related to the engagement dimension also were suggested by all the interviewees as crucial to the internationalization of a university. Those components include forming international partnerships, keeping connection with the alumni, and establishing networks. One of the interviewees mentioned that they have been investing heavily in their alumni network to keep in touch with and hold events for their overseas alumni. They had a huge calendar of events across Asia and also in North America designed to keep their alumni in touch and to hopefully fundraise and arrange projects that they could offer support on campus.

In recent years, there has been a real priority for the university to keep the network of alumni to really help the mission of the university. Fund-raising is one aspect. The other aspect is to encourage alumni to support internships and overseas internship opportunities but also to mentor students who returning home.

> They are great ambassadors of the university. Often you find out they are in influential positions in universities or industry. We have been working very hard with their support to finding internship opportunities for our students. So it is a great way they can give back to the university. It makes sense. And they can give back in so many other ways. It is not just about money. They can give time and particularly they give support for young graduates. There are regime business networks. I think it is not just looking at alumni in terms of their potential of giving money but also the potential to give their time and skills. (Interviewee 5, Australia)

Different universities developed their own approaches and strategies for partnering with HEIs overseas, as illustrated by the deliberation of one PVC,

> Regarding our partnership strategies, we have three layers. The broadest layer is the 500 agreements, 3000 staff all over the place. My approach is just to facilitate it. I do not want any of the university faculty to think the international office is up to strike them, it is just there to help them. That is the first layer. What I mean is that I think good individual researchers will have their own networks and their own knowledge about who are the best people to work on their topic to collaborate. Me, as a representative of the university, my network is limited to the people I know. And my knowledge is limited to the areas that I know. So I cannot advise a microbiologist about who is the best person to cooperate with in Africa. I just do not know that. We have a broader global coverage and we informed global coverage if I let them do their work and I do not tell them what to do. I just help them do their work. I think that is different from almost all the rest of PVCs' approaches.
>
> Next layer is that we have prioritized countries. We have tier 1, tier 2, and tier 3 countries. The top tier is that we have a small number of key partners. I think we have some between 5 to 10. Tier 1 countries are

China, HK, Singapore, Malaysia, the US, and Canada. China is because that is where we get most of our income. Singapore and Malaysia are because that is 25 percent of our students and that is our best alumni network. US and Canada are because of our graduates' collaboration in research. The second tier includes Indonesia, Vietnam, Japan and Korea together. We do stuff there, but they are not as important as the big three. The next tier is actually regions: South Asia, India, Europe, including the UK, the Middle East, and South America. That is a big deal because we invested about $2.5 million over five years in South America, but we do not know results for our efforts there. (Interviewee 7, Australia)

For leading universities, partnerships mean collaborations not only with other similar universities in the world but also influential transnational organizations. The argument made by the recently retired PVC of one participant university best evidences the ambition of Australian universities in playing a leading role in important international affairs.

We have established programs with the international agencies and international governments. We put key people on the committees that affect policy. So, food security and public health, educational reform, so we would put our people on the committees of the World Health Organization, OECD, World Bank, Asian Development Bank. And we spent quite a lot of time on the relationship with those organizations. In addition, every year we have five major international forums in Sydney, like the Australia-China Forum. And every year we had about ten of what we called frontiers knowledge symposia in other countries. We went to Beijing, we have joint day with Beida, and with Tsinghua around an area of mutual interests, like cancer research maybe or engineering, physics, whatever. So, when we go to these groups, we build the international partnerships and then we ask them to continue with projects. (Interviewee 3, Australia)

Finally, culture was reported by a couple of interviewees as an important dimension. It relates to creating a multicultural campus, which gives students and staff exposure to working with people from different mindsets and perspectives. As one of them claimed, 'it is about the fact that we do live in a globalized world with lots of different cultures and therefore, giving our students and staff exposure to experiences of working with people come from a different mindset can help them be successfully when they are baselessly in their professional life as teachers or researchers or politicians. It is about multicultural competence' (Interviewee 1, Australia). His view is echoed by other university leaders; for example, one of them argued that 'students need to have an international experience in which they meet international students, they feel comfortable within different cultures and within the environment' (Interviewee 8, Australia). A multicultural campus does not merely mean having the presence of representatives of different nationalities but also integrating them.

Once the dimensions were identified, the next step was to explore the relationships among them—in other words, whether these dimensions were treated as equally important or were given differential priorities. This issue needs to be addressed cautiously when developing measurements, particularly when the measurement intends to serve a ranking purpose because it will determine the weight of different indicators. Since the indicator set developed in this study does not aim to be used as a ranking system, there is no need to weight the indicators. But exploring the relationship between the dimensions remains crucial, for it is an indispensable part of the conceptual framework, influencing the conceptual structure of the phenomenon being studied and measured.

Interviewees' perceptions diverged on this issue. Only two of them perceived all the dimensions as equally important. Others indicated that the priority given to each dimension depends on the goals of the institution, the perspective, as well as the stage a university is at. For example, one PVC pointed out that

> there is not a straightforward answer to it. It depends through what lens you are looking at the issue. If you talk to our Vice President who is responsible for finance, of course he will say the recruitment is really important. And it actually is because the fees the students bring help us run our university. However, if you look through the lens of our reputation, then of course, the partnerships we have, the research collaborations we have, the alumni base we have are really central to the university in terms of its reputation as a world-class institution. And then if you look

> through the lens of students, the student experience is really important, is one of the most important terms of their lives, the time they are here in the university. The student experience is absolutely critical. And for me, as PVC of International, I am responsible for promoting all of the different pillars equally as they are critical to the university. We certainly take a holistic view here. To make it work those four pillars have to be equally stable. I think universities will be at different stages of their journey. They may focus on one dimension more than others because they do not have the luxury to do all. (Interviewee 5, Australia)

Others argued the profile of the university will determine the priority given to different aspects. As one of the interviewees puts it, 'in our case, we are very strongly identified as a research university. If you take that as the promise, our researchers should be gaining value through international collaboration. That would probably be the most obvious one' (Interviewee 2, Australia).

The prioritized dimensions could also shift with time. In one of the participant universities, as reflected by the PVC, 'for the last ten years, the number one priority has been giving to get international students here. But for me, I took the current role one year ago, and the most important thing for me is to help our researchers have an international research connection. For me, personally, that is the number one. Number two is to make sure that we have study abroad and we increase those numbers. And then international students will be number three' (Interviewee 6, Australia).

Among the diverse views on the priority given to the dimensions, one came to the fore. It is argued by a Vice-Chancellor that weightings should not be applied to the dimensions. This is not because there is no consensus on the proportion that each dimension takes up, but because the result—the internationalization of the university—is expected to be more than the sum of the individual parts. He further illustrated that 'if international students take up 30 percent, international faculty takes up 30 percent, research racks up 30 percent, and institutional relationships account for 10 percent, it's going to add up to 100 percent, whereas actually you want all those things add up to more than the sum of the individual parts' (Interviewee 3, Australia).

Although university leaders perceived the importance of the aspects of internationalization differently, all of them agreed that these dimensions intertwined with each other, and a holistic approach is needed to create an internationalized university. Any single dimension cannot be fully achieved without the inputs of other dimensions. A scrutiny of the interviews shows that 'comprehensive' and 'holistic' are the two words used most frequently by university leaders to describe their institutional approach, which indicates that they take a systematic and deliberate approach to internationalization, and there is a large volume of international work in many areas, which reinforce each other and have intellectual coherence. Several interviewees mentioned the changing of approaches over time. For example, in one participant university, the international model used to be focused exclusively on international students. But now they have stopped thinking in that way and have shifted to a more integrated model (Interviewee 7, Australia). Another newly appointed PVC expressed his intention to change the approach in his institution:

> Initially, practice in this university very much focused on internationalization in the research context and had less of a focus in terms of alumni and fund raising or even teaching and learning. And I think we should treat it in a broad way, having an international element in all main areas. (Interviewee 8, Australia)

Measuring Internationalization Performance in Practice

Australian universities are quite advanced in measuring their internationalization performance. Seven of the nine participant universities have implemented some sort of tracking or assessment of international activities, in a mix of qualitative and quantitative methods. For example, key performance targets were set up in one university, including international student recruitment and satisfaction, exchanges and short-term opportunities, incoming and outgoing students, international staff, research grants, citations, and commercialization of research working with overseas industry partners. Regarding internationalizing curriculum, program reviews were conducted. A high-quality and specific range of indicators were used to monitor the institutional performance of internationalization (Interviewee 5, Australia). Similarly, in other universities Key Performance Indicators (KPIs) and systemic reviews at different levels were employed together to monitor different aspects of the university's international practices. Considering the substantial institutional commitment to internationalization, it is natural for university leaders to ask for measurements. Regardless of the extent to which a university had been tracking and assessing its internationalization performance, all of the interviewees emphasized the importance of having measurements for both evidence-based decision-making and positioning oneself in the internationalized higher education landscape. In the words of one PVC,

> These evidence-based data help inform the approach of our global strategy. For example, it is very powerful if the university wants to change the funding support for outbound mobility. The profile of students going abroad will show who is doing what, where and why, and give the leader levers to shift strategy. This cannot be done without data. (Interviewee 1, Australia)

The information that the data provide can also help universities identify the problems in their current international practice and encourage improvements. As the same PVC illustrated, 'the review of our collaboration with existing partners shows that it is biased to advanced science and technology country partners. It is biased to English-speaking destinations. And it reveals that there is something we have not done adequately' (Interviewee 1, Australia). With her team, she built 13 indicators to measure international collaboration with all the partners, capturing student exchanges, study abroad, course work, recruitment (for volume and for breadth), postgraduate students, joint PhDs, alumni from each partner, sponsorship, joint publications, and projects. By the time that this project was conducted, she was focusing on a possible index to capture the work they do overseas in capacity-building countries; this project was funded by different bodies. It took her team five years to establish the indicator system, working out the definition of each indicator and the data collection protocol. This tool indicates a comprehensive approach in tracking progress in international development.

There are two universities that did not implement any measurements of internationalization. One is because there was no international plan for the university, and the performance in international development had not been systemically monitored. The newly appointed PVC said he was keen to track and assess the university's international activities at different levels. The PVC of the other university with no measurement elaborated on the reason and his considerations for not setting up targets for their international development, which are thought-provoking:

> Because of the history of the university being so decentralized, I think there are lots happening without the central university knowing about them. And I am actually quite comfortable with that because I am confident that all are of high quality. I worked in other universities, where I would be very nervous that a VIP would come to the campus and be taken directly to the school and not be looked after well, not have a good experience, and not get a positive impression of the university if the central office has not been involved in the coordination. That is not the case here. People here are so well connected, and people have such deep and long-lasting links in so many countries and are so influential in terms of policy development and so on. I have no concerns that the international activities which take place without my knowledge are not of high quality. Because there are so many activities every single day, so many visitors, so many collaborations, it would be a pointless task for the central office to know every single activity. It would be counterproductive to try to catch all of that.
>
> What I am trying to do is to review the performance of each unit, looking at how appropriately they are structured and how appropriate their policies are to contribute to the university. That review in particular was not saying 'oh you only have 5000 international students, that's bad.' It was saying 'do you have an effective mechanism for communicating with schools to help them with recruiting students?' And the answer

was no. So that is one recommendation that says we have to have better policy, better systems for communicating with schools. I suppose an additional challenge of a decentralized system is that when you look at your data, and you look at your performance, it is very difficult to figure out who is to blame or who got the credit. We do not spend, at this time, a lot of time looking at KPIs for internationalization. Not yet.

I think the answer is 'not yet' because I do not think that to give the schools targets at this point would be productive. One of the main reasons is that I do not think we have the tools to necessarily meet targets. If we meet the targets, it would not necessarily be because of something we did. I am more concerned at the moment about improving relationships, about developing connections within the university, about building the team, and making sure there is a high-performance team. There is no point in giving people targets if you do not have the tools to meet them. I think that is the first stage for us. There is no point to give schools recruitment targets if the school does not have any control over the activity. (Interviewee 2, Australia)

In addition to a decentralized system, there are other challenges facing the university when attempting to establish effective measurement of internationalization. As one interviewee highlighted, the appropriateness and quality of the proxies of internationalization was one of his concerns. Because of the nature and characteristics of some disciplines, indicators may not be high-quality or meaningful proxies, which can reflect the reality of internationalization. For example, the number of international publications has been commonly used as an indicator; however, it tells very little about the internationalization of research in a case in which the university has researchers who are involved in some mass physics projects like SERN, whose papers have more than 200 authors. They produce thousands of papers a year, but it is difficult to determine rich collaborations in those multi-billion-dollar research projects. Anyone involved in any way appears as an author on the paper. In this regard, weight must be applied to almost all the multi-authored papers, or the number should be refined by discipline analysis before it can be used to draw any meaningful conclusion about the internationalization of research in a university (Interviewee 6, Australia).

Indicators Suggested for Australian Universities

In order to select the appropriate indicators for Australian universities to use to measure their internationalization performance, the questionnaire that lists 57 draft indicators was sent to the interviewed university leaders for distribution to relevant staff. There were 93 responses collected from the nine universities, with 54 useable ones. The demographic information shows over one-third of respondents aged between 50 and 59, followed by over a quarter between 40 and 49. More than half of respondents are female, and nearly one-fifth of respondents have a nationality other than Australian. Slight less than half of respondents worked at the International Office, with another 30% working at the Senior Executive Office. The same rules were applied to the responses to select the appropriate indicators.[1] Forty out of the 57 draft indicators meet the criteria and are included in the final set for universities in Australia, as presented in Table 6.1.

The selected indicators were cross-checked for their feasibility. Nine indicators were cited as feasible by fewer than 70% of respondents, including:

1. R10: Number of co-editorships in international journals,
2. F1: Percentage of international (by nationality) faculty members (full-time equivalent FTE),
3. F2: Number of international scholars visiting for academic purposes,
4. F3: Percentage of faculty (FTE) who were awarded their highest academic qualification by an institution abroad,
5. F4: Percentage of faculty (FTE) proficient in a language other than the primary language of teaching/research,
6. F5: Percentage of faculty (FTE) who have at least one-year overseas experience (excl. degree study),

---

[1] In this project, indicators that are agreed on by more than three-quarters of respondents from each country as 'Very Important' or 'Somewhat Important' are retained in the tailored set for a particular country.

Table 6.1 Final indicators for measuring university internationalization performance (Australia)

Dimension	Indicator	Percentage of respondents rating as 'Very Important' or 'Somewhat Important'
Research	R1: Percentage of research projects involving international partnership and collaboration	100.0
	R5: Percentage of international post-doctoral researchers	96.3
	R4: Number of research centers operated with international partners	94.4
	R6: Proportion of total research income generated by research involving international collaboration	90.7
	R3: Number of research centers focused on international study	88.9
	R9: Percentage of publications cited by SCI, EI, ISTP	77.8
	R8: Number of presentations in international	77.7
	R10: Number of co-editorships in international journals	75.9
Student	S4: Percentage of international higher degree research (HDR) students on campus	100.0
	S6: Percentage of domestic students who have international study experiences	100.0
	S7: Number of incoming international students (incl. exchanges and short-term programs those are no more than an academic year)	98.1
	S1: Percentage of international students (for degree study) on campus in total	96.3
	S2: Percentage of international undergraduate students on campus governments and international agencies)	96.3
	S3: Percentage of international master's (coursework) students on campus	96.3

Dimension	Indicator	Percentage of respondents rating as 'Very Important' or 'Somewhat Important'
	S5: Percentage of international students by region	87.0
	S8: Ratio of outgoing domestic students to incoming international students (no more than an academic year)	83.3
Faculty	F2: Number of international scholars visiting for academic purposes	96.3
	F1: Percentage of international (by nationality) faculty members (full-time equivalent FTE)	87.0
	F5: Percentage of faculty (FTE) who have at least one-year overseas experience (excl. degree study)	83.3
	F6: Percentage of faculty (FTE) who hold a visiting lectureship abroad	83.3
	F4: Percentage of faculty (FTE) proficient in a language other than the primary language of teaching/research	77.7
	F3: Percentage of faculty (FTE) who were awarded their highest academic qualification by an institution abroad	75.9
Curriculum	C8: Number of joint degree programs (Bachelor, Master's and PhD) collaborated with overseas higher education institutions	90.7
	C6: Number of programs with a mandatory period abroad	87.0
	C1: Number of subjects offering foreign language studies	85.2
	C2: Number of subjects involving a partner in other countries	85.2
	C7: Number of subjects on foreign countries/cultures/societies	85.2

(continued)

Table 6.1 (continued)

Dimension	Indicator	Percentage of respondents rating as 'Very Important' or 'Somewhat Important'
Engagement	C11: Number of students who attend joint degree programs collaborated with overseas higher education institutions	81.5
	E2: Number of overseas partners with whom at least one academic activity (mobility, program, research) has taken place	85.2
	E4: Proportion of international (by nationality) alumni relative to the total number of alumni	85.2
	E1: Number of memberships in international organizations and consortia	83.3
	E5: Percentage of alumni working overseas	81.5
	E3: Percentage of partnerships by region (Europe, Africa, Asia, North America, South America, Pacific)	79.6
Governance	G7: Funding to support the international mobility of students	98.1
	G6: Funding for international visiting scholars	92.6
	G8: Funding for international research projects	90.7
	G9: Number of scholarships for international students (all degree levels)	90.7
	G10: Number of scholarships for international post-doctoral researchers	90.7
	G5: Percentage of total budget available (excluding personnel costs) for internationalization activities	88.9
	G3: Percentage of administration staff proficient in more than one working language	79.6

7. F6: Percentage of faculty (FTE) who hold a visiting lectureship abroad,
8. E5: Percentage of alumni working overseas,
9. G6: Funding for international visiting scholars.

It could be noticed that Australian universities were facing particular challenges in monitoring their academic staff's international engagement, which echoes university leaders' view.

Summary

As a migration country, Australia has advantages in internationalizing its higher education sector, and the tolerance for multiple cultures makes Australian universities prevalent destinations for international students, particularly students from Asian countries. The splendid outcomes achieved by Australian universities in recruiting international students contribute significantly to their financial stability and sustainability. The prominent economic incentives for Australian universities to embrace internationalization are partly due to the falling public investment in higher education. Unlike their counterparts in China and Singapore, who enjoy substantial subsidization from the government, universities in Australia are forced to make money out of international student flows to supplement their income. The dependence on international student tuition spurs universities here to take internationalization seriously. The commitment to international engagement manifests itself in almost every aspect of university operation, from leadership to administration, from curriculum to students' experience, from marketing strategy to alumni networks. Moreover, to make sure their internationalization strategies work well; most Australian universities have established tracking systems for international activities and evaluations for the outcomes of these activities. Comprehensive data collection has been implemented to gather information for policy-making and strategy adjustment, complemented by extensive reviews of international performance of different units, departments, and schools within the university. In this respect, universities in other parts of the world could benefit from the experiences of Australian universities in international development and its measurement.

On the other hand, the over-reliance on fee-paying international students has aroused concerns with the slipping quality and devaluation of the degrees. In addition, with the continuing increase in tuition fees and the fluctuations in visa policies, Australian universities have experienced ups and downs in securing the supply of international students. In addition, with the improvement in education and the research capacity of emerging educational hubs in Asia-Pacific regions such as Singapore and China, Asian students who consider overseas study are now provided more options for their destination. The One, Belt One Road initiative launched by the Chinese government in 2013, for instance, creates a favorable environment for Southeast Asian students to pursue degree studies at different levels in China. How to make Australian universities stand out from the competition for international students is an urgent question that deserves policymakers' and university leaders' deliberations. Fortunately, leaders of flagship universities have already taken actions to expand the breadth and depth of internationalization in order to maintain or even increase the appeal of their institutions for international students. A common approach is to reform the curriculum to offer students more flexibility and embed the international and intercultural components into the course at the same time. Universities are also trying hard to encourage more domestic students to spend some time overseas to gain direct international experiences. With the maturity of its internationalization, Australia's leading universities have shown their clear intention to continually be the pioneer in this field.

References

Asian Studies Council. (1988). A national strategy for the study of Asia in Australia. *Asian Studies Review, 12*(2), 85–87.
Australian Bureau of Statistics. (2011). *Australian social trends December 2011: International student*. Retrieved 16 October 2012 from http://www.abs.gov.au/socialtrends.

Back, K., & Davis, D. (1995). Internationalization of higher education in Australia. In J. Knight & H. de Wit (Eds.), *Strategies for internationalization of higher education: A comparative study of Australia, Canada, Europe and the United States of America* (pp. 121–153). Amsterdam: EAIE.

de Wit, H., & Adams, T. (2011). Global competition in higher education: A comparative study of policies, rationales, and practices in Australia and Europe. In H. de Wit (Ed.), *Trends, issues and challenges in internationalisation of higher education* (pp. 29–38). Amsterdam: Centre for Applied Research on Economics and Management Hogeschool van Amsterdam.

Harman, G. (2004). New directions in internationalizing higher education: Australia's development as an exporter of higher education. *Higher Education Policy, 17*(1), 101–120.

Harman, G. (2005). Internationalisation of Australian higher education. In M. Tight (Ed.), *International relations* (Vol. 3, pp. 205–232). Bingley: Emerald Group Publishing Limited.

Krause, K.-L., Coates, H., & James, R. (2005). Monitoring the internationalisation of higher education: Are there useful quantitative performance indicators? In M. Tight (Ed.), *International relations (International perspectives on higher education research)* (Vol. 3, pp. 233–253). Bingley: Emerald Group Publishing Limited.

Marginson, S. (2011). Global position and position-taking in higher education: The case of Australia. In S. Marginson, S. Kaur, & E. Sawir (Eds.), *Higher education in the Asia-Pacific: Strategic responses to globalization* (pp. 375–392). Dordrecht and London: Springer.

Marginson, S. (2012). International education in Australia: The roller coaster. *International Higher Education, 68*(Summer), 11–13.

Marginson, S., & van der Wende, M. (2007). *Globalisation and higher education.* (OECD Education Working Papers, No. 8). OECD Publishing. http://dx.doi.org/10.1787/173831738240.

Murray, D., Hall, R., Leask, B., Marginson, S., & Ziguras, C. (2011). *State of current research in international education.* Melbourne: LH Martin Institute, IEAA, Australian Government Australian Education International.

OECD. (2018). *Education at a glance 2018: OECD indicators.* Paris: OECD Publishing. http://dx.doi.org/10.1787/eag-2018-en.

Rizvi, F. (2004). Globalisation and the dilemmas of Australian higher education critical perspectives on communication. *Cultural and Policy Studies, 23*(2), 33–42.

Stier, J. (2004). Taking a critical stance toward internationalization ideologies in higher education: Idealism, instrumentalism and educationalism. *Globalisation, Societies and Education, 2*(1), 83–97.
Turpin, T., Iredale, R., & Crinnion, P. (2002). The internationalization of higher education: Implications for Australia and its education 'clients'. *Minerva: A Review of Science, Learning and Policy, 40*(4), 327–340.
Universities Australia. (2014). *International links of Australian Universities: Formal agreements between Australian universities and overseas higher education institutions.* Retrieved 3 March 2015 from https://www.universitiesaustralia.edu.au/global-engagement/international-collaboration/international-links#.VVWEGheR_lw.
Universities Australia. (2018). *Data snapshot 2018.* Retrieved 6 January 2019, from file:///C:/Users/e5108961/Downloads/Data%20snapshot%202018%20web.pdf.

7

An Integrated Understanding of University Internationalization Across Nations

The nation-based analysis suggests that, to a large extent, a shared understanding of university internationalization has been established among flagship research universities. The shared understanding highlights both the importance of internationalization and the academic excellence emerging as the main driving force for being internationalized. Moreover, it confirms that internationalization is seen as a multifaceted phenomenon, and a holistic approach has been employed to implement international strategies. The shared understanding also outlines the generic dimensions and components of university internationalization. However, this is not to say that internationalization has been understood and implemented in the same manner in various institutions. Differences are reflected in diverse motives for and priorities on internationalization. National and institutional contexts function as influential factors, contributing to similarities and divergences. Specifically, the national traits are more likely to lead to the variances and the institutional characteristics contribute to both comparability and disparities.

A Conceptual Framework of University Internationalization

Drawing the analysis of the three country cases and the pertinent literature together, a conceptual framework of university internalization considering both researcher and practitioners' perceptions could be established. The integrated conceptual framework highlights the comparable elements existing in policymakers' understanding of the phenomenon and in university practices, including the major academic incentive for institutional internationalization, the holistic approach adopted by universities, and the key dimensions and components involved in institutional international strategies.

The analysis shows that even though the interpretations of university internationalization are diverse, the importance of being internationalized has been widely acknowledged and the ubiquitously recognized magnitude of being internationalized has been largely transformed into institutional commitment in the investigated universities. Although universities are driven by various motives and ideologies toward internationalization, the primary concern, at least in these elite research universities, is the pursuit of academic excellence. This is accordance with Taylor (2010), McBurnie (2000), and Huang (2003)'s claim that the leading motive for HEIs to embark on the internationalization process is to significantly advance the core academic functions of the university. It also reveals that the pursuit of academic excellence intertwines with the aspiration to gain a competitive edge and worldwide reputation and to build world-class universities. In the 3rd Global Survey Report of the International Association of Universities, 'enhancing international profile and reputation' is identified as the third most import reason for the internationalization of HEIs (Beelen, 2011). The university leaders' perceptions corroborated this point. It has been argued by Wang (2008) that the Chinese government has invested heavily on internationalizing universities with the strong conviction to develop a few first-tier universities in China into world-class universities. The findings of this study extended this ambition to other contexts such as Australia and Singapore.

Table 7.1 Key dimensions and components of internationalization in flagship universities

Dimension	Components
Research	Internationally cooperative research programs
	Internationally focused research centers
	International researchers
	Internationally acknowledged research achievements
Student	International students
	Mobility of students
Faculty	International profile of the faculty team
	International perspective and experience of faculty
Curriculum	Courses with an international component
	Joint degree programs
	Students' participation in international studies[a]
Engagement	International networks and partnerships
	International presence of alumni
Governance	Human resources for internationalization activities
	Financial support for internationalization activities
	Infrastructure and facilities[a]
	International presence of the university[a]
Culture	A multicultural campus
	Integration of international and domestic students/staff

[a]Components identified from literature and existing instruments as important to university internationalization

The common dimensions and components (see Table 7.1) outlined in the construct demonstrate that internationalization is seen as a multifaceted phenomenon by university policymakers. Most of the components pointed out by the interviewees have been already identified in previous studies (e.g., see David, 1992; Knight, 1994, 1997). And, the current framework added one more domain—culture to the existing literature. To build international values and achieve cross-cultural understanding and tolerance has been seen as a component of the social missions of higher education (Gopinathan, 2007; Scott, 2005) and one of the rationales for university internationalization (Chan & Dimmock 2008; Knight, 1997; Meiras, 2004). But it is clear in this study that culture constitutes internationalization strategies in itself. Measures need to be taken to encourage the integration of students and staff from diverse backgrounds. It is arguable that in the current context of greater social risk and uncertainty, the cultural dimension deserves more priority to promote a cohesive civic identity, particularly in an ethnically diverse nation like Australia and Singapore.

It is important to bear in mind that every component included in the framework manifests indivisibly in both quantity and quality. Both sides, taken together, convey the full meaning of each component and, thus, the entire framework. The quantity of each component reflects the scale of a university's internationalization activities, while the quality of a component demonstrates the depth of the internationalization activities. International activities at a HEI must reach a certain scale to achieve the goals of international development. However, if no quality assurance applies, the growth in quantity may mean low-end reproduction. Take the *Mobility of students* as an example, which is a major strategy for students to gain international experiences, many universities have invested substantially to create opportunities for students to travel overseas for academic purposes during their program of study. A considerable proportion of students enrolled in flagship universities has participated in short-term exchange programs, improving their intercultural understanding and competence. When only a small minority of students can access these opportunities, their contributions in promoting international values among students are also limited. Once these programs become available to a wider range of students or, in other words, reach a certain scale, it will be necessary to push the transformation from quantity to quality. Policymakers will question with which institutions and in what regions the students are exchanged and what are the short-, medium-, and long-term effects of their exchange experiences on their academic, social, and personal attributes and skills. The quantity and quality sides of every component of university internationalization go hand in hand and, together, determine the performance of a university's internationalization activities.

The internationalization strategies have been implemented in a holistic way according to the interviewees. Both David (1992) and Soderqvist (2007) have predicted that on the way to being internationalized, HEIs would move from an ad hoc to a highly systematic approach, meaning the institutionalization of internationalization. The interviewed policymakers confirmed the projection. The supportive structures, roles and responsibilities, and values are defined, described, agreed, and embedded across the university.

Similarities and Divergences in University Internationalization

Similarities

As identified in this study, academic excellence tends to be the primary motivation for research universities to embrace internationalization. Internationalization is expected to contribute to the enhancement of the quality of research and teaching and learning. This finding may raise questions about Knight's (2013) argument that commercialization is the front and center of the internationalization agenda. The contribution of internationalization to improve educational quality could be fulfilled by strengthening the research capacity of a university. As Marginson (2011a) argues, research plays a determinative role in defining a university's academic quality in both the national and the global systems. Quality could also be achieved by changing the curriculum and teaching approach to produce graduates who are more internationally knowledgeable and interculturally skilled, prepared to live and work in more culturally diverse communities. Fostering appropriate skills and outlooks for graduates has been cited as a key reason for internationalizing universities in the literature by many scholars including McBurnie (2000), Hser (2005), Welch (2002), Knight (1997), and Coelen (2009). In addition, Australia used to be criticized for narrowly focusing on the recruitment of fee-paying overseas students. Consequently, levels of internationalization have been equated with the number of international students on campus, numbers of offshore programs, percentage of revenue earned through international actives, etc. (e.g., see Murray, Hall, Leask, Marginson, & Ziguras, 2011). However, this study suggests that this situation may start changing.

This study has identified comparable elements of university internationalization strategies across institutions and nations. Of the seven generic key dimensions, five (student, faculty, curriculum, research, and governance) have been acknowledged in the literature (see David, 1992; Dewey & Duff, 2009; Knight, 1994, 2004; Liu, 2012; Overton, 1992; Scott, 1992; Windham, 1996). Previously, efforts made to engage a university with the international community were more likely to be seen as a part of the university governance. According to university policymakers, such engagement has been treated as an independent dimension, separated from the governance domain. It has become a crucial pillar of university internationalization strategies with the intention to develop international partnerships and networks, as well as to actively connect with the international alumni. Besides, this research detects *culture* as another generic dimension of university internationalization, overlooked in previous research. It is a common acknowledgment among university leaders that creating a real multicultural campus that enables students and staff to experience working with people from diverse mindsets is a vital and indispensable part of their strategies. In terms of implementing international strategies, this study notices that institutional commitment to internationalization indicates a shift away from sporadic activities without careful planning or programs that take place on a knee-jerk basis on a campus. Instead, it provides empirical evidence to support Hudzik and Stohl's (2009) argument that internationalization has permeated the missions and ethos of an institution, and is no longer a sideshow or an appendage to the institution's main objectives.

Knowing all these characteristics of institutional internationalization, can we conjecture that homogenizing, to a certain extent, is an inevitable trend? Researchers have noticed that we are increasingly facing homogenizing tendencies in the administration, teaching, and research practices of universities (Stromquist, 2007). Different HEIs approach internationalization in various manners, and, within the same university, priorities may be given to different dimensions at different times. However, universities may ultimately employ a holistic approach to internationalization and develop comprehensive strategies, since the key domains of internationalization are closely related. A single dimension can hardly be internationalized without the efforts made in other dimensions. For example, the recruitment of overseas students is one of the main interests of many HEIs. In order to attract international students, an institution is expected to develop courses and relevant services to accommodate the needs of international students. In non-Anglo-Saxon countries, in order to recruit overseas students, it could be necessary for a university to have an internationalized faculty, at least, who can deliver the lesson in English. McBurnie (2000) suggests that internationalizing students' learning experience must be achieved through an internationalized curriculum and a correspondingly wide range of mobility programs. Likewise, Leask (2001) and van Damme (2001) argue that, for an internationalizing curriculum, both international students and staffs are vital aspects of inducing curricular change in the departments. The positive relationship between the internationalization of faculty and the student body has been validated in a study by Horta (2009). Further, without a permanent organizational policy and structure, internationalization could be marginalized or treated as a passing fad (Knight & de Wit, 1995). Drawing the above together, it is reasonable to imagine that HEIs may embrace internationalization in different ways and focus on a particular dimension at a given time; however, in order to attain sustainable internationalization development, a holistic approach highly likely evolves at a mature stage.

Divergences

Although considerable similarities have been observed, internationalization remains far from mature and divergences can be noted in university practices. The major academic motives for internationalization are actually entwined with other incentives in different countries. Thus, it is not surprising that leaders of Australian universities highlighted the economic benefits that the recruitment of international students has brought to the university. In the circumstances of funding reduction, the export of educational service and the revenue generated from international students can help secure a university's financial stability. In this respect, the study provides evidence of the prominent economic factor argued by many researchers (e.g., Altbach & Knight, 2007; Harris, 2008; Marginson, 2012) that have shaped the internationalization agenda in Australian HEIs. These economic incentives influence universities in Singapore in a different way, contributing to the national prosperity and competitiveness in the global economy. This finding supports argument by Coelen (2009), Hser (2005), and Marginson (2011b) in that the internationalization of higher education has become a central concern because of its contributions to the development of human resources and national economy.

For universities in China, the only specified motive for internationalization is to improve educational quality to meet international standards. More than a decade ago, Yang (2002a) argued that internationalization in China meant connecting China's educational practice with mainstream international trends. Initiatives taken by Chinese universities such as recruiting international academic staff or staff who have long-term overseas academic experience have been aimed at approaching world conventions. From this study, it can be seen that this belief has yet been changed much. For many Chinese university leaders, to be internationalized means obtaining an international standing. University practitioners' perceptions empirically verify that internationalization in Chinese HEIs, on the one hand, is driven by externally imposed standards which force them to adopt international (usually Western, and often American) modes of education and administration and, on the other hand, is prompted by the voluntary and even enthusiastic acceptance of the foreign standards of academic excellence (Yang, 2010).

Universities in the three countries studied have developed similar strategies for internationalization; however, the priorities attached to different dimensions are more of an institutional choice. This finding echoes the mainstream argument that the focus of international strategies at any given time varies according to priorities, culture, history, and resources of a university (e.g., see David, 1992; Knight, 2004; Scott, 1992). Generally, in China, the student and faculty dimensions are currently in the spotlight. In Australia and Singapore, internationalizing the student body and research are the central concerns, and the faculty dimension draws less attention. One possible interpretation could be that these two countries have been ethically and culturally diverse for a long time, which has led to a highly internationalized academic team already.

In addition, universities have taken varied approaches and move along various tracks toward an integrated internationalization practice. Many participating universities showed a clear shift in their internationalization arrangements by consistently reviewing and refining their strategies and approaches. For example, universities in China have adopted an approach that is more selective to choose their international partners and develop collaborative activities. Two decades ago, it was common for Chinese universities to have a large number of international partners, with which memorandums of understanding (MoUs) were signed but no concrete collaborations took place. At that time, the quality in internationalization was overwhelmed by the quantity.

With the maturation of policymakers' understanding of internationalization and improvements in capacity, universities in China are now more selective in developing partnerships with overseas HEIs. In-depth collaborations with a smaller number of strategic partners become preferable at the institutional level. At the national level, the number of Sino-foreign collaborations in running schools or educational programs has decreased continually in the past five years due to the raised bar of requirement and regulations. Low-quality or repetitive internationalization activities are no longer encouraged and are seen as a waste of resources in China.

Moreover, Chinese universities have an explicit intention for equal status in collaboration with partners abroad. With the strengthening of the research capacity of the flagship universities in China, as Yang (2014) claims, Chinese universities have reached a new phase of internationalization and global engagement. Specifically, these universities have shifted away from the passive reception of Western knowledge and partnerships with all ranges of HEIs in Western countries in favor of a more discriminating selection of partners and a much-improved balance between importing the foreign knowledge and exporting their owns.

Likely, the shift in internationalization arrangements is observable in Australian universities. A couple of university leaders mentioned that their focus on international collaborations has moved from the matured and highly competitive market to the less-developed one. On the one hand, due to the historical and cultural bond, Australian universities established intensive research collaborations with the UK and the United States. However, emerging Asian countries like China and Singapore were underrepresented in these research networks. This situation is now changing. On the other hand, university policymakers in Australia have been aware of the over-reliance on incoming students from Asia, which resulted in a highly disproportionate international student body. Various strategies and measures have been implemented to promote the recruitment of students from Latin America and Africa to create a well-represented and healthily diversified student body.

The change in approach also manifests itself in university governance. Policymakers from Australia indicated the centralization tendency of university administration. The role of the PVC (international) is expected to bring together several units, making them more powerful and efficient in implementing international strategies, as central leadership is assumed to contribute to better coherence and coordination. Taylor (2004) previously noted this shift; as he states, increased centralization, better communication, and a higher profile within the university are all crucial to more efficient and healthier future internationalization. In Chinese universities, the reverse applied as university leaders pointed to the shift from the top-down to the bottom-up, which illustrates a decentralizing process. The changing of the approach started in the early 2000s remains in progress (see Liao et al., 2008). Schools and departments now enjoy more autonomy and freedom in steering their internationalization arrangements.

As internationalization comes to age, many activities such as short-term exchange programs, recruitment of international faculty members, and internationally collaborative research have become the norm of universities practice. However, internationalization approaches adopted by individual HEIs still vary considerably; universities have their own unique histories, characteristics, and priorities, and they are subject to the available resources when they develop and implement their internationalization strategies. There is no best way that all universities could follow to fulfill their internationalization mission, but each institution has to evolve in its own pace and manner as they know their needs better than any others. The lessons learned in this project indicate that, when resources allow, universities are more likely to develop a wide range of activities with selected strategic partners and explore their unique model and flagship strategies for their international development. Besides, at the initial phase of a university's international agenda, the quantity may come first for fast sprawl, but once it is ready for strategic growth, the quality will become the golden standard for any practices.

National and Institutional Contexts in Shaping University Internationalization

In the extant literature, differences in university internationalization have been largely attributed to the specific internal context of a university and the way it is embedded in the national context (de Wit, 2009). Hence, this section is intended to examine the possible ways in which these contextual factors impact university internationalization and how they contribute to both the similarities and the divergences.

National Contexts

A possible explanation for the prominent economic incentive for internationalization in Australian universities could be the dependency on international student tuition. International education is the third or fourth largest export in Australia. It employs 125,000 people. Earnings from the large cohort of overseas students are high by world standards, but the majority has been invested in local teaching and research due to the reduction of government funding for two decades (Marginson, 2012). Facing the falling public investment on the one hand and confronting the continued regulation on domestic tuition fees and deregulation on the international tuitions on the other (Healey, 2008; Murray et al., 2011), it seems natural for Australian universities to make money out of international student flows for supplementing income.

Singapore is included in this study to provide a distinctive context through which to examine university internationalization. Since its independence from Malaysia in 1965, Singapore—as a city with limited natural resources—has been struggling to position itself on the international stage. Given its small population and the scale of economic industry, deep integration into the community of global trade and an export-led policy have always been the prime directives of the Singaporean government as it designed a national development plan (Gopinathan, 2007). It is in this context that human resources and a high-quality workforce have become the most valuable assets propelling the city-state's economic growth. Consequently, the ruling party, the People's Action Party, has been keen on investing in the higher education sector by recognizing that universities play a crucial role in producing graduate manpower to support the prosperity of the tiny country (Chan, 2013; Daquila, 2013). This helps in understanding the importance of internationalization in attracting global talent to Singapore to fill skill shortages.

The small city-state enables the Singaporean government to play a strong role and become directly involved in the practice of internationalizing universities. The return of investment in higher education is remarkable, justifying the high priority on expansion and diversification of the sector; moreover, the wealth generated by economic growth justifies further investment in universities, particularly in the two elite ones—NUS and NTU (Ashton, Green, James, & Sung, 1999; Brown & Lauder, 2001). Universities in Singapore, unlike their counterparts in Australia, are substantially subsidized by the government, allowing university leaders to treat international students, even the undergraduates, as potential talent rather than a source of income. In addition, because of sufficient government funding, universities in Singapore are able to invite the most prestigious universities in the world to cooperate with them and run educational programs jointly.

China is a country with a distinctive civilization and a long-established education system. Given China's significant position on the global stage, any further discussion of university internationalization should include the Chinese context. As early as in the late Qing period, Chinese scholars were studying Western models of higher education and establishing academic contacts. This development continued through the late imperial period and the nationalist period, and then again up unit the Cultural Revolution when China closed the doors of its universities and higher education languished for a decade. In the 1910s, institutional models were largely Japanese, although the latter had been strongly influenced by German models. The US influences came to be more important in the 1920s, including via the visit of John Dewey and Paul Monroe (Welch & Cai, 2011). After the Chinese Communist Party (CCP) came into power in 1949, Russians replaced departing Americans and Europeans. From 1952, the Chinese higher education system simulated Soviet administration, teaching methods, textbooks, and even classroom design (Yang, 2004). For many years since then, universities in China were run on experience, and under a planning system and 'red-tape' administration (Liu, 2012).

In the long interaction with the Western higher education system, a fundamental conflict emerged between the incompatibility of the Confucianism rooted in Chinese higher education philosophy and the core, classic, and modern ideas of Western university model (Yang, 2010, 2014; Zhang, 2010). China's longstanding traditions never attempted to seek the ontological significance of knowledge; rather, practical demands have always been the highest priority. Contemporary Chinese higher education remains similar (Yang, 2014). The ancient Chinese civil service examination (1300s–1905) has also had an enormous impact on the present practice of universities, wherein the purpose of the examination is to determine whether candidates could be appointed as officials (Zhang, 2010). Unlike the traditional Chinese education philosophy, the pure pursuit of knowledge and truth, the academic and intellectual freedom, and institutional autonomy are authentically appreciated in modern Western universities.

This conflict has become more pronounced as higher education in China has become increasingly internationalized. As the university leaders have argued, internationalization means and requires a change in philosophy and governance approach to operate the university by using internationally prevalent ideas and strategies. The root of this conflict can be traced back to the time of the Opium Wars (1840–1842), when Western education began to emerge in China. The famous compromise between the two sides at the end of the nineteenth century was to let 'Confucian classics constitute the national ideology, whereas Western technologies serve as utilities' (Zhang, 2010). The internationalization of universities in China inclines to this traditional reform philosophy (Cai, 2012). As such, the import of new educational concepts and ideas to China is constrained by ideological and cultural considerations. Under these circumstances, while internationalization has become an instrument by which to improve educational quality of Chinese universities, it is also less likely to result in any fundamental changes in ideology or management.

This study suggests that Chinese universities face more severe challenges than their counterparts in the other two countries in internationalizing the governance of the university. This could be partly determined by the traditional reform philosophy of 'Chinese body and Western use.' Another possible reason could be the long-established highly centralized education system in China (Yang, 2004, 2014). China's central government exercises strong regulation and authority over the higher education system; consequently, education provided at the central and local levels are respectively under its direct administration (Huang, 2007; Yang, 2004). Although some changes have gradually happened in terms of role and function in recent years, with more and increasing influences from foreign models, regulation and orientation by the government have never been diminished (Huang, 2003). Universities in Western countries are traditionally seen as meritocratic communities wherein peers enjoy large degrees of scholarly autonomy from state, society, and markets (Trondal, 2010). However, the independency and autonomy of universities in China could be eroded by the powerful political influence from the central government.

With respect to the internationalization of Chinese universities, which is regarded as a matter of policy (Huang, 2007), the tightly centralized system has led to ineffectiveness in many aspects. For example, in internationalizing the faculty, salaries are not a factor in lessening the attractiveness of Chinese universities. Instead, the difficulties in attracting promising international academic staff in the global market seem to be much more associated with overly bureaucratic recruitment processes. Joint degree programs serve as another example mentioned by the policymakers. Universities in China have promoted the mutual recognition of academic credits and joint degrees with overseas universities, but current legislation so far does not allow Chinese universities to offer joint degrees by themselves; even today, credit transfer among Chinese universities remains problematic not to mention the joint degree practices with foreign HEIs (Cai, 2013; Yang, 2014).

As Yang (2010) argues, modern universities are a foreign transplant to China. Indigenous Chinese higher learning institutions shared only a superficial resemblance with the Western university model. The Chinese case shows that the internationalization of universities in a country with strong central-level regulation and well-established educational philosophy will be a long and arduous process. And, at the current stage, although internationalization as an institution-wide strategy has been implemented in a comprehensive manner, it has yet to touch the core of university operations in China. In addition, political attributes in university administration further impede the effectiveness of internationalization in Chinese universities. Unless the cornerstone can be approached, internationalization of Chinese universities will be largely achieved and maintained at the material level.

Institutional Characteristics

Institutional characteristics that may shape university internationalization include missions and goals, status, and history. While missions and goals of universities contribute to the similarities of institutional motives for being internationalized, they may also result in the differential priorities placed on the dimensions of internationalization strategies. The status of a given university in the national and global higher education systems, to some extent, determines the approach it may adopt to embrace internationalization. Likewise, the special historical elements or origin of an institution could be another factor that influence the institutional strategic priorities.

Although there is tremendous diversity in the attention and priority given to instructional, research, and outreach service missions across institutions, all institutions of higher education arguably engage to some extent in both knowledge creation and dissemination. Large and comprehensive institutions engage in all the missions of instruction and research (Hudzik & Stohl, 2009). The fundamental roles of HEIs emphasize academic excellence as the core value spurring universities in all the three countries to embrace an internationalization agenda. As the policymakers argued, knowledge is the business model of universities. If internationalization has merits to universities, then it is expected to either help generate better knowledge or facilitate the dissemination of knowledge. However, between the roles of education and research, one could outweigh the other in a given university. For example, the instruction has been placed over research in Chinese HEIs. Instead of seeking the truth, Chinese higher education has placed its central focus on utility, in terms of the ruling classes. Chinese higher education within the imperial period stressed solely on the training of scholars with an encyclopedic knowledge based on Confucian values, which in practice served only the aristocracy. Students regarded becoming an official as the only purpose of getting an education (Yang, 2010). This philosophy remains a powerful influence on Chinese university leaders' understanding of the role of higher education and internationalization as well. As a result, the student and faculty dimensions have gained significant attention in Chinese HEIs.

In addition to largely shared goals, universities participating in this study also possess a similar position in the national and the global higher education systems. All of them are placed in the top tier both domestically and globally, a parallel status that enables them to enjoy a worldwide reputation and to access relatively sufficient resources. This helps explain the expectation of internationalization as facilitating the goal of becoming world-class universities. Moreover, the abundance of resources allows them to develop a holistic approach to implementing international strategies, targeting and achieving multidimensional internationalization. If the largely shared missions and status could explain the similarities in their internationalization practice, the histories bonded to individual universities then contribute to the divergent strategic priorities. History carries an institution's most distinctive characters and core values. The origin of a given university may have considerable impact on its strategies for internationalization. For example, one of the Chinese university leaders attributed the close link having developed between his university and HEIs in Taiwan to its 22-year history as the National Central University in the nationalist period (1927–1949). Due to this special tie, Taiwan has become the paramount region for developing partnerships.

The above discussion reduces the vagueness surrounding the impact that national and institutional contexts may have on university internationalization. In the extant literature, such contextual factors have been widely argued as powerful influences in shaping institutional internationalization practice; however, little is known regarding how these factors actually exert their influences.

Implications for Developing Measurements of University Internationalization

The integrated understanding of university internationalization has several implications for measurement development. First, the identified generic dimensions and components demonstrate that internationalization is seen as a multifaceted phenomenon. Given this, the tools developed for measuring internationalization performance are deemed to be comprehensive, thereby capturing different aspects of the phenomenon. A single metric measuring only one dimension of internationalization may not be able to portray the whole picture of internationalization practice in an institution. Some of the existing instruments such as the EMQT, the CIC benchmarking tool, and the indicators developed by van den Besselaar et al. (2012) are designed for assessing a single aspect and may be less capable of reflecting the complexity of the phenomenon. As Hudzik and Stohl (2009) suggest,

> The power of internationalization which permeates an institution has the capacity to strengthen all its parts. This is the paradigm that shapes our approach to thinking about how to assess the internationalization performance. (p. 9)

Secondly, in order to capture all key dimensions of university internationalization, a single instrument may not be adequate. Rather, a combination of different types of measurements could better fulfill the task.

Assessment experts agree on the employment of multiple measures to assess any given outcomes, which can provide a richer picture of the learning and triangulate the insights provided by the different tools (Green, 2012). As shown in the framework, some of the dimensions are more likely to be quantified and gauged by quantitative tools such as indicators. However, for the dimensions that deny quantification, qualitative measures are required to collect information. For example, culture is seen as an indispensable aspect of university internationalization. However, an appropriate quantitative proxy can hardly be found to measure either a multicultural campus or the integration of international and domestic students/staff. Within a dimension, not all the components can be quantified and then measured by indicators. The internationalization of a university's service system is a good example. Here, surveys or panel reviews might be used to elicit meaningful and valid evaluative information. In measuring university internationalization performance, quantitative and qualitative measurements could be combined complementarily, generating comprehensive and accurate information together.

Thirdly, it is clear from the study that universities tend to place different priorities on their internationalization strategies, reinforcing the need to avoid consolidating the various metrics into a single indicator. In order to generate an overall band, weights have to be assigned to the different metrics. Any decisions made by a third party could be arbitrary and fail to fit institutional contexts. Individual universities should be given the right to determine how much a dimension means to them at a particular time. Also, policymakers suggested that the sum of different dimensions should be expected to be more than 100%, again, indicating the inappropriateness of combining the metrics into one barometer. Indeed, weighting of various metrics has been identified in the literature as one of the clouds of uncertainty surrounding every measurement serving a ranking purpose (Coelen, 2009).

Finally, because of the dynamic nature of university internationalization, it is necessary to review any measurements regularly. Keeping measurements updated ensures the validity of an instrument because an assessment tool is valid if it measures that it is supposed to measure—that is, if it adequately measures the underlying concept (Treiman, 2009).

Summary

As internationalization is not a new discourse in the field of higher education, a new understanding of this phenomenon contributes to further theorizing university internationalization. First, the findings of this study suggest that, for the time being, it is better to accept the absence of a universal definition of university internationalization; an understanding of the phenomenon will evolve over time (de Wit, 2002). University leaders tend to narrate internationalization in their own ways. Some of them even question the validity of a single definition since they believe that the definition should reflect the purposes and the characteristics of internationalization in the institution, the nation, and the age. The changing interpretations of the phenomenon may indicate the dynamic nature of university internationalization. Such a nature, to a large extent, suggests that university internationalization, whether concept or phenomenon, can hardly be rigidly defined. Hence, it might be time to stop the disputation over the best definition and accept diverse interpretations. Imposing a particular definition upon all the studies on the phenomenon might not be desirable. Researchers should be allowed to use the term in accordance with their various purposes and contexts.

The conceptual framework established in this study demonstrates that university internationalization is not an intangible concept; rather, it can be constructed. Instead of spending much time on talking about the definition, the focus should be placed on constructing the phenomenon into tangible components. By doing so, the term internationalization will cease to be an umbrella term. As Knight (2013) argues, diploma mills, visa factories, and the lowering academic standards of some private and public education providers are all blamed in the name of internationalization. Indeed, the ambiguity surrounding university internationalization is partly caused by the lack of a clear and robust construct of the phenomenon. Internationalization has been debated by both researchers and university practitioners without either group knowing what it exactly means (Mok, 2007; Stier, 2004; Yang, 2002b). The framework developed in this study may not be the only or the best way to construct the phenomenon, but it certainly helps outline the crucial domains and components, which set the boundaries between internationalization practice and other educational behaviors in the internationalized higher education landscape.

Constructing the phenomenon is also of great importance in developing measurements for university internationalization. If a phenomenon cannot be constructed, then it is less possible for it to be measured. Brown (2009) argues that a conceptual framework provides a formal way to construct a topic area and, thus, to structure and organize the metrics. The identified domains and components of university internationalization help justify the selection of indicators as well as the way that the indicators are organized.

To construct university internationalization, by and large, means to identify the comparable elements of the phenomenon across individual cases and contexts. Internationalization has been taking place in universities in different parts of the world for more than three decades; however, the majorities of existing studies on the phenomenon are case based or focus on the divergence of institutional motives and strategies. As internationalization comes of age, unfortunately, it has yet been adequately theorized. It is by no means to say that the case studies and the research on the variance are of no importance. However, despite what is known about the differences, a shared framework has yet been established to theoretically conceptualize the phenomenon. The findings of this study demonstrate that considerable convergences could be observed in understanding and implementing university internationalization. These notable similarities make it possible to build a shared conceptual framework. The process of internationalization is suggested to be integrated in a systematic and holistic manner in the higher education sector, requiring a complete understanding of its nature and characteristics (Gacel-Avila, 2005).

Finally, the dynamic nature of the phenomenon suggests that the construct of university internationalization is highly likely to be dynamic as well, which needs to be reviewed periodically to ensure its relevance to the current understanding and practice of internationalization. As internationalization is a process, new elements may emerge in the future and need to be added to the construct. For example, researchers (e.g., see David, 1992; Knight, 2004) forecasted the institutionalization of internationalization decades ago. This study shows that governance has actually become an indispensable dimension. With the evolution of the phenomenon, it is reasonable to look forward to the emergence of other new elements.

References

Altbach, P. G., & Knight, J. (2007). The internationalization of higher education: Motivations and realities. *Journal of Studies in International Education, 11*(3–4), 290–305.

Ashton, D., Green, F., James, D., & Sung, J. (1999). *Education and training for development in East Asia: The political economy of skill formation in newly industrialised economies.* London: Routledge.

Beelen, J. (2011). Internationalisation at home in a global perspective: A critical survey of the 3rd global survey report of IAU. *La internacionalización en casa en una perspectiva global: un estudio crítico del Informe del 3.er Estudio Global de la AIU, 8*(2), 249–264.

Brown, D. (2009). *Good practice guidelines for indicator development and reporting.* Paper presented at the third OECD world forum on 'statistics, knowledge and policy': Charting progress, building visions, improving life, Busan, Korea.

Brown, P., & Lauder, H. (2001). The future of skill formation in Singapore. *Asia Pacific Business Review, 7*(3), 113.

Cai, Y. Z. (2012). Traditional reform philosophy and challenges of higher education reforms in China. *International Journal of Humanities and Social Science, 2*(6), 60–69.

Chan, S.-J. (2013). Internationalising higher education sectors: Explaining the approaches in four Asian Countries. *Journal of Higher Education Policy and Management, 35*(3), 316–329.

Chan, W. W. Y., & Dimmock, C. (2008). The internationalization of universities: Globalist, internationalist and translocalist models. *Journal of Research in International Education, 7*(2), 184–204.

Coelen, R. J. (2009). Ranking and the measurement of success in internationalisation: Are they related? In H. de Wit (Ed.), *Measuring success in the internationalisation of higher education* (EAIE Occasional Paper No. 22, pp. 39–47). Amsterdam: European Association for International Education.

Daquila, T. C. (2013). Internationalizing higher education in Singapore: Government policies and the NUS experience. *Journal of Studies in International Education, 17*(5), 626–647.

David, J. L. (1992). Developing a strategy for internationalization in universities: Towards a conceptual framework. In C. B. Klasek, B. J. Garavalia, K. J. Kellerman, & B. B. Marx (Eds.), *Bridges to the future: Strategies for internationalizing higher education* (pp. 177–190). Carbondale, IL: Association of International Education Administrators.

de Wit, H. (2002). *Internationalization of higher education in the United States of America and Europe: A historical, comparative, and conceptual analysis.* Westport, Conn: Greenwood Press.

de Wit, H. (2009). Benchmarking the internationalisation strategies of European and Latin American institutions of higher education. In H. de Wit (Ed.), *Measuring success in the internationalisation of higher education* (pp. 125–135). Amsterdam, The Netherlands: EAIE.

Dewey, P., & Duff, S. (2009). Reason before passion: Faculty views on internationalization in higher education. *Higher Education, 58*(4), 491–504.

Gacel-Avila, J. (2005). The internationalisation of higher education: A paradigm for global citizenry. *Journal of Studies in International Education, 9*(2), 121–136.

Gopinathan, S. (2007). Globalisation, the Singapore developmental state and education policy: A thesis revisited. *Globalisation, Societies and Education, 5*(1), 53–70.

Green, M. F. (2012). *Measuring and assessing internationalization.* Retrieved 21 June 2014 from http://www.nafsa.org/uploadedFiles/NAFSA_Home/Resource_Library_Assets/Publications_Library/MeasuringandAssessingInternationalization.pdf.

Harris, S. (2008). Internationalising the university. *Educational Philosophy and Theory, 40*(20), 346–357.

Healey, N. (2008). Is higher education in really 'internationalising'? *Higher Education, 55*(3), 333–355. https://doi.org/10.1007/s10734-007-9058-4.

Horta, H. (2009). Global and national prominent universities: Internationalization, competitiveness and the role of the state. *Higher Education, 58*(3), 387–405.

Hser, M. P. (2005). Campus internationalization: A study of American Universities' internationalization efforts. *International Education, 35*(1), 35–48.

Huang, F. (2003). Policy and practice of the internationalization of higher education in China. *Journal of Studies in International Education, 7*(3), 225–240.

Huang, F. (2007). Internationalisation of higher education in the era of globalisation: What have been its implications in China and Japan? *Higher Education Management and Policy, 19*(1), 47–61.

Hudzik, K. J., & Stohl, M. (2009). Modelling assessment of the outcomes and impacts of internationalisation. In H. de Wit (Ed.), *Measuring success in the internationalisation of higher education* (EAIE Occasional Paper No. 22, pp. 9–21). Amsterdam: European Association for International Education.

Knight, J. (1994). *Internationalisation: Elements and checkpoints* (CBIE Research No. 7). Ottawa: CBIE.

Knight, J. (1997). Internationalisation of higher education: A conceptual framework. In J. Knight & H. de Wit (Eds.), *Internationalisation of higher education in Asia Pacific countries* (pp. 5–19). Amsterdam: EAIE.

Knight, J. (2004). Internationalization remodeled: Definition, approaches, and rationales. *Journal of Studies in International Education, 8*(1), 5–31.

Knight, J. (2013). The changing landscape of higher education internationalisation—For better or worse? *Perspectives: Policy and Practice in Higher Education, 17*(3), 84–90.

Knight, J., & de Wit, H. (1995). Strategies for internationalization of higher education: Historical and conceptual perspectives. In J. Knight & H. de Wit (Eds.), *Strategies for internationalization of higher education: A comparative study of Australia, Canada, Europe, and the USA* (pp. 5–32). Amsterdam: European Association for International Education.

Leask, B. (2001). Bridging the gap: Internationalizing University Curricula. *Journal of Studies in International Education, 5*(2), 100–115.

Liao, J.-Q., Tan, G.-X., & Zhu, X.-G. (2008). Internationalization and localization of China's higher education. *Journal of Higher Education Management, 2*(2), 1–7 (in Chinese).

Liu, J. (2012). On the internationalization of higher education institutions in China. *Higher Education Studies, 2*(1), 60–64.

Marginson, S. (2011a). Imagining the global. In R. King, S. Marginson, & R. Naidoo (Eds.), *Handbook on globalization and higher education* (pp. 10–39). Cheltenham: Edward Elgar.

Marginson, S. (2011b). Strategizing and ordering the global. In R. King, S. Marginson, & R. Naidoo (Eds.), *Handbook on globalization and higher education* (pp. 394–414). Cheltenham: Edward Elgar.

Marginson, S. (2012). International education in Australia: The roller coaster. *International Higher Education, 68*(Summer), 11–13.

McBurnie, G. (2000). Pursuing internationalization as a means to advance the academic mission of the university: An Australian case study. *Higher Education in Europe, 25*(1), 63–73.

Meiras, S. (2004). International education in Australian universities: Understandings, dimensions and problems. *Journal of Higher Education Policy and Management, 26*(3), 371–380.

Mok, K. H. (2007). Questing for internationalization of universities in Asia: Critical reflections. *Journal of Studies in International Education, 11*(3–4), 433–454.

Murray, D., Hall, R., Leask, B., Marginson, S., & Ziguras, C. (2011). *State of current research in international education*. Melbourne: LH Martin Institute, IEAA, Australian Government Australian Education International.

Overton, J. L. (1992). The process of internationalization at minority institutions. In C. B. Klasek, B. J. Garavalia, K. J. Kellerman, & B. B. Marx (Eds.), *Bridges to the future: Strategies for internationalizing higher education* (pp. 164–176). Carbondale, IL: Association of International Education Administrators.

Scott, R. A. (1992). *Campus developments in response to the challenges of internationalization: The case of Ramapo College of New Jersey (USA)*. Springfield: CBIS Federal.

Scott, P. (2005). Universities and the knowledge economy. *Minerva: A Review of Science, Learning and Policy, 43*(3), 297–309.

Söderqvist, M. (2007). *The internationalization and strategic planning of higher education institutions: An analysis of Finnish ESP strategies*. Finland: Helsinki School of Economics and Administration.

Stier, J. (2004). Taking a critical stance toward internationalization ideologies in higher education: Idealism, instrumentalism and educationalism. *Globalisation, Societies and Education, 2*(1), 83–97.

Stromquist, N. P. (2007). Internationalization as a response to globalization: Radical shifts in university environments. *Higher Education, 53*(1), 81–105.

Taylor, J. (2004). Toward a strategy for internationalisation: Lessons and practice from four universities. *Journal of Studies in International Education, 8*(2), 149–171.
Taylor, J. (2010). The response of government and universities to globalization. In F. Maringe & N. Foskett (Eds.), *Globalisation and internationalisation in higher education: Theoretical, strategic and management perspectives* (pp. 83–96). London: Continuum.
Treiman, D. J. (2009). *Quantitative data analysis: Doing social research to test ideas* (1st ed.). San Francisco, CA: Jossey-Bass.
Trondal, J. (2010). Two worlds of change: On the internationalisation of universities. *Globalisation, Societies and Education, 8*(3), 351–368.
van Damme, D. (2001). Quality issues in the internationalisation of higher education. *Higher Education, 41*(4), 415–441.
van den Besselaar, P., Inzelt, A., Reale, E., de Turckheim, E., & Vercesi, V. (2012). Indicators of internationalisation for research institutions: A new approach. *A report by the ESF member organisation forum on evaluation: Indicators of internationalisation*. Strasbourg Cedex: European Science Foundation.
Wang, Y. (2008). Research on the trend of internationalization of universities in recent decade. *Higher Education in Jiangsu, 3*(Fall), 47–50 (in Chinese).
Welch, A. (2002). Going global? Internationalizing Australian Universities in a time of global crisis. *Comparative Education Review, 46*(4), 433.
Welch, A., & Cai, H.-X. (2011). The internationalisation of China's higher education system. In J. Ryan (Ed.), *China's higher education reform and internationalisation* (pp. 9–33). Abingdon, Oxon and New York: Routledge.
Windham, D. M. (1996). Overview and main conclusion of the seminar. In OECD (Ed.), *Internationalisation of higher education* (pp. 7–29). Paris and Washington, DC: Organization for Economic Co-operation and Development.
Yang, R. (2002a). *Third delight: The internationalization of higher education in China*. New York and London: Routledge.
Yang, R. (2002b). University internationalisation: Its meanings, rationales and implications. *Intercultural Education, 13*(1), 81–95.
Yang, R. (2004). Openness and reform as dynamics for development: A case study of internationalisation at South China University of Technology. *Higher Education, 47*(4), 473–500.

Yang, R. (2010). Chinese ways of thinking in the transformation of China's higher education system. In J. Ryan (Ed.), *China's higher education reform and internationalisation* (pp. 34–47). Hoboken: Taylor & Francis.

Yang, R. (2014). China's strategy for the internationalization of higher education: An overview. *Frontiers of Education in China, 9*(2), 151–162.

Zhang, H.-S. (2010). Higher education reforms and problems in China: Challenges from globalization. In F. Maringe & N. Foskett (Eds.), *Globalisation and internationalisation in higher education: Theoretical, strategic and management perspectives* (pp. 125–137). London: Continuum.

8

An Indicator Set for Benchmarking University Internationalization Performance Across Nations

Having the integrated conceptual framework (see Table 7.1, Chapter 7) helps to move the project one step further. With the generic dimensions and components of university internationalization, it is now possible to select a set of indicators which can be used by universities in different parts of the world to track and assess their performance in international development, not limited to the sampled three nations included in this project. Excluding those elements that deny quantification hence cannot be easily captured by indicators (the *culture* dimension with two components), six dimensions with 17 components of university internationalization are used to organize the indicators in this project. Responses to the questionnaire survey collected from the three countries were put together to select the indicators that have the best capability to be applied across institutional and national contexts. The primary purpose of the analysis is to reduce the number of indicators involved in the final set by identifying the most appropriate indicators agreed to by respondents from all the three countries. There are various ways to determine how many and which indicators should be included in the final set. The decisions made in this study were just one possible scenario. An institutional survey was employed at a later stage to test the data availability of the final indicator set in different universities. In this process, similarities and divergences among different countries in the perceptions of each indicator were detected and dimensional level analysis was performed to show the variances among the six dimensions from national perspectives.

Overview of the Data

The online questionnaire was administered to 17 universities in three countries. A total number of 182 questionnaires were returned, of which there were 129, or 71% usable responses. Table 8.1 shows the number of responses collected from each institution. The number of usable responses from each university ranged from 1 to 14, with a mean of 8.

Table 8.1 Distribution of responses by institution

	Collected	Usable responses
Australian university 1 (AU1)	6	6
Australian university 2 (AU2)	22	10
Australian university 3 (AU3)	4	3
Australian university 4 (AU4)	1	1
Australian university 5 (AU5)	8	5
Australian university 6 (AU6)	24	10
Australian university 7 (AU7)	19	13
Australian university 8 (AU8)	1	1
Australian university 9 (AU9)	8	5
Australian universities in total	*93*	*54*
Singaporean university 1 (SG1)	4	4
Singaporean university 2 (SG2)	13	8
Singaporean universities in total	*17*	*12*
Chinese university 1 (CN1)	8	8
Chinese university 2 (CN2)	15	14
Chinese university 3 (CN3)	16	14
Chinese university 4 (CN4)	8	7
Chinese university 5 (CN5)	10	8
Chinese university 6 (CN6)	15	12
Chinese universities in total	*72*	*63*
Total	*182*	*129*

Table 8.2 shows the distribution of respondents by demographic and professional background. Of the 129 respondents, 32.6% were male. Close to 60% of respondents were middle age, between 30 and 49 years old; one out of five was between 50 and 59, only 3% were over 60, and the rest were younger than 30. Nearly, half of the staff surveyed were Chinese; another one-third were Australian. The Singaporeans comprised 8.5%. Almost one in every ten respondents was an international staff. All the international staffs were in either Australian or Singaporean universities; none worked in the six surveyed Chinese universities. This showed that the professional team in Australian and Singaporean universities was, to some extent, internationalized. However, it remained rare to find international administrative staff in Chinese universities. The majority of respondents worked in the International Office of their institutions, 12.4% in the senior executive office, 6.2% in different faculties or schools, and the remainder in other sectors including marketing, engagement, academic, research office, and the graduate school. Half of the respondents were intermediate professional staff, and about 5% were university leaders (Pro Vice-Chancellor or Deputy Vice-Chancellor). The others were office members. More than half of the surveyed staff were responsible for international partnerships and collaboration, one-third for international student services, nearly a quarter for international student recruitment, 20.9% for student exchanges, almost 15% for international staff recruitment and management, 5.4% for international curriculum, and another quarter of respondents were responsible for other activities rather than the above mentioned. The total was greater than 100% because almost half of the respondents were in charge of more than two areas, and one in every five was responsible for more than three areas at the same time.

When designing the survey instrument, an unbalanced scale was used to rate importance of the draft indicators because of the assumption that the distribution of responses would be skewed, specifically, negatively skewed. According to the descriptive statistics of all 57 indicators (see Appendix C), except the indicator C10 'Number of students registered in programs provided via online learning modes (skewness = 0.363)'; all of the other indicators were negatively skewed, which indicates each of them had relatively few low values.

Table 8.2 Distribution of respondents by demographic and professional background

	$N = 129$	Percentage
Gender		
Female	86	66.7
Male	42	32.6
Missing	1	0.8
Age		
21–29	21	16.3
30–39	47	36.4
40–49	29	22.5
50–59	27	20.9
60 or older	4	3.1
Missing	1	0.8
Nationality		
Australian	43	33.3
Singaporean	11	8.5
Chinese	63	48.8
Others	12	9.3
Department		
International Office	92	71.3
Senior Executive Office	16	12.4
School	8	6.2
Others	12	9.3
Missing	1	0.8
Position		
Deputy Vice-Chancellor (DVC)	**2**	**1.6**
Pro Vice-Chancellor (PVC)	**4**	**3.1**
Office Director	**9**	**7.0**
Deputy Director of the Office	**18**	**14.0**
Sector Chief	**28**	**21.7**
Deputy Sector Chief	**11**	**8.5**
None of these	**56**	**43.4**
Missing	1	0.8
Responsible areas		
International student recruitment	30	23.3
Student exchange	27	20.9
International student services	43	33.3
International partnerships and collaboration	70	54.3
International staff recruitment and management	19	14.7
International curriculum	7	5.4
Others	32	24.8

Indeed, the indicator C10 was the only one that was endorsed as either 'not important' or 'neutral' by more than half of respondents. To get a quick understanding of the data, the four options of responses were combined to two simple categories: important (value = 3 or 4) and less important (value = 1 or 2). It can be noted that of the 57 indicators, 40 were rated as 'important' by more than three-quarters of respondents. Because all the draft indicators stemmed from existing instruments and survived through rigorous selection, it is not surprising that most of them were regarded by respondents as important to a university's internationalization.

In terms of feasibility, when analyzing the data, the four options were merged into three categories: −1 (infeasible), 0 (unknown), and 1 (somewhat feasible or very feasible). The descriptive statistics were shown in Appendix C. The results demonstrated that all 57 indicators were negatively skewed, which justified the employment of an unbalanced scale. For every single indicator, the frequency of the 'unknown' category being chosen varied from 3 to 68. Furthermore, nearly half of the indicators were cited as 'unknown' by more than one-fifth respondents. It confirmed the necessity of including the 'unknown' option in the scale of feasibility. Of the 57 indicators, 32 were rated as either 'very feasible' or 'somewhat feasible' by more than three-quarters of respondents. Feasibility of an indicator is not suggested to be used alone as a criterion to judge the appropriateness of indicators. Only if the indicator is important is it meaningful to examine the feasibility. A feasible but unimportant indicator remains meaningless to be used for measuring university internationalization.

From the Draft Indicators to the Final Set

In determining the indicators to be included in the final set, consensus could not always be achieved. Notable divergences could be observed among the three countries in perceptions of the draft indicators. Nevertheless, decisions had to be made. In this study, to cover internationalization in its widest possible sense, every component in a given dimension is expected to be captured unless all the listed indicators for the component were perceived by the respondent as of no importance. To limit the number of indicators to its minimum to make it cost-effective, only the paramount indicators were included in the final set. Consequently, for each component, the indicator cited by most participants as 'very important' in each country was selected at first.

Selecting the Indicators for Each Component

The Research Dimension

Table 8.3 presents respondents' opinions on 12 indicators which capture four components of the research dimension. Respondents from the three countries reached a consensus on the most important indicator for each component. In measuring *Internationally Cooperative Research Programs*, most respondents cited R1 'Percentage of research projects involving international partnership and collaboration' as a 'very important' indicator in all three countries (34.9% in China, 75.0% in Singapore, and 83.3% in Australia). Two indicators were proposed to measure the component of *Internationally Focused Research Centers*: R3 'Number of research centers focused on international study' and R4 'Number of research centers operated with international partners.' Respondents from all three countries preferred the latter: Respondents from China (30.2%), Singapore (41.7%), and Australia (57.4%) cited R4 as 'very important.' Among the six indicators to measure *Internationally Acknowledged Research Achievements*, most participants from China (34.9%) and Australia (51.9%) favored R9 'Percentage of publications cited by SCI, EI, ISTP.' The three indicators R7 'Number of international conference organized,' R8 'Number of presentations in international conferences (with qualified contribution) per faculty member,' and R9 were all rated by 41.7% of respondents from Singapore. As the only indicator for the *International Researchers* component, nearly two-thirds of Australian participants perceived R5

Table 8.3 Importance of listed indicators in the research dimension by nation

Component	Indicator	Percentage of respondents rating the indicator as 'very important'		
		CN*	SG*	AU*
Internationally cooperative research programs	R1: Percentage of research projects involving international partnership and collaboration	34.9	75.0	83.3
	R2: Percentage of research projects wholly funded by sources outside of host nation (incl. overseas institutions, overseas governments, and international agencies)	19.0	8.3	37.0
	R6: Proportion of total research income generated by research involving international collaboration	17.5	16.7	61.1
Internationally focused research centers	R3: Number of research centers focused on international study	20.6	8.3	31.5
	R4: Number of research centers operated with international partners	30.2	41.7	57.4
International researchers	R5: Percentage of international postdoctoral researchers	20.6	33.3	61.1
Internationally acknowledged research achievements	R7: Number of international conference organized	22.2	41.7	20.4
	R8: Number of presentations in international conferences (with qualified contribution) per faculty member	20.6	41.7	37.0
	R9: Percentage of publications cited by SCI, EI, ISTP	34.9	41.7	51.9
	R10: Number of co-editorships in international journals	33.3	33.3	31.5
	R11: Number of highly cited authors (HiCi) according to Thomson Reuters	22.2	25.0	40.7
	R12: Percentage of patents filed outside the country	9.5	16.7	13.0

CN* = China, SG* = Singapore, AU* = Australia

'Percentage of international postdoctoral researchers' as a very important indicator, while the number reduced to one-third in Singapore and one-fifth in China.

The Student Dimension

The student dimension included two components, captured by eight indicators. For the first component, *International Students*, the data observe divergence in respondents' perceptions. Most participants from China (54.0%) reported S1 'Percentage of international students (for degree study) on campus in total' as 'very important.' In Singapore, two-thirds of respondents cited S1, S2 'Percentage of international undergraduate students on campus,' and S5 'Percentage of international students by region (Europe, Africa, Asia, North America, South America and Pacific)' as 'very important.' 83.3% of Australian respondents, however, preferred S4 'Percentage of international higher degree research (HDR) students on campus,' endorsing it as 'very important.' For the second component, *Mobility of Students*, 55.6% of respondents from China, 83.3% from Singapore, and 49.6% from Australia identified the indicator S6 'Percentage of domestic students who have international study experiences' as the most important indicator. Table 8.4 shows respondents' opinions from different countries on the eight indicators.

The Faculty Dimension

Of the 57 draft indicators, seven measured the two components in the faculty dimension, *International Profile of the Faculty Team* and *International Perspective and Experience of Faculty*. As illustrated in Table 8.5, participants from different countries showed diverse attitudes toward what they considered the most appropriate indicators for the two components. For the *International Profile of the Faculty Team*, China (39.7%) and Singapore (58.3%) shared similar opinions, regarding F1 'Percentage of international (by nationality) faculty members' as the most important indicator, while participants from Australia appreciated F2 'Number of international visiting scholars for academic

Table 8.4 Importance of listed indicators in the student dimension by nation

Component	Indicator	Percentage of respondents rating the indicator as 'very important'		
		CN	SG	AU
International students	S1: Percentage of international students (for degree study) on campus in total	54.0	66.7	68.5
	S2: Percentage of international undergraduate students on campus	41.3	66.7	64.8
	S3: Percentage of international Master (coursework) students on campus	41.3	41.7	63.0
	S4: Percentage of international higher degree research (HDR) students on campus	46.0	41.7	83.3
	S5: Percentage of international students by region (Europe, Africa, Asia, North America, South America, and Pacific)	27.0	66.7	59.3
Mobility of students	S6: Percentage of domestic students who have international study experiences (incl. exchanges and short-term programs that are no more than an academic year)	55.6	83.3	79.6
	S7: Number of incoming international students (incl. exchanges and short-term programs that are no more than an academic year)	47.6	75.0	68.5
	S8: Ratio of the outgoing domestic students to the incoming international students (no more than an academic year)	23.8	58.3	44.4

Table 8.5 Importance of listed indicators in the faculty dimension by nation

Component	Indicator	Percentage of respondents rating the indicator as 'very important'		
		CN	SG	AU
International profile of the faculty team	F1: Percentage of international (by nationality) faculty members (full-time equivalent FTE)	39.7	58.3	50.0
	F2: Number of international visiting scholars for academic purposes	27.0	41.7	64.8
International perspective and experience of faculty	F3: Percentage of faculty (FTE) who were awarded their highest academic qualification by an institution abroad	34.9	25.0	25.9
	F4: Percentage of faculty (FTE) proficient in a language other than the primary language of teaching/research	34.9	0.0	33.3
	F5: Percentage of faculty (FTE) who have at least one-year overseas experience (excl. degree study)	28.6	25.0	44.4
	F6: Percentage of faculty (FTE) who hold a visiting lectureship abroad	14.3	25.0	37.0
	F7: Percentage of faculty (FTE) who had international experience for academic purposes in the past academic year	14.3	25.0	29.6

purposes' more, with half of them regarding F2 as 'very important.' For *International Perspective and Experience of Faculty*, more than one-third of participants from China cited F3 'Percentage of faculty (FTE) who were awarded their highest academic qualification by an institution abroad' and F4 'Percentage of faculty (FTE) proficient in a language other than the primary language of teaching/research' as very important indicators. There was 44.4% of Australian respondents regarded F5 'Percentage of faculty (FTE) who have at least one-year overseas experience' as 'very important.' In Singapore, respondents showed no preference toward F3, F5, F6, or F7, as a quarter of respondents categorized these indicators as 'very important.'

The Curriculum Dimension

Table 8.6 presents participants' perceptions of the 11 indicators measuring the curriculum dimension. Within this dimension, three components were distinguished. For *Courses with an International Component*, Singapore and Australia shared similar opinions, identifying C2 'Number of subjects involving a partner in other countries' as the most important indicator. One-third of Singaporean respondents and over half of Australian respondents cited C2 as 'very important.' Respondents from China, however, cited C5 'Number of subjects offered in a foreign language' as more suitable to measure this component.

All three countries highly valued indicator C8 'Number of joint degree programs collaborated with overseas higher education institutions' as the only indicator for *Joint Degree Programs*. Two-thirds of Singaporean respondents, over half of Australian respondents, and one-third of Chinese respondents rated C8 as 'very important.'

For *Students' Participation in International Studies*, respondents from Singapore (50.0%) and Australia (35.2%) agreed that C11 'Number of students who attend joint degree programs collaborated with overseas higher education institutions' was the most important. Chinese participants, however, favored C9 'Number of students registered in subjects taught in a foreign language,' with 14.3% rating it as 'very important.'

Table 8.6 Importance of listed indicators in the curriculum dimension by nation

Component	Indicator	Percentage of respondents rating the indicator as 'very important'		
		CN	SG	AU
Courses with an international component	C1: Number of subjects offering foreign language studies	12.7	25.0	44.4
	C2: Number of subjects involving a partner in other countries	34.9	33.3	51.9
	C3: Number of programs available through online learning modes	12.7	16.7	24.1
	C4: Number of programs available for offshore delivery	14.3	25.0	31.5
	C5: Number of subjects offered in a foreign language	50.8	8.3	24.1
	C6: Number of programs with a mandatory period abroad	9.5	25.0	44.4
	C7: Number of subjects on foreign countries/cultures/societies	12.7	16.7	44.4
Joint degree programs	C8: Number of joint degree programs (Bachelor, Masters, and PhD) collaborated with overseas higher education institutions	33.3	66.7	51.9
Students' participation in international studies	C9: Number of students registered in subjects taught in a foreign language	14.3	16.7	27.8
	C10: Number of students registered in programs provided via online learning modes	0.0	8.3	14.8
	C11: Number of students who attend joint degree programs collaborated with overseas higher education institutions	12.7	50.0	35.2

The Engagement Dimension

The engagement dimension included five indicators measuring two components, as shown in Table 8.7. For *Institutional Networks and Partnerships*, respondents from China and Australia agreed that indicator E2 'Number of overseas partners with whom at least one academic activity (mobility, program, research) has taken place' was the most important. One-third of Chinese and 63.0% of Australian participants reported E2 as 'very important.' Two-thirds respondents from Singapore also highly appreciated this indicator, citing it as 'very important.' In comparison with E2, however, more than four-fifths Singaporean participants appreciated E3 'Percentage of partnerships by region' more.

Compared to E5 'Percentage of alumni working overseas,' the analysis showed that in both China (22.2%) and Singapore (83.3%) most respondents agreed on E4 'Proportion of international (by nationality) alumni relative to the total number of alumni' for assessing *International Presence of Alumni*. Participants from Australia held an opposite opinion, however, with 44.7% endorsing E5 as 'very important' compared to 40.7% for E4.

The Governance Dimension

The last governance dimension included 14 indicators measuring four components. Table 8.8 shows participants' opinions on these indicators. For *Human Resources for Internationalization Activities*, slightly less than one-third of Chinese respondents agreed that G3 'Percentage of administration staff proficient in more than one working language' is very important. In Singapore, the same proportion (33.3%) of participants cited G3 and G2 'Percentage of administration staff with international experience (minimum 3 months)' as 'very important.' 20.4% of Australian participants also rated G3 and G2 as 'very important.' Attitudes varied toward the most important indicator for the *Financial Support* component. Both China (31.7%) and Australia (81.5%) agreed

Table 8.7 Importance of listed indicators in the engagement dimension by nation

Component	Indicator	Percentage of respondents rating the indicator as 'very important'		
		CN	SG	AU
Institutional networks and partnerships	E1: Number of memberships in international organizations and consortia	22.2	33.3	31.5
	E2: Number of overseas partners with whom at least one academic activity (mobility, program, research) has taken place	33.3	66.7	63.0
	E3: Percentage of partnerships by region (Europe, Africa, Asia, North America, South America, Pacific)	28.6	83.3	57.4
International presence of alumni	E4: Proportion of international (by nationality) alumni relative to the total number of alumni	22.2	83.3	40.7
	E5: Percentage of alumni working overseas	17.5	33.3	44.7

Table 8.8 Importance of listed indicators in the governance dimension by nation

Component	Indicator	CN	SG	AU
Human resources for internationalization activities	G1: Percentage of international staff (by nationality) in institutional senior management team	4.8	25.0	18.5
	G2: Percentage of administration staff with international experience (minimum 3 months)	27.0	33.3	20.4
	G3: Percentage of administration staff proficient in more than one working language	30.2	33.3	20.4
	G4: Percentage of administration staff who have participated in international exchange programs	22.2	16.7	11.1
Financial support for internationalization activities	G5: Percentage of total budget available (excluding personnel costs) for internationalization activities	30.2	58.3	57.4
	G6: Funding for international visiting scholars	17.5	16.7	51.9
	G7: Funding to support the international mobility of students	31.7	58.3	81.5
	G8: Funding for international research projects	23.8	66.7	74.1
	G9: Number of scholarships for international students (all degree levels)	28.6	41.7	63.0
	G10: Number of scholarships for international postdoctoral researchers	28.6	41.7	51.9
Infrastructure and facilities	G11: Percentage of library collection in other languages	28.6	0.0	11.1
International presence of the university	G12: Number of participations in fairs abroad	6.3	25.0	18.5
	G13: Number of languages in which the university Web site can be read	19.0	8.3	27.8
	G14: Number of committee activities in international professional associations	17.5	8.3	14.8

Percentage of respondents rating the indicator as 'very important' on G7 'Funding to support the international mobility of students,' while two-thirds of Singaporean respondents favored G8 'Funding for international research projects,' reporting it as 'very important.'

Only one indicator (G11 'Percentage of library collection in other languages') was identified for measuring *Infrastructure and facilities* component. While, more than a quarter of Chinese respondents regarded it as 'very important,' no one in Singapore thought the indicator was very important, and only 11.1% of Australian participants agreed on its importance. For the *International Presence* component, Chinese (19.0%) and Australian (27.8%) respondents agreed on G13 'Number of languages in which the university Web site can be read' as 'very important.' Singaporean respondents, however, chose G12 'Number of participations in fairs abroad' as their first choice, a quarter of whom citing it as 'very important.'

Determining the Final Indicator for Each Component

The above analysis shows that there was not always full consensus among the three countries on the most important indicator for each component. In this case, the author calculated Gamma correlation to determine whether the alternative indicator could be accepted. Usually, $G > 0.4$ indicates a strong positive relationship between the two variables (Connolly, 2007), suggesting that the alternative indicator may be used. If $0 < G < 0.4$, however, the positive relationship between the two variables is relatively weak and the alternative choice is not acceptable (Connolly, 2007). Table 8.9 summarizes the most cited indicator for each component in the three countries.

Of the 17 components, the three countries agreed on the final indicators for eight components: *Internationally cooperative research programs* (R1); *Internationally focused research centers* (R4); *International researchers* (R5); *Internationally acknowledged research achievements* (R9); *Mobility of students* (S6); *Courses with an international component* (C8); *Human resources for international activities* (G3); and *Infrastructure and facilities* (G11). In order to determine the final indicator for the remaining nine components, the author employed Gamma correlation to suggest solutions.

Table 8.9 Indicators cited by most respondents as 'very important' for each component

Dimension	Component	Indicator CN	Indicator SG	Indicator AU
Research	Internationally cooperative research programs (R1, R2, R6)	R1	R1	R1
	Internationally focused research centers (R3, R4)	R4	R4	R4
	International researchers (R5)	R5	R5	R5
	Internationally acknowledged research achievements (R7, R8, R9, R10, R11, R12)	R9	R7/R8/R9	R9
Student	International students (S1, S2, S3, S4, S5)	S1	S1/S2/S5	S4
	Mobility of students (S6, S7, S8)	S6	S6	S6
Faculty	International profile of the faculty team (F1, F2)	F1	F1	F2
	International perspective and experience of faculty (F3, F4, F5, F6, F7)	F3/F4	F3/F5/F6/F7	F5
Curriculum	Courses with an international component (C1, C2, C3, C4, C5, C6, C7)	C5	C2	C2
	Joint degree programs (C8)	C8	C8	C8
	Students' participation in international studies (C9, C10, C11)	C9	C11	C11
Engagement	International networks and partnerships (E1, E2, E3)	E2	E3	E2
	International presence of alumni (E4, E5)	E4	E4	E5
Governance	Human resources for internationalization activities (G1, G2, G3, G4)	G3	G2/G3	G2/G3
	Financial support for internationalization activities (G5, G6, G7, G8, G9, G10)	G7	G8	G7
	Infrastructure and facilities (G11)	G11	G11	G11
	International presence of the university (G12, G13, G14)	G13	G12	G13

For *International Students*, both China and Singapore agreed on S1 'Percentage of international students (for degree study) on campus in total,' while Australia chose S4 'Percentage of international higher degree research (HDR) students on campus.' Therefore, Gamma correlation between S1 and S4 determined whether Australia could accept S1. Since $G = 0.698$, the identified positive relationship between the two indicators is relatively strong, meaning that Australian respondents who rated S4 as 'very important' also tended to rate S1 the same way. Hence, S1 is acceptable as an alternative in Australia. Similarly, F1 is acceptable in Australia ($G = 0.455$) as an alternative of F2 in measuring *International Profile of the Faculty Team*, while E4 ($G = 0.744$) could replace E5 to measure *International Presence of Alumni*. In China, C2 ($G = 0.698$) is acceptable as an alternative to C5 in measuring *Courses with an international component*; C11 ($G = 0.589$) can substitute for C9 in measuring *Students' Participation in International Studies*. In Singapore, since E2 ($G = 1.0$) can perfectly predict E3, E2 is therefore acceptable to measure *International Networks and Partnerships*. Also, G7 ($G = 1.0$) is a good substitute for G8 as the indicator for *Financial Support for Internationalization Activities*.

In the case of the *International Perspective and Experience of Faculty* component, the common overlap between China and Singapore was F3, while Singapore and Australia shared overlap with F5. In this circumstance, the author calculated the Gamma values between F3 and F5 in both China and Australia to make the final decision. Since $G < 0.4$, F3 is not accepted as an alternative in Australia. In China, however, the G value is 0.647, which means F5 could be used to predict F3, suggesting F5 as the indicator for *International Perspective and Experience of Faculty*.

Gamma correlation analysis thus helped the research move one step closer to the final indicator set, resulting in the draft set shown in Table 8.10. One exception to this, however, is the *International Presence of the University* component due to the weak positive relationship ($G < 0.4$) between G12 and G13, thus making G13 unacceptable in Singapore. In this case, the Gamma correlation analysis failed to suggest the final indicator, thus requiring further decision-making. At this stage, another decision was made to exclude G11 'Percentage

Table 8.10 Draft final indicator set

Dimension	Component	Indicator
Research	Internationally cooperative research programs (R1, R2, R6)	R1
	Internationally focused research centers (R3, R4)	R4
	International researchers (R5)	R5
	Internationally acknowledged research achievements (R7, R8, R9, R10, R11, R12)	R9
Student	International students (S1, S2, S3, S4, S5)	S1
	Mobility of students (S6, S7, S8)	S6
Faculty	International profile of the faculty team (F1, F2)	F1
	International perspective and experience of faculty (F3, F4, F5, F6, F7)	F5
Curriculum	Courses with an international component (C1, C2, C3, C4, C5, C6, C7)	C2
	Joint degree programs (C8)	C8
	Students' participation in international studies (C9, C10, C11)	C11
Engagement	International networks and partnerships (E1, E2, E3)	E2
	International presence of alumni (E4, E5)	E4
Governance	Human resources for internationalization activities (G1, G2, G3, G4)	G3
	Financial support for internationalization activities (G5, G6, G7, G8, G9, G10)	G7
	International presence of the university (G12, G13, G14)	G12/G13

of library collection in other languages,' the only indicator measuring *Infrastructure and Facilities*, based on its insignificance in both Singapore (0.0%) and Australia (11.1%). Consequently, the final set does not include this component since no appropriate indicators could be identified to measure it.

The Feasibility of the Indicators

The 17 indicators included in the draft set were crosschecked with their feasibility. Of the 17 draft indicators, 12 were reported by more than three-quarters respondents in each country as feasible to be collected[1] (see Table 8.11). The three countries might encounter varying degrees of difficulties in recording the other five indicators. For example, 41.7% of respondents from Singapore perceived R9 'Percentage of publications cited by SCI, EI, ISTP' as less feasible to be tracked. For F5 'Percentage of faculty (FTE) who have at least one-year overseas experience,' more than two-fifths of participants in both Singapore and Australia expressed their concerns with its feasibility. About one-third of surveyed staff members from Singapore and Australia believed the data of G7 'Funding to support the international mobility of students' could be difficult to gather. Approximate 35% of Chinese participants expressed concern about the feasibility of G12 'Number of participations in fairs abroad,' and one-third of respondents in both China and Singapore regarded G13 'Number of languages in which the university Web site can be read' as a less feasible indicator.

Other Possible Indicators

For each dimension, respondents were asked in the open-ended question to suggest appropriate indicators other than the listed ones, which

---

[1]Here, a feasible indicator means the respondents rated it as either 'somewhat feasible' or 'very feasible.'

Table 8.11 Feasibility of the 17 draft indicators

Indicator	CN	SG	AU
R1: Percentage of research projects involving international partnership and collaboration	93.7	91.7	92.6
R4: Number of research centers operated with international partners	92.1	83.3	83.3
R5: Percentage of international postdoctoral researchers	79.4	83.3	90.7
R9: Percentage of publications cited by SCI, EI, ISTP	87.3	58.3	75.9
S1: Percentage of international students (for degree study) on campus in total	98.4	100	96.3
S6: Percentage of domestic students who have international study experiences (incl. exchanges and short-term programs those are no more than an academic year)	100	100	88.9
F1: Percentage of international (by nationality) faculty members (full-time equivalent FTE)	95.2	75.0	85.2
F5: Percentage of faculty (FTE) who have at least one-year overseas experience (excl. degree study)	87.3	58.3	59.3
C2: Number of subjects involving a partner in other countries	87.3	83.3	74.1
C8: Number of joint degree programs (Bachelor, Masters, and PhD) collaborated with overseas higher education institutions	90.5	91.7	81.5
C11: Number of students who attend joint degree programs collaborated with overseas higher education institutions	76.2	83.3	75.9
E2: Number of overseas partners with whom at least one academic activity (mobility, program, research) has taken place	93.7	83.3	87.6
E4: Proportion of international (by nationality) alumni relative to the total number of alumni	74.6	100	81.5
G3: Percentage of administration staff proficient in more than one working language	84.1	75.0	70.4
G7: Funding to support the international mobility of students	90.5	66.7	68.5
G12: Number of participations in fairs abroad	65.1	75.0	42.6
G13: Number of languages in which the university Web site can be read	66.7	66.7	81.5

Percentage of respondents rating the indicator as feasible to be collected they believed need to be taken into account. Analysis of these open questions resulted in a number of new indicators. The criteria used in this study to examine the eligibility of indicators were applied to these suggested new indicators to judge if they can meet the requirements.

In regard to the research dimension, 12 new indicators emerged from the responses:

- China

  - NR1 Number of influential international awards won by faculty
  - NR2 Impact factor of each published article
  - NR3 Number of awards won in international competitions

- Singapore

  - NR4 Number of agreements signed to pursue near future research collaboration

- Australia

  - NR5 Number of research agreements/MOUs
  - NR6 Number of invited speaks
  - NR7 Number of invited research fellow
  - NR8 Number of joint research supervisions with foreign institutions
  - NR9 Number of membership of foreign scholarly societies
  - NR10 Number of leadership roles in international scholarly societies
  - NR11 Percentage of academic staff working on internationally oriented research
  - NR12 Number of commercial transaction including contracts with internationally based organizations

Among the 12 indicators, NR1, NR6, NR7, and NR11 are less intelligible since the definition of the four indicators could be ambiguous and might cause confusions in calculating the data. For example, consensus could hardly be achieved on defining 'influential international awards.' Other emerged indicators are related to a university's internationally acknowledged research achievements. For example, the indicators NR2

'Impact factor of each published article' and NR3 'Number of awards won in international competitions' are indicative of the visibility and quality of research in the global community. So are NR9 and NR10. Some of the suggested indicators attempt to measure the aspects of research internationalization that had already been covered by the draft indicators. For example, NR4 and NR5 intend to evaluate the international collaboration in research, which could be captured by the draft indicator R1 'Percentage of research projects involving international partnership and collaboration.' The indicator NR8 'Number of joint research supervisions with foreign institutions' meets all the criteria and suggests a new component of the research dimension—internationally joint research supervision, which could be taken into consideration in further studies.

Respondents suggested eight new indicators to measure the student dimension:

* China
  - NS1 Number of awards won by students in the international competitions
  - NS2 Percentage of students participating in the international conference
  - NS3 Percentage of undergraduate students participating in the international competitions
  - NS4 Percentage of international student by discipline (science and engineering, humanities, social science, and medicine)
* Australia
  - NS5 Percentage of HDR students undertaking research that includes international fieldwork
  - NS6 Percentage of HDR students presenting at international conferences
  - NS7 Number of students participating in international events (conferences and competitions)
  - NS8 Number of domestic events in which students engage with foreign visitors

Most of the proposed indicators focus on various types of international experiences of students, such as NS2, NS3, NE5, NS6, and NS7. These indicators could be integrated into the existing indicator S6 'Percentage of domestic students who have international study experience (incl. exchange and short-term programs those are no more than an academic year).' Taking the diverse forms of international experience presented in these new indicators into account, the original scope of S6 could be extended to include international conferences, competitions, and fieldworks. The only concern with the broadened scope of S6 is the feasibility to collect the data. The change of definition of S6 may result in different opinions on its feasibility. The suggested indicators NS1 and NS8 are less capable of meeting the requirement of unambiguity because neither 'international competitions' nor 'domestic events' could be easily scoped and defined. Respondents proposed NS4 to measure the distribution of international students across disciplines. It satisfies all the criteria for indicators and could make complement to the existing indicators that measure the international profile of the student body.

The respondents suggested five new indicators for the faculty dimension, all of which meet the criteria:

* China

    – NF1 Percentage of international faculty members titled Professor
    – NF2 Number of supervised international students per faculty member
    – NF3 Percentage of supervised students who had overseas academic experience per faculty member
    – NF4 Percentage of international faculty members by title

* Australia

    – NF5 Percentage of faculty members with at least one degree awarded by an institution abroad

They have the potential to make contributions to a more detailed and in-depth evaluation of the internationalization of faculty in a particular HEI. The indicator NF5 'Percentage of faculty members with at least one degree awarded by an institution abroad' deserves special attention, which resembles the draft indicator F3 'Percentage of faculty (FTE) who were awarded their highest academic qualification by an institution abroad.' China and Singapore perceived F3 as the most important indicator to measure *International Perspective and Experience of Faculty*. It, however, turned out to be the least important indicator in Australia. If NF5 could be used to substitute for F3, there might be a possibility in changing Australian participants' opinions and achieve a higher level of agreement among countries.

No other indicator was proposed for the curriculum dimension. In measuring the engagement dimension, responses suggested three new indicators:

- China

  - NE1 Number of overseas branches/research institutes
  - NE2 Place in the international league tables

- Australia

  - NE3 Percentage of international alumni contribute back to their university with time, expertise or funds

Indeed, some existing instruments include NF1. The reason for eliminating it from the draft indicator list was because the overseas branch is not a generic component of university internationalization and may not be appropriate to be used for comparative assessment across institutions and countries. The indicator NE2 does not meet the criterion of intelligibility. The disputation on which international league tables would be used as the reference could be foreseen. Theoretically, NE3 is an even better indicator than the draft indicator E4 'Proportion of international (by nationality) alumni relative to the total number of alumni' in measuring the engagement of international alumni. But technically, it could be really difficult to scope the contributions made by international alumni and to generate valid data.

For governance dimension, respondents suggested another five indicators in addition to the 14 listed:

- China
    - NG1 Percentage of administration staff who participated in international conferences in the past academic year
    - NG2 Number of international activities that university leaders attended in the past academic year
    - NG3 Percentage of administration staff engaged with international affairs
    - NG4 Frequency of university Web site updated in other languages
- Australia
    - NG5 Funding to support international mobility of professional and academic staff

Among the five, the expression of NG2 is ambiguous. The interpretation of 'international activities' could vary from university to university. NG3 was identified as an indicator in Chen, Zeng, Wen, Weng, and Yu (2009) study. But in the interview, several participants indicated that the number of staff involved in institutional international activities or the size of the International Office is not a key factor that influences the internationalization performance of a university. Therefore, it was removed from the list. The other three indicators—NG1, NG4, and NG5—satisfy all the requirements and could be regarded as complementary indicators for institutions to use.

Because the importance and feasibility of all these newly emerged indicators were not tested by university practitioners, it would not be appropriate to include them in the final indicator set. Those new indicators that meet all criteria could be considered as potential complements to the indicator set established in this study. And several of them contributed to the adjustment of the draft indicators.

Finalizing the Indicator Set

Development of the indicator set was now close to completion but several issues had to be settled. First, the feasibility of the indicator F5 'Percentage of faculty (FTE) who have at least one-year overseas experience' needed to be secured, particularly in Australia and Singapore, where less than 60% of respondents reported it as feasible. In the case that F5 was not feasible, the best substitute indicators had to been decided. It could be either F3 'Percentage of faculty (FTE) who were awarded their highest academic qualification by an institution abroad' or the new indicator NF5 'Percentage of faculty members with at least one degree awarded by an institution abroad.' Second, a decision had to be made regarding the best indicator for the *International Presence of University* component (either G12 or G13). Third, as suggested in the previous section, the scope of the indicator S6 'Percentage of domestic students who have international study experience (incl. exchange and short-term programs that are no more than an academic year)' could be extended to integrate the new indicators NS2, NS3, NE5, and NS6, embracing all types of international academic experience. The feasibility to collect the data of S6 given the extended scope needed to be tested. Finally, because R9 'Percentage of publications cited by SCI, EI, ISTP' and G7 'Funding to support the international mobility of students' were cited as feasible by fewer than two-thirds of respondents from Singapore, the extent to which the data for the two indicators could be collected had to be further examined.

University leaders who were interviewed in the first phase were invited again as consultants to help finalize the indicator set by sharing their judgment on the above issues. A review form (see Appendix D) including the draft indicator set and five questions was distributed to the interviewees via email. Of the 17 interviewees, nine (one from Singapore, two from China, and six from Australia) returned the completed review form. The returned feedback showed that with respect to the feasibility of F5 'Percentage of faculty who have at least one-year overseas experience,' four respondents assumed that it is infeasible to collect the data. Two others suggested it could be collected but the value would not be worth the effort. A majority of respondents agreed with NF5 'Percentage of faculty members with at least one degree awarded by an institution abroad' as a substitute for F5 to measure the international perspective and experience of faculty. Given this, in the final indicator set, the new indicator NF5 was used to replace the original indicator F5. For the indicator to capture the *International Presence of the University* component, a majority of respondents argued that neither of the two suggested indicators (G12 'Number of participations in fairs abroad' and G13 'Number of languages in which the university Web site can be read') was quality or suitable. One respondent commented, 'both of the two indicators are useful for recruitment purposes but bigger issues like research are missed by both. Recruitment is just a subset of an organization' (Respondent 1). Another respondent showed his concern with the terminology of G12, saying that 'the definition of the participation in fairs abroad will be controversial' (Respondent 6). In relation to the indicator G13, he argued that 'you can have a huge international presence and a monolingual Web site as University of Oxford.' Given the above consideration, the author excluded the component from the final indicator set. It is not suggesting that the *International Presence of the University* is of no importance to a university's internationalization or it should not be taken into account in measuring institutional internationalization performance. The reason for excluding the component aligns with the lack of appropriate indicator to accurately capture it.

The extension of the scope of S6 to include all types of academic experience was overwhelmingly welcome. As the consultant suggested, it is inappropriate to limit the academic experience within the semester to yearlong exchanges. Other types of activities should be recognized and embraced. Only one respondent reported that there would be difficulties in collecting the data for the new indicator. None of the respondents believed that it would be difficult to collect the data for R9 'Percentage of publications cited by SCI, EI, ISTP.' The same happened to G7 'Funding to support the international mobility of students.' In addition, two respondents suggested a better wording of the indicator G7, as the 'proportion of students funded by university for international academic experiences.' Because it could be difficult to determine the scope of 'funding,' which might include different resources and mix with the funding for research and education projects as well, the change will reduce the ambiguity of the expression of the indicator (Respondent 6 and 7). The feedback from the nine consultants led to the finalization of the indicator set. The final set (presented in Table 8.12) includes 15 indicators capturing 15 components of university internationalization.

Table 8.12 The final set of indicators for measuring university internationalization

Dimension	Element	Indicator
Research	Internationally cooperative research programs	Percentage of research projects involving international partnership and collaboration
	Internationally focused research centers	Percentage of research centers operated with international partners
	International researchers	Percentage of international postdoctoral researchers
	Internationally acknowledged research achievements	Percentage of publications cited by SCI, EI, ISTP
Student	International students	Percentage of international (by nationality) students (for degree study) on campus in total
	Mobility of students	Percentage of students who have international academic experiences (incl. all types of academic-related experience no more than an academic year)[a]
Faculty	International profile of the faculty team	Percentage of international (by nationality) faculty members (FTE)
	International perspective and experience of faculty	Percentage of faculty members (FTE) with at least one degree awarded by an institution abroad[a]
Curriculum	Courses with an international component	Number of subjects involving a partner in other countries
	Joint degree programs	Number of joint degree programs (all degree levels) collaborated with overseas institutions
	Students' participation in international studies	Number of students who attend joint degree programs collaborated with overseas higher education institutions

(continued)

Table 8.12 (continued)

Dimension	Element	Indicator
Engagement	International networks and partnerships	Number of overseas partners with whom at least one academic activity has taken place
	International presence of alumni	Percentage of international (by nationality) alumni
Governance	Human resources for internationalization activities	Percentage of administration staff proficient in more than one working language
	Financial support for internationalization activities	Proportion of students who have international academic experiences funded by university relative to the total number of students who have international academic experiences[a]

[a]The expression of the indicator was modified from the original one

National Divergences in Perceptions of the Final Indicators

In addition to selecting the most appropriate indicators to be included in the final set, the data generated by the questionnaire also provided an opportunity to explore if there were any divergences between respondents from different countries in relation to their perceptions of the indicators. The analysis suggested that although respondents from all three countries agreed on the final indicators, considerable differences could be observed in their opinions on the 15 indicators.

Differences in Importance

The researcher conducted a Kruskal–Wallis test to identify any differences between countries in their perceived importance of the 15 final indicators. The alternative and null hypotheses are as follows:

- H1: There are differences between participants from different countries in relation to the importance they rated for Indicator$_x$ ($x = 1, 2, \ldots 15$).
- H0: There are no differences between participants from different countries in relation to the importance they rated for Indicator$_x$ ($i = 1, 2, \ldots 15$).

An Asymp. Sig. (p) smaller than 0.05 implies a divergence between respondents from different countries in relation to their perceived importance of an indicator, in which case the research would accept the alternative hypotheses (H1) (Connolly, 2007). Otherwise, the research would accept null hypotheses. The results of the Kruskal–Wallis test observed evidence of differences in 8 of the 15 indicators, listed as follows (see Table 8.13):

- R1 ($p = 0.000$, Kruskal–Wallis $H = 30.168$, df $= 2$)
- R4 ($p = 0.02$, Kruskal–Wallis $H = 7.789$, df $= 2$)
- R5 ($p = 0.000$, Kruskal–Wallis $H = 26.495$, df $= 2$)

Table 8.13 Perceptions of the importance of the seven identified indicators by nation

Indicators		Country		
		China (%)	Singapore (%)	Australia (%)
R1 Percentage of research projects involving international partnership and collaboration	1 Not important	0.0	0.0	0.0
	2 Neutral	6.3	0.0	0.0
	3 Somewhat important	58.7	25.0	16.7
	4 Very important	34.9	75.0	83.3
R4 Number of research centers operated with international partners	1 Not important	0.0	8.3	0.0
	2 Neutral	7.9	0.0	5.6
	3 Somewhat important	61.9	50.0	37.0
	4 Very important	30.2	41.7	57.4
R5 Percentage of international postdoctoral researchers	1 Not important	4.8	0.0	0.0
	2 Neutral	28.6	8.3	3.7
	3 Somewhat important	46.0	58.3	35.2
	4 Very important	20.6	33.3	61.1
S6 Percentage of domestic students who have international study experiences (incl. exchanges and short-term programs those are no more than an academic year)	1 Not important	0.0	0.0	0.0
	2 Neutral	3.2	8.3	0.0
	3 Somewhat important	41.3	8.3	20.4
	4 Very important	55.6	83.3	79.6
C11 Number of students who attend joint degree programs collaborated with overseas higher education institutions	1 Not important	0.0	8.3	5.6
	2 Neutral	25.4	8.3	13.0
	3 Somewhat important	61.9	33.3	46.3
	4 Very important	12.7	50.0	35.2
E2 Number of overseas partners with whom at least one academic activity (mobility, program, research) has taken place	1 Not important	0.0	0.0	5.6
	2 Neutral	9.5	0.0	9.3
	3 Somewhat important	57.1	33.3	22.2
	4 Very important	33.3	66.7	63.0

Indicators		Country		
		China (%)	Singapore (%)	Australia (%)
E4 Proportion of international (by nationality) alumni relative to the total number of alumni	1 Not important	1.6	0.0	3.7
	2 Neutral	19.0	0.0	11.1
	3 Somewhat important	57.1	16.7	44.4
	4 Very important	22.2	83.3	40.7
G7 Funding to support the international mobility of students	1 Not important	0.0	0.0	0.0
	2 Neutral	6.3	8.3	1.9
	3 Somewhat important	61.9	33.3	16.7
	4 Very important	31.7	58.3	81.5

- S6 ($p = 0.012$, Kruskal–Wallis $H = 8.914$, $df = 2$)
- C11 ($p = 0.031$, Kruskal–Wallis $H = 6.940$, $df = 2$)
- E2 ($p = 0.019$, Kruskal–Wallis $H = 7.929$, $df = 2$)
- E4 ($p = 0.000$, Kruskal–Wallis $H = 15.517$, $df = 2$)
- G7 ($p = 0.000$, Kruskal–Wallis $H = 27.576$, $df = 2$)

With these findings, it could be further examined the specific differences in perceiving the eight indicators by conducting a Mann–Whitney U test for the three pairs of countries: China and Singapore, Singapore and Australia, and China and Australia. One problem in conducting multiple Mann–Whitney U tests is that it increases the chances of making a Type I error. To address this problem, a stricter level of statistical significance to make sure the overall level remains no higher than 5% (Connolly, 2007). In this study, thus the three Mann–Whitney U tests were conducted with a statistical significance level of $5/3 = 1.7\%$ ($p = 0.017$).

The results of Mann–Whitney U tests showed that respondents from China and Singapore shared similar opinions for most of the eight indicators, with divergences in perceiving R1 ($p < 0.017$, Mann–Whitney $U = 220.500$, $Z = 2.581$) and E4 ($p < 0.017$, Mann–Whitney $U = 134.000$, $Z = 3.863$). As Table 8.13 demonstrates, Singapore appreciated R1 much more than China, with three-quarters of respondents rating R1 as 'very important' compared to 34.9% from China. Over half of Chinese participants classified R1 as 'somewhat important' rather than 'very important.' Respondents from China and Singapore also gave E4 different degrees of importance: A significant majority of Singaporean participants endorsed it as 'very important,' compared to only slightly more than one-fifth of Chinese participants. Like R1, most respondents from China (57.1%) agreed that E4 is a 'somewhat important' indicator. The data observed few variances between Singapore and Australia, with identified divergences only for E4 ($p < 0.017$, Mann–Whitney $U = 178.000$, $Z = 2.673$). As shown in the cross-table, 83.3% of Singaporean participants rated E4 as 'very important,' in comparison with only 40.7% of Australian participants. There are 14.8% of Australian respondents deemed it either 'neutral' or 'not important,' while no one from Singapore categorized E4 into these two groups.

The data observed remarkable differences, however, between China and Australia. The Mann–Whitney U tests show that of the eight indicators, five had an Exact Sig. (p) smaller than 0.017: R1 ($p = 0.000$, Mann–Whitney $U = 859.500$, $Z = 5.307$); R4 ($p = 0.005$, Mann–Whitney $U = 1246.000$, $Z = 3.793$); R5 ($p = 0.000$, Mann–Whitney $U = 839.000$, $Z = 5.067$); S6 ($p = 0.005$, Mann–Whitney $U = 1280.500$, $Z = 2.804$); and G7 ($p = 0.000$, Mann–Whitney $U = 856.500$, $Z = 5.271$). Australia valued all five indicators more than China. More than four-fifths of Australian respondents cited R1 as 'very important' compared to 34.9% in China. Most Chinese participants regarded R1 as 'somewhat important.' Similarly, more than half of respondents from Australia rated R4 as a 'very important' indicator, in comparison with less than one-third of Chinese participants. A considerable amount of Chinese respondents (33.4%) denied the importance of R5, reporting it as either 'not important' (4.8%) or 'neutral' (28.6%). Only 3.7% of respondents from Australia, however, deemed R5 as 'neutral,' and no one rated it as 'not important.' There are over two-fifths of Chinese participants gave S6 moderate importance, while nearly four-fifths of respondents in Australia thought it 'very important.' For indicator G7, the majority of Chinese participants endorsed it as 'somewhat important' with slightly less than one-third categorizing it as 'very important.' More than four-fifths of Australian respondents, in contrast, agreed that G7 is a 'very important' indicator.

Differences in Feasibility

Since the scale involves an 'unknown' option, the data regarding feasibility should be treated as nominal rather than ordinal. The non-parametric tests employed in the importance section cannot thus apply to nominal variables. In order to explore the difference between country and the feasibility of each indicator which respondents perceived, a Chi-square test was employed, the hypotheses of which are as follows:

- H1: There is a difference between country and the feasibility of Indicator$_x$ ($x = 1, 2, \ldots 15$).
- H0: There is no difference between country and the feasibility of Indicator$_x$ ($x = 1, 2, \ldots 15$).

Two basic conditions need to be met when using a Chi-square test:

- No more than 20% of cells in the contingency table should have expected values less than five.
- No cell has an expected value of less than one.

Considering the small numbers within the 'infeasible' category of each indicator, a decision was made to merge the 'infeasible' and 'unknown' categories into one group called 'less feasible' in order to meet the two conditions while conducting the Chi-square test. Similarly, 'highly feasible' and 'somewhat feasible' were combined into one category as 'feasible.' Cramer's V was calculated to measure the effect size. Table 8.14 presented respondents' perceptions of the feasibility for each of the 15 indicators. The Chi-square test resulted on detected differences in two indicators: R9 ($p = 0.046$, $\chi^2 = 6.143$, $df = 2$) and F5 ($p = 0.029$, $\chi^2 = 7.062$, $df = 2$). The effect size of the two indicators is medium (Cramer's $V > 0.2$). As shown in the cross-table, participants regarded R9 as highly feasible for collection in both China (87.3%) and Australia (75.9%). Over two-fifths of participants from Singapore, however, cited it as 'less feasible,' assuming difficulties in gathering the data for R9. Regarding F5, slightly less than half of respondents from Singapore (41.7%) and Australia (40.7%) indicated concerns with its feasibility. In contrast, 87.3% of participants from China believed F5 to be a feasible indicator. R1, S1, and S6 did not meet the conditions for the Chi-square test, as half of the cells have expected count less than 5. With the assistance of the cross-table, however, the researcher noticed no obvious difference among the three countries regarding the feasibility of the three indicators. In each of the three countries, about 90% of respondents endorsed these indicators as feasible. Similarly, no striking discrepancies could be observed among the three countries in their participants' opinions on the feasibility of the other 10 indicators.

Table 8.14 Perceptions of the feasibility of the 15 indicators

Indicator		Country		
		China (%)	Singapore (%)	Australia (%)
R1 Percentage of research projects involving international partnership and collaboration	Less feasible	6.3	8.3	7.4
	Feasible	93.7	91.7	92.6
R4 Number of research centers operated with international partners	Less feasible	7.9	16.7	16.7
	Feasible	92.1	83.3	83.3
R5 Percentage of international postdoctoral researchers	Less feasible	20.6	16.7	9.3
	Feasible	79.4	83.3	90.7
R9 Percentage of publications cited by SCI, EI, ISTP	Less feasible	12.7	41.7	24.1
	Feasible	87.3	58.3	75.9
S1 Percentage of international (by nationality) students (for degree study) on campus in total	Less feasible	1.6	0.0	3.7
	Feasible	98.4	100	96.3
S6 Percentage of domestic students who have international study experiences (incl. exchanges and short-term programs those are no more than an academic year	Less feasible	0.0	0.0	11.1
	Feasible	100	100	88.9
F1 Percentage of international (by nationality) faculty members (FTE)	Less feasible	4.8	25.0	14.8
	Feasible	95.2	75.0	85.2
F5 Percentage of faculty who have at least one-year overseas experience (FTE)	Less feasible	12.7	41.7	40.7
	Feasible	87.3	58.3	59.3
C2 Number of subjects involving a partner in other countries	Less feasible	12.7	16.7	25.9
	Feasible	87.3	83.3	74.1
C8 Number of joint degree programs (all degree levels) collaborated with overseas higher education institutions	Less feasible	9.5	8.3	16.7
	Feasible	90.5	91.7	83.3

(continued)

Table 8.14 (continued)

Indicator	China (%)		Singapore (%)		Australia (%)	
C11 Number of students who attend joint degree programs collaborated with overseas higher education institutions	23.8	Less feasible	16.7	Less feasible	24.1	
	76.2	Feasible	83.3		75.9	
E2 Number of overseas partners with whom at least one academic activity (mobility, program, research) has taken place	6.3	Less feasible	0.0	Less feasible	14.8	
	93.7	Feasible	100		85.2	
E4 Proportion of international (by nationality) alumni relative to the total number of alumni	25.4	Less feasible	0.0	Less feasible	18.5	
	74.6	Feasible	100		81.5	
G3 Percentage of administration staff proficient in more than one working language	15.9	Less feasible	25.0	Less feasible	29.6	
	84.1	Feasible	75.0		70.4	
G7 Funding to support the international mobility of students	9.5	Less feasible	33.3	Less feasible	13.0	
	90.5	Feasible	66.7		87.0	

Importance of the Six Dimensions by Nation

In addition to understanding how respondents in the three countries perceived individual indicators, it also was interesting to know their opinions of different dimensions at a more aggregated level. In doing so, six new variables were calculated, presenting the importance of each dimension. The six new variables were defined as the mean score of indicators in each dimension. For example, the new research dimension variable (Dimension_R) was defined as Mean (R1 + R2 + ... + R12). As suggested by Boone and Boone (2012), the new dimension variables were created by calculating a composite score from more than four Likert-type items; therefore, the composite score could be treated as interval data. The mean of each new variable was used to measure the importance of the dimension accordingly.

As shown in Table 8.15, the student dimension was regarded as the most important, regardless of the country that respondents came from. And, accord was achieved among the three countries that the curriculum dimension was regarded as the least important. International engagement also was highly appreciated in all three countries. The faculty dimension was much more valued in China than in Singapore and Australia. The three countries shared similar opinions on the research and governance dimensions. Australia showed a remarkably similar pattern to Singapore, with the only disagreement between the two countries being on the importance of the faculty and governance dimensions. In Singapore, the faculty dimension was less valued than the governance one. Respondents from Australia perceived them

Table 8.15 Importance of six dimensions by nation

China		Singapore		Australia	
Variable	Mean	Variable	Mean	Variable	Mean
Dimension_S	3.2718	Dimension_S	3.5938	Dimension_S	3.6042
Dimension_F	3.1224	Dimension_E	3.5	Dimension_E	3.2519
Dimension_E	3.0413	Dimension_R	3.1111	Dimension_R	3.2222
Dimension_R	3.0172	Dimension_G	3.0952	Dimension_G	3.1825
Dimension_G	2.9853	Dimension_F	3.0238	Dimension_F	3.0304
Dimension_C	2.8874	Dimension_C	2.8258	Dimension_C	2.9461

in the opposite way. China presented a distinct attitude toward the six dimensions. This pattern is consistent with Chinese university leaders' opinions on the differential priorities given to the dimensions of internationalization. As discussed in Chapter 4, Chinese policymakers regarded student and faculty as the two paramount dimensions and placed them on the top of other dimensions. They explained that this is because the core mission of Chinese HEIs is to nature talents. The findings of the staff survey evidenced the Chinese understanding of the role of HE from another perspective.

Availability of Data

This project proceeded one step further after the establishing the indicator set, to test the data availability for the indicators. To know whether the data of suggested indicators are available at universities is important for the utility of the instrument. An institutional survey including the final 15 indicators was distributed to the participant universities that agreed to be involved in the third phase investigation. The aim of the institutional survey was not to test the final instrument but to explore the availability of data. Of the 17 universities, nine consented to participate in the institutional survey and eight returned the survey. They were Universities 1, 5, 7, 8, and 9 in Australia and Universities 12, 13, and 14 in China. Neither of the two universities in Singapore agreed to participate in the final phase or returned the survey. Consequently, this study could provide little information regarding the data availability in Singaporean universities. The eight universities showed considerable variance in terms of the availability of data. The number of available indicators varied from 1 to 15 in different institutions. Of the five Australian universities, data for the 15 indicators were less ready to be reported in Universities 1 and 8, compared to the other three. Among the three institutions in China, two of them recorded the data to a fuller degree. In general, compared with their counterparts in Australia, universities in China had developed relatively comprehensive statistics in relation to internationalization. This was in accordance with the findings of the interview.

The results of the institutional survey also showed that the most ready to be collected indicator was S1 'Percentage of international (by nationality) students (for degree study) on campus in total,' which had already been tracked in all eight universities. The data for the indicator S6 'Percentage of students who have international academic experiences (incl. all types of academic-related experience no more than an academic year)' and NF5 'Percentage of faculty members (FTE) with at least one degree awarded by an institution abroad*' were also highly available in different institutions, reported by seven and six universities, respectively. Indicators R1, R9, C8, E2, E4, and G7 came next, recorded in five of the eight universities, respectively. Fewer universities were able to report indicators R4 'Percentage of research centers operated with international partners operated with formal international partners,' C2 'Number of subjects involving a partner in other countries,' and G3 'Percentage of administration staff proficient in more than one working language.' The data for the three indicators were only collected in two surveyed universities. In general, indicators measuring the student and engagement dimensions had been already recorded in most of the participant institutions. More difficulties were encountered in collecting and reporting the data for the indicators capturing the curriculum and governance dimensions.

According to the results of the staff survey and the feedback from the university leaders, it was believed that all 15 indicators were feasible to be collected in the participant universities. However, the institutional survey findings showed that the data were not ready to be reported. The reasons for the absence of data could be diverse. Firstly, in some universities, measuring internationalization performance had not yet become a routine practice and thus data in relation to university international activities might not be regularly collected and tracked. When they were asked to complete the survey, no data were available to report. Secondly, universities might employ different indicators to monitor and assess their internationalization performance. In this case, the data that the survey asked for were different from those that were available in individual institutions. To calculate the required data, considerable efforts might be needed to synthesize the existing data. It would be costly in time and human resources; therefore, the university determined to leave the answer to the question blank. Similarly, the indicators were designed to measure internationalization performance at the institutional level. Hence, in some universities, particularly those in Australia where the administration system was much more decentralized, the data might not be available at the central level. Finally, considering that some institutions might be concerned about revealing the data to external parties, even though the data were available, they might choose not to report and share the data.

To put the final indicator set into practice, three related issues had to be addressed: feasibility, availability, and accessibility. Feasibility is related to practitioners' perceptions of whether the data for the indicators could be collected given the time and cost. Availability refers to the readiness of the data to be reported. And accessibility examines the extent to which the data are available to the public. The two surveys used in this study investigated both the feasibility of the indicators and the availability of data. Availability is a precondition of accessibility. Because the result of the institutional survey suggested a relatively low availability of data in a majority of the Australian universities, it was likely that few of the data would be publicly accessible. The survey also showed better availability of data in universities in China. However, it does not mean the data could be accessed via public resources such as national databases or university Web sites. Indeed, almost all of data relevant to institutional internationalization were internally available. It had not yet been a common exercise for HEIs in China to be accountable to the public and to reveal adequate information with respect to university governance and operation.

In returning the institutional survey, some respondents also gave their feedback on the issues with data generation and collection. Concerns were shown on the terminology of the indicators. Given the various institutional and national contexts, the same indicator actually could be interpreted in different ways and consistency could hardly be achieved. The indicator used to measure the international networks and partnerships: 'Number of overseas partners with whom at least one academic activity has taken place' serves an example. The definition of 'academic activity' was not clear enough and could be understood in diverse ways, as respondents reported. Even the indicators that seemed self-defined could be problematic in terminology. A respondent from University 9 commented that the indicator 'percentage of research projects involving international partnership and collaboration' was confusing. The scope of the research project needed to be rigorously defined. To calculate the data for this indicator, explicit instruction was required in regard to what types of projects should be included.

In addition to the terminology, the respondents suggested the necessity to standardize the calculation procedure of each indicator. To obtain reliable data and yield valid comparisons between institutions, a uniform data collection procedure is necessary for individual universities to follow. For some indicators, such as the 'percentage of international (by nationality) alumni,' both the number of each year and the accumulative number could be calculated. Without clear instructions, universities might make their own interpretations and decisions. Accuracy of the data was another concern of respondents. Because some indicators could be collected only through a self-completed questionnaire, the data generated in this manner might not be entirely accurate. University 5 gave an example in the survey. The data of the indicator 'percentage of administration staff proficient in more than one working language' were reported by the Human Resources Department through a staff questionnaire, and employees were not obliged to identify if they spoke more than one language. All the issues related to data collection shed light on the direction of further work to improve the current indicator set before it could be widely implemented. These concerns and suggestions are extremely valuable as they reflect the complexity in developing valid measurement for university internationalization, particularly to serve a benchmarking purpose. This complexity is definitely not exclusive to the assessment of internationalization but commonly exists in any practices of performance measurement and evaluation. There may never be an ideal tool which is capable of generating perfectly accurate performance information; however, researchers and practitioners still need to maximize the validity and reliability of the instruments as the information gathered by these instruments sometimes plays a decisive role in decision-making. In order to avoid misleading data, from the designing to the implementation, a cautious and rigorous manner needs to be applied throughout the process.

Characteristics of the New Instrument

The key features of the new instrument fruited in this project are summarized as:

- A quantitative measurement,
- Measuring achievements and effects rather than plans,
- An institutional level measurement,
- An all-round measurement,
- A cross-border measurement,
- A feasible measurement to be implemented, and
- Measuring what is valued about internationalization.

Similar to the tools developed by Horn, Hendel, and Fry (2007) and Chen et al. (2009), the indicators included in the new instrument are all quantitative in nature, thus, presenting quantifiable assessment for university internationalization performance. It is designed to measure facts about internationalization instead of policies, plans, or perceptions. Unlike in some other instruments, indicators examining institutional policies, for example, 'what is the institutions' stated policy (goals and objectives) for internationalization,' are included; the new instrument focuses on the concrete achievements. Considering that not all the policies and plans could be transformed into solid material commitment, measurements are expected to reflect what has been taking place in the university to attain internationalization instead of what is planning to be achieved (Hudzik & Stohl, 2009). Too often, internationalization is used as a dressing term in the university's mission statement without any investments to implement and realize it. Consequently, it is not surprising to have a gap between internationalization aspiration and the reality (Foskett, 2010). While policymakers could simply believe internationalization is the good and the right thing to do, in practice, however, the extent to which such keenness is converted into actions is another thing. Given this, in order to demonstrate that internationalization is not a 'paper commitment' in a given institution, the indicator set is developed to reveal the degree of internationalization that has been reached in a particular university.

As discussed previously, instruments have been developed to provide measurements on various levels, including program (e.g., MINT), department/school/faculty (e.g., IMS 2020), and institution (e.g., IMPI). Like most existing instruments, the indicator set developed in this project is designed to provide institutional level measurement. Although some tools like the one developed by Brandenburg and Federkeil (2007) claim to serve multi-level assessments, in practice, it is challenging to have one instrument implemented at different levels. Because measurement is closely related to goals and missions, internationalization goals of different departments and programs may vary in many aspects and cannot be assessed by using a same set of indicators. Some existing tools are designed for measuring a single or several aspects of university internationalization but cannot draw a whole picture. For example, the EMQT provides an assessment of academic and student mobility exclusively, as does the CIC benchmarking tool. As internationalization has been recognized as a multifaceted phenomenon, single dimension measurement can hardly reflect the complexity of the issue. Hence, the new indicator set, functioning as an all-round measurement, is able to capture six dimensions of university internationalization, covering most of the crucial domains of the phenomenon.

The majority of available measurements for internationalization are nationally focused such as the ACE and CIC benchmarking tools for universities in America, the Osaka University Project for HEIs in Japan, and the indicator set developed by Chen et al. (2009) for Chinese universities. Although recent cross-border instruments like IMPI have been developed to fit a regional context, an internationally applicable measurement has yet been established. The new indicator set measures the generic and comparable components of university internationalization, which are relevant to research intensive universities in most countries. The involvement of universities in three countries with distinctive social cultural backgrounds gives the new instrument considerable potentials to be applied in other national contexts than the three sampled ones in this project. Therefore, this instrument is capable of serving the benchmarking purpose for research universities across the world in regard to their internationalization performance. When applying this indicator set to other types of HEIs (e.g., teaching intensive universities or community colleges), a review is required to remove the irrelevant dimensions and components (e.g., the research or engagement dimension) from the framework.

In comparison with most existing measurements, the major difference of this new instrument is the number of indicators included in the set. In many of the available tools, cross-border measurements in particular, a large number of indicators are employed. For example, there are 186 indicators in the CHE project. In the MINT project, 257 indicators are developed, and IMPI project offers results with over 500 indicators. The continuous growth in the number of indicators has been noticed by other researchers (see Beerkens et al., 2010), who have argued that the increased number of indicators leads to a very complex indicator system that is less likely to be usable. Nonetheless, while such an instrument can provide universities a comprehensive and detailed assessment, it will require tremendous human and capital resources to put the complicated tools into practice. Indeed, many appealing assessment models are impractical, either due to their cost or on methodological grounds. It is no good proposing an assessment model that will be burdensome or unaffordable in terms of money or time (Hudzik & Stohl, 2009). Still, one may argue that it is not necessary for universities to track all the hundreds of indicators provided by a single instrument; rather, one needs to choose those that best fit its own needs. In this case, however, the instrument may not be able to serve the inter-institutional comparison purpose that they aim to, for it is less likely that individual universities will select the same set of indicators.

The indicator set covers internationalization in its widest possible sense; meanwhile, it strikes a balance between comprehensiveness and utility. As Stecher and Koretz (1996) suggest, sufficient indicators should be used to ensure a degree of sophistication. However, the tool would not be practical in its application if too many indicators were included. Thus, uniting the need for sufficient nuance and the need for conciseness within a single tool is a challenge, and, considering the both sides, the tool developed in this project came up with a compromise. The new instrument also sets normative values with respect to university internationalization. The dimensions and components captured by the indicator set are valued by policymakers in their international practices as well as in theory. Given that the indicators included in the set are agreed upon by university practitioners from different institutions and countries as determinative of a university's internationalization performance, the new instrument arguably has the capacity to measure what should be measured in relation to internationalization.

Using the New Instrument to Inform and Improve University Internationalization Practice

The use of indicators primarily intends to serve three main purposes: characterizing the nature of a system (Dickson & Lim, 1991; Gaither, 1994; Selden, 1985; Shavelson, 1991; Sizer, Spee, & Bormans, 1992), informing policy-making (Dickson & Lim, 1991; Gaither, 1994; Oakes, 1986; van den Besselaar, Inzelt, Reale, de Turckheim, & Vercesi, 2012), and contributing to the accountability of a system (Hudzik & Stohl, 2009; Jenkins-Deas, 2009). The new indicator set is expected to help inform and improve university internationalization practice in all three aspects.

Characterizing the Nature of University Internationalization

The new instrument provides a toolset capable of monitoring and assessing university internationalization performance on an ongoing basis via a coherent system of key indicators. It could generate evidence for the achievements of a university has made, helping them move beyond vague descriptions of their internationalization status. In addition to providing accurate and precise information to illustrate the condition of performance, a good set of indicators, as Shavelson (1991) suggests, is expected to contribute to practice improvement. With the data provided by the set, a spider diagram could be generated to reflect a given university's performance in the six dimensions of internationalization, thereby helping policymakers understand the current pattern of their practice. For example, universities in Australia could be a high achiever in the student dimension, particularly in the component of international students' recruitment, while Singaporean universities may show a strong profile in the curriculum dimension and the student exchange component.

By identifying the pattern of practice, the strengths and weaknesses of a particular HEI's internationalization could be revealed. If the pattern is observed over time, then any changes of the pattern could be captured. Meanwhile, the pattern could also signal any potential risks existing in the current practice. For example, if a university has an extremely high percentage of international students, it may indicate that the university relies overwhelmingly on revenue gained from oversea student recruitment. And this could be a latent risk that may threaten the financial stability of the institution.

The use of indicators ultimately involves comparisons—against oneself, a norm or others (Dickson & Lim, 1991; Gaither, 1994; Jarratt, 1985; Ogawa & Collom, 1998; Selden, 1985; Sizer et al., 1992). Since the indicator set is a cross-border measurement tool, information provided by the instrument may help universities obtain a clear picture of their current position in comparison with other institutions in their own regions and in other parts of the world. Through such comparisons, good practices in internationalization could be identified and universities can learn from them. Policymakers can also observe trends and issues in internationalization strategies that emerge from such a comparative analysis. In the case of a comparison with institutions from other regions, universities can learn about the opportunities and challenges of cooperation with institutions in that region. Comparing oneself with others could suggest comparative strengths and weaknesses and offer insights. Moreover, comparison across universities could also illustrate distinctive institutional characteristics, revealing general patterns of university internationalization practice in a particular country or region, which enables the identification of diverse models of internationalization in different nations/regions at the aggregated level.

As Hudzik and Stohl (2009) argue, comparison metrics have advantages and disadvantages. On the positive side, a standardization of assessment across institutions is required for meaningful comparisons of some key indicators. On the other hand, too much reliance on standard measures across institutions may lead to the minimizing of diversity and the homogenization of institutional internationalization practice. Thus, when using the indicator set for comparison purposes, policymakers should be cautious. Internationalization is not a goal in itself (de Wit, 2011a; Green, 2012; Krause, Coates, & James, 2005); therefore, it will be meaningless to chase the numbers only. The recruitment of international students may be considered as a good example. Australian universities have achieved a substantial presence in the international student market; however, this has been achieved at a considerable cost, such as declining staff-student ratios and declining morale among many staff members (Stromquist, 2007). The comparison with others may provide references and insights, but it may not be used as the criterion to evaluate the effectiveness or quality of internationalization practice in a particular university. Deliberately, there is no weight assigned to each indicator included in the new set, which prevents it being used as a ranking tool. The users of the new indicator set need to bear in mind that this tool does not aim at imposing hierarchical ranking or reputational competition in the field of internationalization. Instead, the comparisons enabled by the tool should be used to identify strengths and weakness for improvement purpose. By leaving the meaning-making right to the users of the tool, it shows full respect to diverse institutional profiles.

Informing Evidence-Based Decision-Making

While measurement for internationalization is essential to be able to discern progress or retrogression (Dumont & Robert, 2010), assessment is never the end; rather, it should initiate improvements. In this regard, indicators may serve as policy tools that help policymakers improve their institution's performance (Lashway, 2001; Pollard, 1989). The new instrument gives policymakers a way to make evidence-based decisions and steer strategies with respect to internationalization. As international pursuit requires a substantial commitment of institutional financial and human resources and may be an opportunity cost in some other areas, it is critical to know objectively and in measurable terms that internationalization produces value in desired directions in order to garner support beyond rhetoric (Hudzik & Stohl, 2009; Knight, 2001). Only with objective information about internationalization practice and effects can wise decisions be made on funding allocation and budget planning. By knowing the weaknesses in practice, more resources can be directed to the weak areas to make improvements. For those domains that do not meet the institutional targets, possible reasons could be analyzed and measures could be taken accordingly. Moreover, the data can also tell if achievements have been made in the desired direction. As the example given by a university leader, the data about the students going abroad indicate that students prefer to exchange to English-speaking countries. And if the outbound mobility toward Asian countries is to be encouraged, the funding strategy might be changed to advocate Asian-oriented exchange programs. These data give policymakers levers to shift strategy.

While it is necessary to be cautious about the policy-related expectations of indicators, such indicators should not be the determinant factor in policy development; rather, the fruit of indicators will be more directly a contribution to policymakers' cognition than to their decision (Shavelson, 1991). Raw numbers rarely speak for themselves nor constitute an accountability system, but require careful interpretation. No matter how sophisticated the data collected, they cannot substitute for informed human judgment (Lashway, 2001; Oakes, 1986). With the information provided by the indicator set, policymakers could understand their strengths and weaknesses in internationalization practice. Before changes can be made however, it is the responsibility of policymakers to figure out what they exactly want regarding internationalization. While it might be ideal to develop a comprehensive range of strengths in all domains, this could run counter to institutional strategic priorities. Subject to available resources, university leaders are expected to use the data in a wise way to develop policies. Otherwise, it is possible to be misled by the data. For example, how does one determine the optimum number of international students for different universities? In the late 2000s, some universities began to take the view that they were reaching capacity, and some began to refine their international students recruitment policies to emphasize greater quality or an improved balance between undergraduate and postgraduate enrolments, or even, to shun further growth altogether. Other universities had, and still have, capacity for further growth (Murray, Hall, Leask, Marginson, & Ziguras, 2011). Thus, it should be noted that the strategic outlook of a HEI should in no way be subordinate to seeking the short-term improvement of individual key figures.

Improving Accountability

Indicators also serve as the basis for holding an education system accountable (Blank, 1993; Meyer, 1995). It is clear from this study that tracking and recording the data about internationalization performance has yet to become common practice in universities in Australia. Only recently has internationalization become an institution-wide strategy, integrated into the core areas of university operation. With the recognition of its magnitude, there will be increasing demands for more sophisticated information in relation to international performance. The new instrument is expected to stimulate a more regular data collection mechanism, by which internal and external accountability regarding internationalization can be shaped. If faculty and staff are expected to buy into the notion of internationalization, then it is necessary to demonstrate quantifiable achievements through evaluative measures that articulate its benefits to the institution, to students, and to the community as a whole, using objective data. If internationalization efforts are expected to justify financial support, then these efforts must prove their worth through ongoing assessment. Externally, the data provided by the indicator set could inform others outside the institution. On the one hand, as Beerkens et al. (2010) point out, institutions might have to show that they are international in order to be eligible for certain funding sources or to be considered for accreditation. On the other hand, the Internet has ensured that the general public has access to various information of a university, which may help students and parents to better know about the university in making their decision about where to study. As internationalization itself has become an important part of education quality, in students' future decision-making about the place to study, information in relation to a university's internationalization might be taken into account. For example, a university that can offer opportunities for international exchanges or offer a multicultural learning environment could be more appealing to prospective students. If such data could be open to the public, they may impact students and parents' choice.

Limitations of the New Instrument

The indicator set developed in the current study adds more choices for universities to measure their internationalization performance. Despite the many advantages this set offers, users need to be aware of its limitations. First, it is not possible to measure all valued aspects of university internationalization using the indicator set. Moreover, qualitative measures of internationalization have not yet been adequately incorporated into the new indicator set. Given the quantitative nature of indicators, the new tool cannot assess components that defy quantification. For example, culture is seen as an indispensable dimension included in the conceptual framework of university internationalization; however, numbers capture neither the integration of international and domestic students/staff nor a multicultural campus easily. Indeed, while most would agree that indicators could describe key aspects and features of the phenomenon being measured, they do not explain everything about an entity (Oakes, 1986). It is better to regard indicators modestly, as signals or guides, rather than as absolute measures (Bottani, Delfau, Hutmacher, & Desmond, 1991; Sizer et al., 1992), since it is not possible to substitute for comprehensive, in-depth evaluations. Some components of university internationalization stand out, whereas others are difficult to assess using the indicator set despite knowing that they are conceptually important. Ideally, depicting a full picture of institutional internationalization performance requires measures for both the quantity and quality of every component. Take the *International Student* component as an example; it is equally important to know how many international students on campus in total, as captured by the indicator of the new instrument, and the distribution of the students from different regions/countries, even the quality of the incoming students. Likewise, to evaluate a university's international collaborations in research, the indicator (percentage of research projects involving international partnership and collaboration) only assesses quantity. Thus, it provides no information about influences or achievements of the collaborative research, which indicate the quality of the research collaboration. The quantitative side of each component indicates the scale of internationalization activities and the qualitative side mirrors the depth. Taken together, both sides convey the component fully, just like the two sides of a coin. With the new instrument, one could examine only the quantitative side of a university's internationalization performance. Other qualitative measures, such as evaluation rubrics, are necessary to capture the components that defy quantification and reflect the depth of institutional internationalization performance in every aspect.

Secondly, the new tool may not be capable of drawing an exhaustive picture of university internationalization performance or showing all relevant details. In order to maximize the utility of the indicator set, subtlety is sacrificed by limiting the number of indicators to 15. For each component, only one indicator is selected to capture it. However, rarely can a single indicator by itself provide adequate information (Cuttance, 1994; Oakes, 1986; Pollard, 1989). In the three separate sets of indicators proposed for the three countries, respectively, more than one indicator are included to measure a single component, which are more likely to generate sophisticated information about internationalization.

Thirdly, although the new instrument intends to be internationally applicable, its relevance has been only verified in three national contexts. When time and resources allow, it would be helpful to test the validity and relevance of the tool in other contexts, including American, European, other Asian countries, etc. Also, since all the participant institutions are flagship universities, the tool is more capable of serving large comprehensive research universities. Adjustments may be necessary in order to accommodate the need of other types of HEIs. For example, for teaching intensive institutions, the research dimension included in the indicator set may be less relevant. For research-only institutes that do not recruit undergraduates, the curriculum dimension may need to be removed.

Another limitation of the current indicator set is related to the measurement level. Since the unit of measurement is the entire institution, it may mask differences of internationalization performance in various disciplines. Increased internal differentiation within various faculties even departments has led to varied degrees of internationalization (Trondal, 2010; Yang, 2004). Precisely, the so-called 'hard' sciences are often assumed to be generally more internationally oriented than the 'soft' sciences (Kyvik & Larsen, 1997; Yang, 2003). Hard science tends to be global in the sense that research results are not influenced by the country or region where the research is undertaken. Therefore, in these disciplines, such as experimental physics, there are significant opportunities for international collaboration. On the other hand, some research subjects are situated in a social, cultural, bio-topical, and geographical context that makes the research results particularly regionally oriented (Trondal, 2010). Due to the more varied ideologies and paradigms inherent in these fields, opportunities to cooperate with international partners or to win grants from external resources are much more limited (Yang, 2003). As a result, the extent of internationalization is usually much less in social sciences and humanities.

Finally, the current indicator set remains in progress. Before it can be widely implemented in universities, the terminology of each indicator and the calculation procedure have to be standardized in order to produce valid and reliable comparable information. It is important that a valid, complete, and consistent definition is developed for each indicator. While some indicators may appear simple and easy to be understood, they could actually be interpreted in various ways. For example, 'international faculty members' can be defined by nationality, passport, place of birth, or even the primary language used. Even for a self-defined term like 'research project,' boundaries need to be set to define the scope of the term. The vagueness around expression might raise problems for universities to collect accurate data. If the statistics produced by different definitions or calculation procedures were used to make comparisons between peer institutions, the conclusion would be unreliable and potentially erroneous. The limitations of the indicator set do not reduce the usefulness of the instrument. In contrast, they help set boundaries and remind the audience to be cautious when using the tool to draw any conclusions and to inform decision-making.

Obstacles to Implementing the New Instrument

It is also clear from the study that universities in different countries may face various obstacles in putting the indicator set into practice. The main challenge for universities in Australia could be the collection of data because of the decentralized administration system there. Universities have already been tracking and synthesizing data of a wide range of performance indicators regarding both research and teaching and learning. And the new indicator set means a greater workload on the staff in different offices and departments. Although the number of indicators included in the set is restricted to the minimum to reduce the burden to university administration, in order to generate the information at the institutional level, considerable input from almost all units across the campus is necessary. Neither of the two participant Singaporean universities provided the data for the indicators. One possible interpretation could be that very few data were ready to be reported. It is reasonable to foresee that, like their counterparts in Australia, the major challenge to implementing the new instrument in Singapore could be generating the required data. Compared to their counterparts in Australia and Singapore, universities in China have already established a relatively comprehensive statistics about internationalization. Thanks to the highly centralized system, it is less difficult to collect and record data at the central level. However, this information has yet to be effectively used to inform decision-making. Instead, they are regarded as the annual summary of the work of the International Office. If the data are not linked to policy and strategy development, they are numbers, not measurements. Interpreting the data and making them serve analytical and evaluative purposes could be the lesson for Chinese university leaders.

Summary: A Reflection on Measuring University Internationalization

The new instrument, together with other existing tools, indicates that, in relation to university internationalization, inputs and outputs rather than outcomes are more likely to be tracked and measured. All the components captured by the indicator set are either inputs or outputs of university internationalization activities but not outcomes. There have been witnessed a tendency in performance management in public organizations that to narrowly frame performance and focus mainly on visible inputs/outputs, which are easy to be measured by indicators, but do not have much to do with quality of research and teaching (Pietrzak & Pietrzak, 2016). Hudzik and Stohl (2009) argue that inputs are the resources (money, people, policies, etc.) available to support internationalization efforts, like the components of financial and human resources support included in the indicator set. Outputs are the amount and types of work or activity undertaken in support of internationalization efforts, such as the student mobility, joint degree programs, and the internationally cooperative research projects. Here, outputs could be understood as the direct results of university international practice. What are the outcomes? They are the impacts or end results. The expected outcomes of internationalization include the enhancement of general educational and research quality, the intercultural competence of students, the employability of graduates, the lifting of reputation of the institution, etc. Specifically, the intercultural competence of students could mean knowledgeable global perspectives, so that students can embrace the diversity, commonalities, and interdependence of the world's people, nations, and environmental systems (Papp, 2008). The employability of graduates is possibly influenced by their intercultural engagement skills, which enable them to communicate and interact effectively and appropriately with people of different nationalities and cultures. Internationally oriented education also intends to foster global citizenship attitudes, with which students are willing to support the common good of the world community, concerning human rights and the welfare of others and the sustainability of natural systems and species (Papp, 2008). Given these, either the students' mobility programs or the internationalization of curriculum is not the objective in itself but the means to achieve the outcomes (de Wit, 2010).

Clearly, institutional internationalization performance and the outcomes it achieves could be related to each other; however, no cause–effect relationship can be simply inferred between the efforts and results. Connections between inputs and outcomes are only partially mediated by institutional outputs. There are also few, if any, linear relationships between inputs/outputs and outcomes—nonlinear marginal returns on further investment are the rule (Green, 2012; Hudzik & Stohl, 2009). In other words, the presence and quality of a given set of international activities like the number of or the participation in internationally cooperative programs do not tell institutions about its success in producing inter-culturally competent students. Indeed, students may acquire global learning through experiences other than the opportunities provided by the institution (de Wit, 2011b). The intercultural competence of a student, for example, could be obtained through international exchange programs or internationally focused courses, or it could be gained from the student's family background if some of the family members come from different countries. Every measurement designer faces the challenge to prove the cause and effect relationship between inputs/outputs and outcomes. Internationalization outcomes, to some extent, are influenced by international efforts made by universities. However, many other factors may have their respective impacts on the outcomes as well. If outcome measurements are the really important measures and what the policymakers are keen for, are inputs/outputs measures still needed? One reason for including some input and output measures, as Hudzik and Stohl (2009) suggest, is that they help monitor the health and effectiveness of the process to make sure progress has been made toward achieving the intended outcomes. Appropriate inputs and outputs are supposed to contribute to satisfactory outcomes. For example, if it is believed that intercultural competence could be gained from exchange programs, sufficient opportunities should be created to support student mobility. The other reason to have input/output measures is that without parameters of internationalization, by no means can the cause–effect relationship between inputs/outputs and outcomes be verified.

Why it is so difficult to measure outcomes of university internationalization? Unlike the core missions of HEIs, research, teaching and learning and service, internationalization is not the goal in itself, and it can hardly be separated from the core pillars of university operation. It is supposed to add value to the core areas of universities. In this regard, internationalization should be seen as a process factor. It is a means toward other ends. A university's performance in the core areas such as research and teaching and learning is relatively less difficult to assess, for the outcome could be directly linked to activities. For example, research activities taking place on campus determine the quality or impacts of research. The linear cause–effect relationship between the inputs/outputs and outcomes of research activities is more easily demonstrated. However, when it comes to internationalization, it is by no means meaningful to launch more international activities if the contribution of internationalization to the core missions of universities cannot be justified. Internationalization functions as a mediator. Its impacts on the ultimate educational products (e.g., graduates and research outcomes) have to be realized through other venues like research or teaching/learning activities. This explains the fundamental difficulty in measuring university internationalization. Since internationalization is embedded with the core functions of HEIs, it is extremely challenging to identify the direct impact of internationalization on the results. Any improvement of outcomes could be caused by the changes of the venue (e.g., research, teaching and learning, engagement activities) or the mediator (internationalization).

References

Beerkens, E., Brandenburg, U., Evers, N., van Gaalen, A., Leichsenring, H., & Zimmermann, V. (2010). *Indicator projects on internationalisation: Approaches, methods and findings—A report in the context of the European project 'Indicators for Mapping & Profiling Internationalisation' (IMPI).* Gütersloh: CHE Consult GmbH.

Blank, R. K. (1993). Developing a system of education indicators: Selecting, implementing, and reporting indicators. *Educational Evaluation and Policy Analysis, 15*(1), 65–80.

Boone, H. N., & Boone, D. A. (2012). Analyzing Likert data. *The Journal of Extension, 50*(2), 1–5. https://joe.org/joe/2012april/tt2.php.

Bottani, N., Delfau, I., Hutmacher, W., & Desmond, N. (1991). Lessons gained from the OECD/CERI international educational indicators project. In J. Hewton (Ed.), *Performance indicators in education: What can they tell us?* (pp. 35–42). Brisbane: Australian Conference of Directors-General of Education.

Brandenburg, U., & Federkeil, G. (2007). *How to measure internationality and internationalisation of higher education institutions! Indicators and key figures*. Gütersloh: Centre for Higher Education Development.

Chen, C.-G., Zeng, M.-C., Wen, D.-M., Weng, L.-X., & Yu, Z. (2009). The establishment of indicator system for the evaluation of internationalisation of research universities in China. *Peking University Education Review, 7*(4), 116–135 (in Chinese).

Connolly, P. (2007). *Quantitative data analysis in education: A critical introduction using SPSS*. Abingdon, Oxon and New York: Routledge.

Cuttance, P. (1994). Monitoring educational quality through performance indicators for school practice. *School Effectiveness & School Improvement, 5*(2), 101–126.

de Wit, H. (2010). *Internationalisation of higher education in Europe and its assessment, trends and issues*. The Hague, The Netherlands: NVAO.

de Wit, H. (2011a). Law of the simulative arrears? In H. de Wit (Ed.), *Trends, issues and challenges in internationalisation of higher education* (pp. 7–23). Amsterdam: Centre for Applied Research on Economics and Management Hogeschool van Amsterdam.

de Wit, H. (2011b). Internationalization misconceptions. *International Higher Education, 64*(Summer), 6–7.

Dickson, G. S., & Lim, S. (1991). *The development and use of indicators of performance in educational leadership*. Paper presented at the International Congress for School Effectiveness and Improvement, Cardiff, Wales.

Dumont, S. E., & Robert, A. P. (2010). The internationalization of U.S. universities—Are we making progress? *International Educator (1059–4221), 19*(4), 52–55.

Foskett, N. (2010). Global markets, national challenges, local strategies: The strategic challenge of internationalization. In F. Maringe & N. Foskett

(Eds.), *Globalisation and internationalisation in higher education: Theoretical, strategic and management perspectives* (pp. 35–50). London: Continuum.

Gaither, G. (1994). *Measuring up: The promises and pitfalls of performance indicators in higher education* (ASHE-ERIC Higher Education Report No. 5). Washington, DC: George Washington University.

Green, M. F. (2012). *Measuring and assessing internationalization*. Retrieved 21 June 2014, from http://www.nafsa.org/uploadedFiles/NAFSA_Home/Resource_Library_Assets/Publications_Library/Measuring%20and%20Assessing%20Internationalization.pdf.

Horn, A. S., Hendel, D. D., & Fry, G. W. (2007). Ranking the international dimension of top research universities in the United States. *Journal of Studies in International Education, 11*(3), 330–358.

Hudzik, K. J., & Stohl, M. (2009). Modelling assessment of the outcomes and impacts of internationalisation. In H. de Wit (Ed.), *Measuring success in the internationalisation of higher education* (EAIE Occasional Paper No. 22, pp. 9–21). Amsterdam: European Association for International Education.

Jarratt, R. (1985). *Report of the steering committee for efficiency studies in universities*. London: Committee of Vice-Chancellors and Principles.

Jenkins-Deas, B. (2009). The impact of quality review on the internationalisation of Malaysian university-college, Canada: A case study. In H. de Wit (Ed.), *Measuring success in the internationalisation of higher education* (EAIE Occasional Paper No. 22, pp. 111–124). Amsterdam: European Association for International Education.

Knight, J. (2001). Monitoring the quality and progress of internationalization. *Journal of Studies in International Education, 5*(3), 228–243.

Krause, K.-L., Coates, H., & James, R. (2005). Monitoring the internationalisation of higher education: Are there useful quantitative performance indicators? In M. Tight (Ed.), *International relations* (International Perspectives on Higher Education Research, Vol. 3, pp. 233–253). Bingley: Emerald Group Publishing Limited.

Kyvik, S., & Larsen, I. M. (1997). The exchange of knowledge: A small country in the international research community. *Science Communication, 18*(3), 238–264.

Lashway, L. (2001). *Educational Indicators: ERIC Digest*. Eugene, OR: Eric Clearinghouse on Educational Management.

Meyer, R. H. (1995). *Educational performance indicators: A critique*. Madison, WI: Institute for Research on Poverty.

Murray, D., Hall, R., Leask, B., Marginson, S., & Ziguras, C. (2011). *State of current research in international education*. Melbourne: LH Martin Institute, IEAA, Australian Government Australian Education International.

Oakes, J. (1986). *Educational indicators: A guide for policymakers.* CPRE Occasional Paper Series. Washington, DC: Center for Policy Research in Education.

Ogawa, R., & Collom, E. (1998). *Educational indicators: What are they? How can schools and school districts use them?* Riverside: California Educational Research Cooperative, University of California.

Papp, D. S. (2008). Strategic perspectives on internationalizing a University. *Presidency, 11*(3), 22–22.

Pietrzak, M., & Pietrzak, P. (2016). The problem of performance management at public universities. In M. Orszulak (Ed.), *Global challenges of management control and reporting* (pp. 191–201). Wrocław: Uniwersytet Ekonomiczny we Wrocławiu.

Pollard, J. S. (1989). *Developing useful educational indicator systems* (Insights on Educational Policy and Practice. Number 15). Austin, TX: Southwest Educational Development Lab.

Selden, R. W. (1985). *Educational indicators: What do we need to know that we don't know now?* Washington, DC: National Center for Education Statistics.

Shavelson, R. J. (1991). *What are educational indicators and indicator systems? ERIC/TM digest.* Washington, DC: Eric Clearinghouse on Tests, Measurement Evaluation.

Sizer, J., Spee, A., & Bormans, R. (1992). The role of performance indicators in higher education. *Higher Education, 24*(2), 133–155.

Stecher, B. M., & Koretz, D. (1996). *Issues in building an indicator system for mathematics and science education.* Santa Monica, CA: Rand Corp.

Stromquist, N. P. (2007). Internationalization as a response to globalization: Radical shifts in university environments. *Higher Education, 53*(1), 81–105.

Trondal, J. (2010). Two worlds of change: On the internationalisation of universities. *Globalisation, Societies and Education, 8*(3), 351–368.

van den Besselaar, P., Inzelt, A., Reale, E., de Turckheim, E., & Vercesi, V. (2012). *Indicators of internationalisation for research institutions: A new approach* (A report by the ESF member organisation forum on evaluation: Indicators of internationalisation). Strasbourg Cedex: European Science Foundation.

Yang, R. (2003). Globalisation and higher education development: A critical analysis. *International Review of Education, 49*(3), 269–291.

Yang, R. (2004). Openness and reform as dynamics for development: A case study of internationalisation at South China University of Technology. *Higher Education, 47*(4), 473–500.

9

The Future of University Internationalization

Modern universities are facing unprecedented challenges within the globalized context, as they are expected to reform teaching and research to meet twenty-first-century requirements, including fostering students' global citizenship attitudes and intercultural competence, and solving issues concerning the international community. Further, the knowledge economy emphasizes higher education's role in maintaining and improving a nation's competitiveness, and accordingly, universities are expected to serve national economic development better. For those in many developed nations, reductions in public funding also require them to operate more efficiently and innovatively. Thus, the emerging global landscape requires universities to reposition themselves both nationally and globally to obtain a 'competitive edge.' In addition, the growing importance of universities' social mission encourages them to engage with local communities more actively. Therefore, to respond to these challenges, universities must be more internationalized.

University policymakers recognize internationalization's vital role in universities' successful performance in the new era. Internationalization requires substantial institutional investment, as it no longer means simply having a large number of international students on campus or a wide range of overseas partners, but instead, a comprehensive strategy that takes nearly all core pillars of university operation into account. Policymakers are invited to think about internationalization as multidimensional and dynamic, rather than narrow or static. However, this does not mean that they must embrace all dimensions simultaneously. Rather, they need to prioritize internationalization's different aspects according to their own needs and targets. Given limited capital and human resources, it may be a luxury for a university to develop strength in all domains. Further, contextual factors, including national and institutional cultural background and characteristics, shape internationalization's practice in different universities powerfully. Thus, strategic priorities may shift over time, and, ultimately, internationalization may be approached holistically.

Transformation from Structural to Cultural Diversity—Universities' Cultural Mission

Most forecasts in recent years have claimed that interactions across borders will increase in almost all spheres in life and that higher education is a sector of society in which this is especially frequent and important. As argued above, the widespread use of the term 'internationalization' is based on the assumption that growth is endemic. However, views on the extent we will achieve internationalization vary (Teichler, 2017). Particularly, the forces that motivate the internationalization process keep changing, which adds uncertainty to the future of university internationalization. As a recent issue of *The Economist* (January 26, 2019) indicated, globalization, as the major driving force of the internationalization process, has slowed from light speed to a snail's pace in the past decade for several political and commercial reasons and has resulted in a new era of sluggishness or 'slowbalization.' The golden age of globalization from 1990 to 2010 was something to behold. Commerce soared as the cost of shipping goods, phone calls became cheaper, tariffs were cut, and finance liberalized. All of these factors that facilitated globalization have changed, as the cost of transporting goods has stopped falling and multinational firms have found that local rivals outcompete them frequently. In particular, activity is shifting toward services, which are more difficult to sell across borders. Slowbalization will lead to stronger links within regional blocs. For example, supply chains in North America, Europe, and Asia are sourcing more firms closer to home. In Asia and Europe, most trade is intra-regional already, and the share has risen since 2011. This intensified regionalization manifests itself not only in the commercial domain, but also in educational sectors. As a number of researchers have observed, this trend has led to stronger cross-border cooperation among neighbors, not only in Europe (Teichler, 2009; Wächter, 2008), but in some other regions of the world as well (see, for example, Yonezawa, Kitamura, Meerman, & Kuroda, 2014). As one of modern HE's key functions is to facilitate economic and social development, these changing global forces will bring new requirements for universities that result in different responses. Universities' international development is no exception, as the struggle among global, national, and local powers has been, and will continue to, shape it.

Universities' ability to fulfill their cultural mission will determine internationalization's fate to a large extent. As internationalization has matured, the focus of research in the field has shifted from understanding the phenomenon to investigating its effects. Internationalization in higher education is expected to confer benefits in four broad spheres: academic, economic, political, and cultural, among which the cultural benefits are desired most. Universities long have served as key cultural mediators in encounters between global and national cultures (Scott, 2005) with the goal to establish international values, cross-cultural understanding and tolerance, and greater global awareness in the wider community (Chan, 2008; Knight, 1997). Internationalization opens new possibilities for universities to fulfill their cultural mission, as it has increased the opportunities for people of different cultures to meet dramatically, primarily by increasing the rate of transnational mobility. Over the past three decades, the number of students enrolled in higher education in foreign countries has risen from 0.8 million worldwide in 1975 to 4.6 million in 2015 (OECD, 2017), a more than fivefold increase. Educating students from abroad is viewed as an important mechanism for countries to appreciate 'what makes each other tick,' and to '…build bridges and create cultural understanding, reducing the likelihood of war and terrorism and binding people together in ways that are helpful for peace and prosperity' (Chankseliani, 2018, p. 58).

According to Spencer-Oatey and Dauber (2015), university internationalization will experience four stages. The first is pre-internationalization, in which a campus is culturally homogeneous. Then, it evolves to the second stage in which most universities are currently—structural internationalization. This stage features culturally diverse students and staff, but limited intercultural interaction and integration. With the efforts of all staff and students and commitment of sustainable resources, university internationalization is expected to move forward to the third stage, in which a culturally diverse campus community with high levels of intercultural interaction and integration develops. Ultimately, universities will arrive at the final stage, competency internationalization, which fosters interculturally competent staff and students. The large number of international students on campuses contributes to the structural diversity of universities in major Western countries, such as the United States, UK, and Australia. However, it may be inaccurate to assume that structural diversity leads automatically to intercultural understanding. Both Allport's (1954) and Putman's (2007) works demonstrate that simply being in the vicinity of different people does not result in meaningful, intercultural learning. A recent British Council report indicated that simply having a diverse student body does not signify that the education, or even the campus, is multicultural in nature.[1] Integrating domestic and international students in both academic and social activities is the key to achieve desirable cultural understanding. Unfortunately, a number of studies have argued repeatedly that meaningful interaction between international and domestic students in higher education communities remains far

---

[1] British Council. (2014). *Integration of international students. A UK perspective*. Available at http://www.britishcouncil.org/education/ihe/knowledge-centre/student-mobility/report-integration-internationalstudents.

from the reality (e.g., see Healey, 2017; Teichler, 2017; Yvonne, Lynne, & Nazneen, 1997). Intercultural engagement and understanding generally do not occur naturally, but need to be nurtured and developed intentionally. Universities have great potential to encourage meaningful intercultural relationships' development (Kudo, Volet, & Whitsed, 2017). Having a diverse population provides favorable conditions to build intercultural understanding, but efforts need to be made timely to facilitate the transformation from structural to cultural diversity.

Students from different cultures—both international and domestic—are 'cultural carriers' who bring diverse ideas, values, experiences, and behaviors to the learning environment (Segall, Dansen, & Poortinga, 1990). In Bourdieu's (1984) words, students' 'cultural capital' can be used to drive learning. Students learn '…when shaken by new facts, beliefs, experiences and viewpoints' (Conklin, 2004, p. 38), which allows them to comprehend that there are multiple, equally legitimate ontologies that they need to respect (Chen & Starosta, 1997; Chiu, Lonner, Matsumoto, & Ward, 2013). Properly managed, this 'ontological shock' can be directed to facilitate growing self-awareness and better understanding of their own construction of reality (Healey, 2017). As the famous Chinese philosopher, Liang Shuming (1893–1988), remarked, 'People will never gain a clear understanding if they only remain within the structures of their own society; if only they first look to others and then at themselves, then they will immediately understand' (1921/1990). However, both international and domestic students' cultural values, particularly that of the former, are underestimated considerably and left unexploited largely in the current internationalized higher education environment. There are two reasons for this. On the one hand, students are unaware of their cultural capital, while on the other, universities provide inadequate support to use students' cultural capital to foster intercultural understanding. Universities can fulfill their cultural mission only when student and staff's cultural capital is recognized, respected, and exploited fully. In 1993, political scientist Samuel Huntington wrote the following about the future:

> It is my hypothesis that the fundamental source of conflict in this new world will not be primarily ideological or primarily economic. The great

divisions among humankind and the dominating source of conflict will be cultural. (p. 22)

The internationalized higher education landscape either could intensify or reduce intercultural conflicts, and fortunately, the outcome is in our hands. A truly internationalized university of the future will have to measure its success not only with respect to such structural factors as the number or proportion of international students and staff, but also by its ability to implement an agenda for integration that will facilitate and increase students and staff's global spirit. As pointed out in the previous chapter, this also is the fundamental challenge measurement developers face. Both integration and global spirit are difficult to measure. It is more likely to be detected in the atmosphere than in hard facts. One may observe it more closely by walking on the campus, talking to students, and interviewing the President than by looking at such statistics as the percentage of foreign students on campus. Actually, these figures could be highly misleading if not interpreted properly; they may tell the user certain things, but integration or global spirit is not necessarily one of them (Hertig, 2016).

Uncertainties Cloud the Future of University Internationalization

In addition to fulfilling their cultural mission, other uncertainties cloud the fate of university internationalization. For those countries that rely highly on exported education to bring revenues to HEIs, such as the UK and Australia, internationalization's prosperity depends largely on the supply of international students. On the one hand, while the growing capacity of major source countries' higher education—i.e., those of Asian nations—means they could accommodate more tertiary students at home, there is a question whether there is continuity in the number of outgoing students for degree studies. Because of concern about the negative consequences of 'brain drain' that could lead source countries to lose talent, it has been observed that nearly all developing countries have committed substantially to expand their higher education systems to increase tertiary education's accessibility to the masses and retain a talented workforce. On the other hand, fears have grown that internationalization might conflict frequently with quality, and economic rationales might undermine academic approaches, thus losing higher education internationalization's core values, such as 'international understanding' and 'global spirit' (Teichler, 2017). The 'degree mill' has been criticized for decades, and international students' high dropout rate and low satisfaction with their learning experiences remain key challenges that numerous universities in major host countries face. Harsh criticism of economization is widespread in academia, and it is expressed vividly often, as, for example—'From the pursuit of knowledge to the pursuit of revenue' (Reisberg & Rumbley, 2014; Kehm & de Wit, 2005). Moreover, many observers have noted an increasing emphasis is placed on 'competition' rather than 'cooperation.' A growing nationalistic or even imperialistic undercurrent of internationalization policies or 'hegemonic internationalization,' a term Scott (2015) coined, has been witnessed that refers to gaining financial, economic, and political advantages at the expense of other countries through intelligent internationalization policies and activities in higher education. It can be anticipated that the competition for international students will become even fiercer because of more emerging 'education hubs' as destination choices and expanded, quality higher education systems in Asian countries, which are the primary sources of international students today. Whether major host countries can retain their ability to attract a large number of overseas students depends on the additional value that international experiences can provide them. A degree from an overseas HEI may not be adequate to persuade students to travel across continents to pursue their studies, but their real influence and learning outcomes may.

A number of nations that were international student source countries previously, and now are attempting to build their own brands to achieve the transformation from source to destination countries, such as Singapore and China, have their own problems in internationalization waiting to be resolved. The national government subsidizes universities, particularly the flagship institutions in both countries, heavily, and provides generous scholarships to increase their universities' attractiveness to international students. Taking China as an example, after the launch of the One Belt One Road initiative enormous financial aid has been poured into recruiting students from neighboring South and Central Asian countries, and the eligibility for the government scholarship is not at all strict. This financial investment has achieved splendid outcomes already, as the number of incoming students from the countries targeted has soared. However, it may be hyper-optimistic to claim that China has become an appealing study destination based on these figures. In a recent study, Professor Liu Jin and I conducted on the One Belt One Road country students' motives for choosing to study at universities in China, the financial aid provided rather than the quality of education was the primary motivation the students surveyed reported.[2] When asked whether they would recommend China as a destination for other students or evaluate their learning experiences at the current university highly, only a minority of participants responded positively. It is difficult to predict how far China, as an emerging education hub, can go without offering international students substantial funding. To test the real outcomes of these initiatives designed to build their brands, universities in these countries have to be put on the 'market' and compete with all the players in the global higher education landscape under the same terms and conditions.

Finally, if university internationalization has a future, it has to prove its relevance to all members involved in global higher education. Clearly, there are leaders and followers in the process of internationalization. Major Western countries, the education exporters, have led the international development of higher education and the emerging hubs are the followers who would like to catch up and identify their own positions on the internationalization map. However, there are other players in addition to the leaders and followers: the 'marginalizers.' These have the least visibility in the global community, their voices have been heard rarely, and the international community has neglected their role for years. Universities in small states and in the most underdeveloped areas fall into this group and never are a priority on the university

---

[2] This study has not been published yet, and the data currently are available only to the project members.

international development research agenda. Further, the sporadic studies on them have failed to attract the attention of leading scholars in this field. Universities in these marginalized countries have many concerns about embracing internationalization. As internationalization requires substantial financial and human resources, the lack of government funding slows their pace in joining the global family. Subject to such limited resources, their more urgent challenges are to improve their education and research quality to meet 'international standards.' Indeed, internationalization provides them a shortcut to build capacity. However, being unable to obtain a place on the internationalization agenda may result in a widening gap between these universities and their counterparts who have been on the international track in both quality and quantity for a long while. It must be admitted that little is known about these universities and their struggles to engage in internationalization. A better understanding of these issues not only is theoretically important to research on this phenomenon, but also practically important to the universities themselves and their counterparts in other countries, as there are many possibilities and opportunities waiting to be discovered and explored. How should these countries place themselves and their universities in the global landscape? Which pathway do they prefer—internationalization or regionalization? What does internationalization mean to them? What global, regional, and local forces are involved in their engagement in international development? All of these questions are interesting, challenging, and worthy of further investigation.

Challenges in Internationalization Facing Universities in All Countries

Regardless of whether they are leaders, followers, or marginalizers, some common challenges face all participants in internationalization. With the growing number of international students on campuses, a significant number of scholars have highlighted the challenges associated with student diversity and the potential for negative outcomes, both for the students and the institution, including increased stereotyping, hardening of prejudicial attitudes toward other groups, and intergroup hostility (Asmar, 2005; Henderson-King & Kaleta, 2000; Rothman, Lipset, & Nevitte, 2003; Wood & Sherman, 2001; Yu & Moskal, 2018). The key concern is international students' influence on both their own and domestic students' learning experiences. Do international students contribute to, or inhibit, education on campus? According to Healey (2017), it is not at all clear that recruiting international students enhances a university's ability to produce high-quality teaching and research. In the English-speaking world, faculty and domestic students often complain that large numbers of international students in the classroom affect the learning experience adversely, as the latter's weaker English language skills and different learning styles make it difficult for them to engage in group discussions and problem-centered learning (Barron, Gourlay, & Gannon-Leary, 2010). Similarly, Chankseliani (2018) argued that increasing diversity on campus is not always viewed as beneficial to learning and teaching, particularly when the international student body includes a disproportionately high number of a specific group of students. As an extreme, but not unusual, example given in her study, an MSc in Management taught on an Australian campus where 80% of the students are native Chinese speakers and stated that it is unlikely to be a satisfactory experience for anyone, faculty, or domestic or Chinese students. This percentage of international students is not uncommon at the postgraduate level in some disciplines in Australia and the UK. Although international students are an important revenue source for universities, they do not want an entire classroom of foreign students, particularly non-native speakers. Universities want to ensure that there is a good mix of students from different national backgrounds. It is feared that a high proportion of foreign students in the classroom will cause a 'backlash from home students,' especially in a class in which the majority are non-native English speakers. For some universities, it may be a challenge to achieve a good mix of students from all over the world and avoid the situation in which one international student group dominates the campus (Chankseliani, 2018). It would be arbitrary to suggest one single right number for a good international-domestic student ratio. However, according to Chankseliani's study, as soon as an institution's international student body exceeds 15%, they will begin to skew the student experience overall, primarily for domestic students. Balanced numbers also are suggested to be a key indicator of successful internationalization.

The difficulties with large numbers of international students are by no means intended to deny the huge potential contributions that this cohort can make to academic, social, and cultural life on campus. Indeed, in Spencer-Oatey and Dauber's (2015) study, statistical analysis revealed that the experience of both mixed nationality friendships and mixed nationality group work is associated positively with students' perceptions that they are developing the skills needed to work effectively in international contexts. What I am trying to emphasize here is that large numbers of international students do not necessarily yield the educational benefits desired, particularly when the domestic and international students exist independently and ignore each other. The benefits that being educated with culturally diversified cohorts brings rely largely on the 'ontological shock' when a student first comes into contact with a group that shares an alternative ontology (Healey, 2017). When one begins to realize that the other group has a different, but equally valid, worldview, self-awareness grows. Paradoxically, it is the case often that the larger the cohort of international students on a campus, the more likely they are to form self-sufficient cliques and not integrate with their domestic counterparts (Healey, 2017; Wang, Harding, & Mai, 2012). This is because humans are tribal by nature, and integrating tribes to reap the benefits of internationalization requires hard work. International experiences' effects on students' competence, views, and attitudes need to be achieved through in-depth cultural interaction and engagement. Universities are advised to begin prioritizing this mission more, particularly as these changes are the most desirable outcomes of internationalization and employers have identified them as the top skill they seek.

Another tension in the internationalization process that needs to be addressed cautiously is that between the desire for a global or cosmopolitan profile and the preservation of national identity (e.g., see Yonezawa & Shimmi, 2015). This tension seems more prominent in small, developing, or non-Western countries, but developed Western nations also face it commonly, as internationalization, to some extent, has become the byword of homogenization and loss of diversity. To integrate themselves into the global higher education landscape, universities around the world are more likely to adopt internationally prevalent practices, norms, values, and English as the instruction language, which the hegemony of Western theoretical knowledge shapes largely. The dominant role of English in Western universities' rules of commercialization and ranking practices reinforces academic dependency and Western superiority further (Choi, 2010; Kim, 2005; Marginson, 2004; Singh, 2011; Yang, 2011). The result often is the emergence and reproduction of hierarchical intellectual partnerships and unequal exchanges at all levels, which raises questions concerning national identity (Ha, 2013). If we look at many of the developing countries that have suffered from the humiliations of Western colonialism, it is understandable that they fear the potential 'academic colonization' that internationalization may bring. The colonization experience has twisted their citizens' psychology and produces two opposite reactions: one of complete self-denigration and worship of all things Western, and the other of total rejection, exclusion, and even hatred of the West (Fei, 2015). Many counties have debated the conflict between being internationalized and preserving one's own national identity intensively, and it has become the primary reason that many countries are reluctant to internationalize their higher education systems.

Not all scholars see the loss of national identity as an inevitable consequence of internationalization. On the contrary, some of them believe the contact with, and understanding of, other civilizations and cultures create opportunities to intensify one's national identity and foster cultural self-awareness (Fei, 2015; Liang, 1921). Fei's (2015) Cultural Self-awareness theory points out one way to resolve the conflict. As he argued, cultural self-awareness means that those who live within a specific culture have a true understanding of it, know from where it derived, the way it developed and is evolving, and its unique features (p. 50). Acquiring this self-awareness is not easy and will take a long time because it means knowing one's own culture first and then understanding the many cultures one encounters. Thereafter, it may be possible to find one's place in this culturally diverse world, and through conscious adaptation, absorb the strengths of others.

There are many signs that nations around the world all want to know more about their own cultures and are asking questions about themselves: Why do we live like this? What does it mean? How should we live and what are our goals? How do we achieve them? (Fei, 2015, p. 110)

The cultural contacts that accompany international communications and exchanges create a favorable environment for people to deepen their understanding of other cultures, and through recognition of the differences between themselves and others, people can achieve a better understanding of themselves, who they are, and who they would like to be.

Another challenge that requires both researchers and practitioners' attention is higher education internationalization's effect on social equity. The increased global demand for tertiary education, the reduced transportation and communication costs, and the internationalization of labor markets for highly skilled people combined have led to dramatic growth in student mobility during the recent past. Yet there has been no discussion of equitable access and what this might mean in the international context with respect to this large group of international students (Naidoo, 2007). As no nation has achieved universal access to higher education, and the higher education sector consumes enormous public resources, whether taxpayers want to support universities that are educating so many overseas students remains a problem. In nations where the host country's government, like that of China, subsidizes international students substantially, complaints are not unusual because of the contrast between the ease with which international students obtain generous scholarships and the difficulties domestic students from disadvantaged backgrounds have obtaining educational loans. The low quality of some international students worsens the conflicts, as it has been found that many overseas students who are awarded scholarships are neither academically competent nor culturally and socially engaged with their domestic counterparts. In a country in which higher education remains a scarce resource, it is reasonable for the public to ask whether the investment in recruiting international students has achieved desirable outcomes. The accessibility to higher education is one side of the equity issue, while the other is higher education's quality. Given that internationalization could yield various benefits for tertiary students, whether students at different universities benefit equally from international experiences raises another equity issue. Recognizing the risk that an emphasis on internationalization may deepen social inequalities between wealthier and poorer students unintentionally, many universities have developed 'short-cycle' mobility opportunities (e.g., international summer schools, field trips, study tours, internships) that are much more accessible to lower income, more risk averse students. This focus on short-cycle mobility is coupled typically with the introduction of an income-contingent travel scholarship, which is restricted to low-income students and designed to make short-cycle opportunities affordable (Healey, 2017). In addition to providing disadvantaged students financial aid for overseas experiences, more efforts are required to create an internationalized and multicultural environment on campus by integrating international and intercultural elements into curricula and engaging students from diverse cultural backgrounds to ensure that internationalization is accessible to all students. Without leaving one's own country, which normally is costly, students can be exposed to international experiences, and 'internationalization at home' has been implemented at flagship universities around the world already. However, it may not be an easy commitment for local universities with limited financial flexibility. In any case, internationalizing the curriculum or running multilingual courses requires investment in financial and human resources, which could be a luxury for universities that are struggling to enhance their quality and build their capacity. Although internationalization is one of HEIs three missions, not all universities prioritize it in their operation and development. Therefore, there remains a long way to go before the benefits of internationalization can reach all students, regardless of their socioeconomic status.

Better Performance Measures for Universities

As institutional investments in internationalization continue to increase, better measures of universities' internationalization performance are required to demonstrate achievements and justify and focus on further investment. In addition, because of accountability pressures, universities need to provide clear information both to internal stakeholders and the public about their institution's performance in internationalization. Because monitoring and measuring institutional internationalization performance is still in its infancy, more and better data are needed to develop valid and effective measures. The challenges for universities and measurement designers are multi-faceted. Moreover, these challenges are not specific to measuring internationalization alone, but also relate to performance measures in other domains. As universities play increasingly diverse roles in modern society, institutional policymakers face the challenge of measuring their institutions' performance effectively in more dimensions than before. Research has shown that performance measures are used most frequently to evaluate financial resources management, research performance, and teaching quality in universities, but are used least for universities' third missions such as community service and internationalization (Alach, 2017). The lessons learned in developing robust measures of internationalization may offer insights into efforts made to assess university community engagement and capacity building, for example.

Because of the increasing importance of university rankings and league tables, a danger observed with the current university performance measurement system is the shift from an interpretative measuring system to a mechanical one—success in prevailing performance indicators overrides the actual outcomes that the indicators are designed to portray (e.g., see Kallio, Kallio, & Grossi, 2017). Comparing and even ranking HEIs impel the construction and use of common 'yardsticks,' the gradations along which these entities can be placed. Yet, unlike length, height, and width, these 'yardsticks' are used to measure very complex, often multi-faceted, fast-changing, contextually varied, and even conceptually contentious phenomena. By necessity, the use of such unidimensional metrics to compare and rank anything simplifies what are otherwise complex and dynamic realities. Yet these metrics not only are pervasive, but they are used constantly to make daily choices and even complex decisions (Marope & Wells, 2013). Being aware fully of the isomorphic effects that rankings have imposed in the development of HEIs, the intention of the indicator set developed in this project is not to invent another league table to intensify the mania for rankings. Rather, university policymakers need necessary skills to understand the data the measurement generates and use them wisely to inform their policies and decisions. As the tool may provide comparative information, one university may find it lags behind with respect to international student recruitment or internationally cooperative course development, for example. However, it is not advisable to change the marketing plan immediately to catch up with others' numbers. Internationalization is expected to contribute to an institution's strategic goal overall; therefore, universities should by no means seek to improve key figures if they are irrelevant or conflict with their strategic outlook.

Another challenge in implementing performance measures in the higher education sector is related to the reality that many activities at universities, including internationalization, require collective efforts, and therefore, cannot be measured at the individual level. This fact conflicts with the basic idea of managerial doctrines, which is to implement the organizational strategy all the way down to the grassroots level by measuring individual-level performance. However, management-by-results (MBR) scarcely can be applied to measure university's performance in its third missions, as in many cases, failure or unsatisfactory results cannot be attributed to a specific person. Thus, while the result is obvious, the problem's source is difficult to determine.

The hesitation and resistance encountered in the process of developing measures for internationalization's performance in this study also highlights the reason why universities are particularly unresponsive to performance management. First, universities traditionally are seen as loosely coupled organizations (e.g., see Weick, 1976), which means that their units or departments typically are independent of other units and departments' functions. Consequently, it is difficult to manage and coordinate, never mind control, university organizations with traditional administrative control mechanisms (Modell, 2003; Rautiainen & Järvenpää, 2012). Second, the traditional ideals of academic freedom often conflict with performance management's ideologies. Some have opposed what are viewed as quasi-market and neoliberal approaches' intrusion into a non-market field (Curtis, 2008; Forrester, 2011; Kallio & Kallio, 2014). The attitude toward performance management in the higher education sector also is sensitive to cultural and national context. For example, performance management in universities has been promoted and adopted in major Western countries since the beginning of the twenty-first century. However, it remains a new concept and approach in China. Although China's public universities have mandated increasing performance management requirements recently, their scope is limited compared to that of their Western counterparts. Despite such hesitation and resistance, it can be predicted that performance management will be implemented in HEIs as well as other public sectors to a greater and more intensified extent, given that they consume considerable public wealth and resources. This challenges researchers to design effective and efficient tools, and universities to use those measures wisely and strategically to measure performance in the best way possible.

References

Alach, Z. (2017). The use of performance measurement in universities. *International Journal of Public Sector Management, 30*(2), 102–117. https://doi.org/10.1108/IJPSM-05-2016-0089.

Allport, G. (1954). *The nature of prejudice*. Cambridge, MA: Perseus Books.

Asmar, C. (2005). Politicising student difference: The Muslim experience. In M. Tight (Ed.), *International relations* (pp. 129–157). Oxford, UK: Elsevier.

Barron, P., Gourlay, L. J., & Gannon-Leary, P. (2010). International students in the higher education classroom: Initial findings from staff at two post-92 universities in the UK. *Journal of Further and Higher Education, 34*(4), 475–489.

Bourdieu, P. (1984). *Distinction: A social critique of the judgment of taste*. Cambridge, MA: Harvard University Press.

Chan, D. K. K. (2008). Revisiting post-colonial education development: Reflections on some critical issues. In M. Marson (Ed.), *Comparative education bulletin: Special issue: Education and development in post-colonial societies* (pp. 21–36). Hong Kong: Comparative Education Society of Hong Kong.

Chankseliani, M. (2018). Four rationales of HE internationalization: Perspectives of U.K. universities on attracting students from former Soviet countries. *Journal of Studies in International Education, 22*(1), 53–70.

Chen, G.-M., & Starosta, W. J. (1997, January). A review of the concept of intercultural sensitivity. *Human Communication, 1*, 1–16.

Chiu, C.-Y., Lonner, W. J., Matsumoto, D., & Ward, C. (2013). Cross-cultural competence: Theory, research, and application. *Journal of Cross-Cultural Psychology, 44*(6), 843–848. https://doi.org/10.1177/0022022113493716.

Choi, K. C. (2010). 'Weep for Chinese university': A case study of English hegemony and academic capitalism in higher education in Hong Kong. *Journal of Education Policy, 25*(2), 233–252.

Conklin, W. (2004). A diversity case gold mine: The affirmative action amicus briefs. *Diversity Factor, 12*(1), 30–39.

Curtis, B. (2008). The performance-based research fund: Research assessment and funding in New Zealand. *Globalisation, Societies and Education, 6*(2), 179–194.

Fei, X.-T. (2015). *Globalization and cultural self-awareness*. Heidelberg: Springer-Verlag.

Forrester, G. (2011). Performance management in education: Milestone or millstone? *Management in Education, 25*(5), 112–118.

Ha, P. L. (2013). Issues surrounding English, the internationalisation of higher education and national cultural identity in Asia: A focus on Japan. *Critical Studies in Education, 54*(2), 160–175.

Healey, N. M. (2017). Beyond 'export education': Aspiring to put students at the heart of a university's internationalisation strategy. *Perspectives: Policy and Practice in Higher Education, 21*(4), 119–128. https://doi.org/10.1080/13603108.2017.1286399.

Henderson-King, D., & Kaleta, J. A. (2000). Learning about social diversity: The undergraduate experience and intergroup tolerance. *Journal of Higher Education, 71*(2), 142–164.

Hertig, H. P. (2016). *Universities, rankings and the dynamics of global higher education: Perspectives from Asia, Europe and North America*. London: Palgrave Macmillan.

Huntington, S. P. (1993). The clash of civilizations? *Foreign Affairs, 72*(3), 22–49.

Kallio, K.-M., & Kallio, T. J. (2014). Management-by-results and performance measurement in universities—Implications for work motivation. *Studies in Higher Education, 39*(4), 574–589.

Kallio, K.-M., Kallio, T. J., & Grossi, G. (2017). Performance measurement in universities: Ambiguities in the use of quality versus quantity in performance indicators. *Public Money & Management, 37*(4), 293–300. https://doi.org/10.1080/09540962.2017.1295735.

Kehm, B., & de Wit, H. (2005). *Internationalisation in higher education: European responses to the global perspective*. Amsterdam: European

Association for International Education (EAIE) and European Association for Institutional Research (EAIR).

Kim, T. (2005). Internationalisation of higher education in South Korea: Reality, rhetoric, and disparity in academic culture and identities. *Australian Journal of Education, 49*(1), 1–28.

Knight, J. (1997). Internationalisation of higher education: A conceptual framework. In J. Knight & H. de Wit (Eds.), *Internationalisation of higher education in Asia Pacific countries* (pp. 5–19). Amsterdam: EAIE.

Kudo, K., Volet, S., & Whitsed, C. (2017). Thematic review: Intercultural relationship development at university: A systematic literature review from an ecological and person-in-context perspective. *Educational Research Review, 20*, 99–116. https://doi.org/10.1016/j.edurev.2017.01.001.

Liang, S.-M. (1921/1990). Substance of Chinese culture (SUBS-CC). In S. B. Zhang (Ed.), *Liang Shuming quanji* [Collections of Liang Shuming] (pp. 3–16). Jinan: Shandong People's Press.

Marginson, S. (2004). Don't leave me hanging on the Anglophone. *Higher Education Quarterly, 58*(2/3), 74–113.

Marope, P. T. M., & Wells, P. J. (2013). University rankings: The many sides of the debate. In P. T. M. Marope, P. J. Wells, & E. Hazelkorn (Eds.), *Rankings and accountability in higher education: Uses and misuses* (pp. 7–19). Paris: UNESCO.

Modell, S. (2003). Goals versus institutions: The development of performance measurement in the Swedish university sector. *Management Accounting Research, 14*(4), 333–359.

Naidoo, R. (2007). *Higher education as a global commodity: The perils and promises for developing countries*. London: The Observatory on Borderless Higher Education.

OECD (2017). *Education at a glance 2017: OECD indicators*. Paris: OECD Publishing. http://dx.doi.org/10.1787/eag-2017-en.

Putnam, R. D. (2007). E Pluribus Unum: Diversity and community in the twenty-first century. *Scandinavian Political Studies, 30*(2), 137–174.

Rautiainen, A., & Järvenpää, M. (2012). Institutional logics and responses to performance measurement systems. *Financial Accountability & Management, 28*(2), 164–188.

Reisberg, L., & Rumbley, L. E. (2014). Redefining academic mobility: From the pursuit of scholarship to the pursuit of revenue. In A. Maldonado-Maldonado & R. M. Basset (Eds.), *The forefront of international higher education: A Festschrift in Honor of Philip G. Altbach* (pp. 115–126). Dordrecht: Springer.

Rothman, S., Lipset, S. M., & Nevitte, N. (2003). Racial diversity reconsidered. *Public Interest, 151*(Spring), 25–38.

Scott, P. (2005). Universities and the knowledge economy. *Minerva: A Review of Science, Learning and Policy, 43*(3), 297–309.

Scott, P. (2015). Dynamics of academic mobility: Hegemonic internationalisation or fluid globalisation. *European Review, 23*(1), 55–69.

Segall, M. H., Dansen, P. R., Berry, J. W., & Poortinga, Y. H. (1990). *Human behavior in global perspective: An introduction to cross-cultural psychology*. New York: Pergamon.

Singh, M. (2011). Learning from China to internationalise Australian research education: Pedagogies of intellectual equality, 'optimal ignorance' and the ERA journal rankings. *Innovations in Education and Teaching International, 48*(4), 395–405.

Spencer-Oatey, H., & Dauber, D. (2015). *How internationalised is your university? From structural indicators to an agenda for integration* (GlobalPAD Working Papers). Available at GlobalPAD Open House. http://www.warwick.ac.uk/globalpadintercultural.

Teichler, U. (2009). Student mobility and staff mobility in the European higher education area beyond 2010. In B. K. Kehm, J. Huisman, & B. Stensaker (Eds.), *The European higher education area: Perspectives on a moving target* (pp. 183–201). Rotterdam and Taipei: Sense.

Teichler, U. (2017). Internationalisation trends in higher education and changing role of international student mobility. *Journal of International Mobility, 2015*(1), 177–216.

Wächter, B. (2008). Mobility and cooperation in the European higher education area. In K. Maria (Ed.), *Beyond 2010: Priorities and challenges for higher education in the New Decade* (pp. 13–42). Bonn: Lemmens.

Wang, Y., Harding, R., & Mai, L.-W. (2012). Impact of cultural exposure on young Chinese students' adaptation in a UK business school. *Studies in Higher Education, 37*(5), 621–639.

Weick, K. E. (1976). Educational organizations as loosely coupled systems. *Administrative Science Quarterly, 21*(1), 1–19.

Wood, T. E., & Sherman, M. J. (2001). Is campus racial diversity correlated with educational benefits? *Academic Questions, 14*(3), 72–88.

Yang, R. (2011). Self and other in the Confucian cultural context: Implications of China's higher education development for comparative studies. *Springer Science + Business Media B.V.* Retrieved from http://www.voced.edu.au/content/ngv49014.

Yonezawa, A., Kitamura, Y., Meerman, A., & Kuroda, K. (2014). *Emerging international dimensions in east Asian higher education*. Dordrecht: Springer.

Yonezawa, A., & Shimmi, Y. (2015). Transformation of university governance through internationalization: Challenges for top universities and government policies in Japan. *Higher Education, 70*(2), 173–186.

Yu, Y., & Moskal, M. (2018). Missing intercultural engagements in the university experiences of Chinese international students in the UK. *Compare: A Journal of Comparative and International Education*. https://doi.org/10.1080/03057925.2018.1448259.

Yvonne, A., Lynne, M. H., & Nazneen, M. (1997). Ending the international-domestic dichotomy: New approaches to a global curriculum for the millennium. *Journal of Social Work Education, 33*(2), 389–401.

Appendix A: Data Collection Instruments Used in This Project

Interview Protocol

Project: Measuring University Internationalization: Indicators Across National Contexts

Time of Interview:
Date of Interview:
Interviewee:
Position of Interviewee:
Venue:

[Thank the participant for accepting the interview]
[On request, describe the project, telling the interviewee about (a) the purpose of the study, (b) the individuals and sources of data being collected, (c) what will be done with the data to project the confidentiality of the interviewee, and (d) how long the interview will take.]
[Have the interviewee read the sign the consent form.]

[Ask the interviewee if he/she has any questions about the purpose of the research or interview]
[Turn on the tape recorder]

Warm-up Questions:

1. Can you describe your role as the [interviewee's position] at the moment?
   Notes:

2. Before you became the [interviewee's position], what other experience did you have in relation to university internationalization?
   Notes:

Main Questions:

1. Can you describe the administration system in your institution for international activities?
   Notes:

2. In what way do you think internationalization benefits your institution?
   Notes:

3. Thinking about your institution, in your opinion, what does university internationalization mean?
   Notes:

4. According to your understanding of internationalization, what do you think are the key dimensions of university internationalization?
   Notes:

5. Do you think these dimensions are equally important or they should be given differential priorities?
   Notes:

6. Is there any particular internationalization initiative in your institution that you would like to highlight?
   Notes:

7. How international performance is monitored, measured, or evaluated in your institution?
   Notes:

8. Finally, is there anything else you would like to share with me in relation to your institution's international strategies or policies?
   Notes:

[Thank the interviewee for their time and participation in the interview. Assure them of the confidentiality of the responses and ask for cooperation and support for the next phase of questionnaire data collection.]

Appendix A: Data Collection Instruments Used in This Project

Questionnaire Survey

Appendix A: Data Collection Instruments Used in This Project

UNIVERSITY INTERNATIONALIZATION INDICATORS

To Start With: A Few Questions About You and Your Current Job

1. What is your age?
- ○ 21-29
- ○ 30-39
- ○ 40-49
- ○ 50-59
- ○ 60 or older

2. What is your gender?
- ○ Female
- ○ Male

3. What is your nationality? (you can choose more than one answer)
- ☐ Australian
- ☐ Singaporean

Other (please specify)
[   ]

4. Which institution do you work in?
- ○ University of Queensland
- ○ University of Sydney
- ○ University of Western Australia
- ○ University of Adelaide
- ○ University of New South Wales
- ○ National University of Singapore
- ○ Australian National University
- ○ University of Melbourne
- ○ Nanyang Technological University
- ○ Macquarie University
- ○ Monash University

5. What department do you work in?
- ○ Senior Executive Office
- ○ International Office
- ○ Other (please specify)

[   ]

UNIVERSITY INTERNATIONALIZATION INDICATORS

6. Are you currently in any of the following roles?

○ Vice Chancellor
○ Deputy Vice-Chancellor
○ Pro Vice-Chancellor
○ Office Director
○ Deputy Director of the Office
○ Section Leader
○ Deputy Section Leader
○ None of these

7. Which area/s are you currently responsible for? (you can choose more than one answer)

☐ International student recruitment
☐ Student exchange
☐ International student services
☐ International partnership and collaboration
☐ International staff recruitment and management
☐ International curriculum
☐ Other (please specify)

Appendix A: Data Collection Instruments Used in This Project

UNIVERSITY INTERNATIONALIZATION INDICATORS
Your Opinions on Indicators of University Internationalization

In this study, six key dimensions of university internationalization have been identified. They are research, student, faculty, curriculum, engagement and governance and organisational support. In the following sections, possible indicators of each dimension are listed, and you are asked to give your opinions on both the importance and the feasibility of each indicator.

UNIVERSITY INTERNATIONALIZATION INDICATORS
Research Dimension

*8. Considering the following research related indicators,

1) To what extent do you think the following indicators ought to be taken into account when measuring the degree of university internationalization?

2) To what extent do you think the following indicators are feasible in your institution given the time, cost and the availability of data?

	1) Importance	2) Feasibility
a. Percentage of research projects involving international partnership and collaboration		
b. Percentage of research projects wholly funded by sources outside of host nation (incl. overseas institutions, overseas governments and international agencies)		
c. Number of research centers focused on international study		
d. Number of research centers operated with international partners		
e. Percentage of international post-doctoral researchers		
f. Proportion of total research income generated by research involving international collaboration		
g. Number of international conferences organised		
h. Number of presentations in international conferences (with qualified contribution) per faculty member		
i. Percentage of publications cited in SCI, EI, ISTP		
j. Number of co-editorships in international journals		
k. Number of highly cited authors (HiCI) according to *Thomson Reuters*		
l. Percentage of patents filed outside the country		

9. Other than the indicators listed above, are there any other indicators you think should be taken into account when measuring the research dimension of university internationalization?

Appendix A: Data Collection Instruments Used in This Project   303

UNIVERSITY INTERNATIONALIZATION INDICATORS
Continued: Student Dimension

*10. Considering the following student related indicators,

1) To what extent do you think the following indicators ought to be taken into account when measuring the degree of university internationalization?

2) To what extent do you think the following indicators are feasible in your institution given the time, cost and the availability of data?

	1) Importance	2) Feasibility
a. Percentage of international students (for degree study) on campus in total		
b. Percentage of international undergraduate students on campus		
c. Percentage of international Master (coursework) students on campus		
d. Percentage of international higher degree research (HDR) students on campus		
e. Percentage of international students by region (Europe, Africa, Asia, North America, South America and Pacific)		
f. Percentage of domestic students who have international study experiences (incl. exchange and short-term programs those are no more than an academic year)		
g. Number of incoming international students (incl. exchange and short-term programs those are no more than an academic year)		
h. Ratio of the outgoing domestic students to the incoming international students (no more than an academic year)		

11. Other than the indicators listed above, are there any other indicators you think should be taken into account when measuring the student dimension of university internationalization?

UNIVERSITY INTERNATIONALIZATION INDICATORS
Continued: Faculty Dimension (Academic Staff)

*12. Considering the following faculty related indicators,

1) To what extent do you think the following indicators ought to be taken into account when measuring the degree of university internationalization?

2) To what extent do you think the following indicators are feasible in your institution given the time, cost and the availability of data?

	1) Importance	2) Feasibility
a. Percentage of international (by nationality) faculty members (full-time equivalent FTE)		
b. Number of international visiting scholars for academic purposes		
c. Percentage of faculty (FTE) who were awarded their highest academic qualification by an institution abroad		
d. Percentage of faculty (FTE) proficient in a language other than the primary language of teaching/research		
e. Percentage of faculty (FTE) who have at least one-year overseas experience (excl. degree study)		
f. Percentage of faculty (FTE) who hold a visiting lectureship abroad		
g. Percentage of faculty (FTE) who had international experience for academic purposes in the past academic year		

13. Other than the indicators listed above, are there any other indicators you think should be taken into account when measuring the faculty dimension of university internationalization?

UNIVERSITY INTERNATIONALIZATION INDICATORS
Continued: Curriculum Dimension

*14. Considering the following curriculum related indicators,

1) To what extent do you think the following indicators ought to be taken into account when measuring the degree of university internationalization?

2) To what extent do you think the following indicators are feasible in your institution given the time, cost and the availability of data?

	1) Importance	2) Feasibility
a. Number of subjects offering foreign language studies		
b. Number of subjects involving a partner in other countries		
c. Number of programmes available through online learning modes		
d. Number of programmes available for off-shore delivery		
e. Number of subjects offered in a foreign language		
f. Number of programmes with a mandatory period abroad		
g. Number of subjects on foreign countries/cultures/societies		
h. Number of joint degree programs (Bachelor, Masters and PhD) collaborated with overseas higher education institutions		
j. Number of students registered in subjects taught in a foreign language		
k. Number of students registered in programmes provided via online learning modes		
l. Number of students who attend joint degree programs collaborated with overseas higher education institutions		

15. Other than the indicators listed above, are there any other indicators you think should be taken into account when measuring the curriculum dimension of university internationalization?

UNIVERSITY INTERNATIONALIZATION INDICATORS

Continued: Engagement Dimension

*16. Considering the following engagement related indicators,

1) To what extent do you think the following indicators ought to be taken into account when measuring the degree of university internationalization?

2) To what extent do you think the following indicators are feasible in your institution given the time, cost and the availability of data?

	1) Importance	2) Feasibility
a. Number of memberships in international organisations and consortia		
b. Number of overseas partners with whom at least one academic activity (mobility, program, research) has taken place		
c. Percentage of partnerships by region (Europe, Africa, Asia, North America, South America, Pacific)		
d. Proportion of international (by nationality) alumni relative to the total number of alumni		
e. Percentage of alumni working overseas		

17. Other than the indicators listed above, are there any other indicators you think should be taken into account when measuring the engagement dimension of university internationalization?

UNIVERSITY INTERNATIONALIZATION INDICATORS

Continued: Governance and Organisational Support Dimension

*18. Considering the following governance and organisational support related indicators,

1) To what extent do you think the following indicators ought to be taken into account when measuring the degree of university internationalization?

2) To what extent do you think the following indicators are feasible in your institution given the time, cost and the availability of data?

	1) Importance	2) Feasibility
a. Percentage of international staff (by nationality) in institutional senior management team		
b. Percentage of administration staff with international experience (minimum 3 months)		
c. Percentage of administration staff proficient in more than one working language		
d. Percentage of administration staff who have participated in international exchange programs		
e. Percentage of total budget available (excluding personnel costs) for internationalization activities		
f. Funding for international visiting scholars		
g. Funding to support the international mobility of students		
h. Funding for international research projects		
i. Number of scholarships for international students (all degree levels)		
j. Number of scholarships for international post-doctoral researchers		
k. Percentage of library collection in other languages		
l. Number of participations in fairs abroad		
m. Number of languages in which the university website can be read		
n. Number of committee activities in international professional associations		

UNIVERSITY INTERNATIONALIZATION INDICATORS

19. Other than the indicators listed above, are there any other indicators you think should be taken into account when measuring the governance and organisational support dimension of university internationalization?

Appendix B: A Summary of the Characteristics of Existing Instruments

© The Editor(s) (if applicable) and The Author(s), under exclusive licence to Springer Nature Switzerland AG 2019
C. Y. Gao, *Measuring University Internationalization*,
Palgrave Studies in Global Higher Education,
https://doi.org/10.1007/978-3-030-21465-4

Project/Study	Context and audience	Purposes	Unit of measurement	Dimensions	Source of indicators	Data collection
IQRP (Knight & de Wit, 1999)	• A wider variety of country/cultural contexts • Both university and non-university sectors/small and large institutions/comprehensive and specialized institutions/private and public institutions	Self-evaluation	Institution	Seven dimensions: • Context • Internationalization policies and strategies • Organizational and support structures • Academic programs and students • Research and scholarly collaboration • Human resources management • Contracts and services	Experts from IMHE/OECD and ACA	• Self-assessment report • Peer review report
Internationalization of higher education: performance assessment and indicators (Paige, 2005)	• Japan • Different types of HEIs	Multi-purposes (self-evaluation and benchmarking)	Institution	Ten dimensions: • University leadership for internationalization • Internationalization strategic plan • Institutionalization of international education • Infrastructure—professional international education units and staff • Internationalized curriculum • International students and scholars • Study abroad • Faculty involvement in international activities • Campus life—co-curricular programs • Monitoring the process	Experts	
Measuring internationalization at research universities (Green, 2005) (ACE)	• The United States • Research universities	Multi-purposes (comparison and classification)	Institution	Six dimensions: • Articulated commitment • Academic offerings • Organizational infrastructure • External funding • Institutional investment in faculty • International students and student programs	Experts	Institutional survey

Appendix B: A Summary of the Characteristics ...

Project/Study	Context and audience	Purposes	Unit of measurement	Dimensions	Source of indicators	Data collection
Monitoring the internationalization of higher education: are there useful quantitative performance indicators? (Krause, Coates, & James, 2005)	• Australia • Different types of HEIs	Merely research purpose	Institution	Five dimensions: • The strategic dimension • The teaching and curriculum dimension • The student dimension • The faculty dimension • The research dimension	Experts	N/A
Osaka University Project (Furushiro, 2006)	• Japan • Different types of HEIs	Self-evaluation	Institution	Eight dimensions: • Mission, goals, and plans of the university • Structure and staff • Budgeting and implementation • International dimension of research activities • Support system, information provision, and infrastructure • Multifaceted promotion of international affiliation • Internationalization of the university curriculum • Joint programs with external organizations	Experts	N/A
The strategy of internationalization in universities: a quantitative evaluation of the intent and implementation in UK universities (Ayoubi & Massoud, 2007)	• The UK • Different types of HEIs	Classification	Institution	Three variables: • Percentage of overseas students to the total number of students in each university • Percentage of overseas income to the total income of a university • Percentage of market share of overseas first-year students to the total overseas market share	Variables were chosen according to the availability in public nationwide statistics	Publicly accessible data (from Higher Education Statistics Agency [HESA], 2001)

Project/Study	Context and audience	Purposes	Unit of measurement	Dimensions	Source of indicators	Data collection
How to measure internationality and internationalization of higher education institutions! Indicators and key figures (Brandenburg & Federkeil, 2007) (CHE)	• Germany • Different types of HEIs	Multi-purposes (self-evaluation, benchmark, and ranking)	Institution and Department	Three dimensions: • Overall aspects • Academic research • Teaching and studies	• Experts • Stakeholders (representatives from 4 different universities and a group of students)	
Ranking the international dimension of top research universities in the United States (Horn, Hendel, & Fry, 2007)	• The United States • Research universities	Ranking	Institution	Five dimensions: • Student characteristics • Scholar characteristics • Research orientation • Curricular content • Organizational support	Experts	Publicly accessible data (public database and institutions' web sites)
Trends and indicators of Taiwan's higher education internationalization (Chin & Ching, 2009)	• Taiwan • Different types of HEIs	No specified purposes	Institution	Twelve dimensions: • Institutional commitments • Strategic planning • Funding • Institutional policy and guidelines • Organizational infrastructure and resources • Academic offerings and curriculum • Internet presence • Faculty and staff development • International students and scholars • Study abroad • Campus life • Performance evaluation and availability	• Experts • Stakeholders (3 scholars, 22 internationalization officers, and 35 international students)	N/A

Appendix B: A Summary of the Characteristics ...

Project/Study	Context and audience	Purposes	Unit of measurement	Dimensions	Source of indicators	Data collection
The survey and evaluation indicators for internationalization of research universities in China (Chen, Zeng, Wen, Weng, & Yu, 2009)	• China • Research and quasi-research universities	Multi-purposes (comparison and ranking)	Institution	Five dimensions: • Strategic planning and organizational structure • Structural characteristics and the exchange of personnel • Teaching and research • Infrastructures and facilities • Exchange of output	Statistical analysis (PCA)	Institutional survey
MINT Project (van Gaalen, 2009)	• EU • Different types of HEIs	Multi-purposes (self-evaluation and benchmarking)	Multi-levels (institution, department, program)	Five dimensions: • Policy and goals • Activities • Service • Key figures • Output • Outcomes	Experts	Institutional survey
Internationalization of German universities—concepts and collection of profile data (DAAD, 2010)	• Germany • Different types of HEIs	Multi-purposes (self-evaluation and benchmarking)	Institution	Seven dimensions: • Student and staff • ERASMUS students • International study programs • Offshore educational programs • ERASMUS lectures • Fellows and award winners of the Humboldt Foundation • International funding	Experts	Institutional survey
IMPI Project (Beerkens et al., 2010)	• European • Different types of HEIs	Multi-purposes (self-evaluation and benchmarking)	Institution	Nine dimensions: • Students • Staff • Administration • Funding and finance • Curriculum and academic services • Research • Promotion and marketing • Non-academic services, and campus and community life • Other	• Experts • Stakeholders (from six metalevel institutions)	Institutional survey

Project/Study	Context and audience	Purposes	Unit of measurement	Dimensions	Source of indicators	Data collection
EMQT Project (Managing Committee of the EMQT Project, 2011)	• European • Different types of HEIs • Students' associations • Quality assurance agencies • European Commission • Ranking agencies • The ICT centers of HEIs	Self-evaluation	Institution	Two dimensions: • Student mobility • Staff mobility	• Experts • Stakeholders (from partner institutions)	Institutional survey
Indicators of internationalization for research institutions: a new approach (van den Besselaar, Inzelt, Reale, de Turckheim, & Vercesi, 2012)	• European • Funding agencies • Research performing organizations	Self-evaluation	Institution	One main dimension of research and several components	• Experts • Stakeholders (from member organizations)	N/A
IMS 2020 Project (Gajowniczek & Schlabs, 2013)	• International • Medical schools/faculties	Multi-purposes (benchmarking and accreditation)	School/faculty	Six dimensions: • Institution • Student • Staff • Curriculum • Research • Global health service	• Experts • Stakeholders (from member organizations)	Online toolbox
CIC international mobility benchmark (Potts, Ramirez, & Huckel, 2013)	• The United States • Research universities	Benchmarking	Institution	One major dimension: • Student learning mobility	• Experts • Stakeholders (from member organizations)	Institutional survey

References

Ayoubi, R. M., & Massoud, H. K. (2007). The strategy of internationalization in universities: A quantitative evaluation of the intent and implementation in UK universities. *International Journal of Educational Management, 21*(4), 329–349.

Beerkens, E., Brandenburg, U., Evers, N., van Gaalen, A., Leichsenring, H., & Zimmermann, V. (2010). *Indicator projects on internationalisation: Approaches, methods and findings: A report in the context of the European project 'Indicators for Mapping & Profiling Internationalisation' (IMPI)*. Gütersloh: CHE Consult GmbH.

Brandenburg, U., & Federkeil, G. (2007). *How to measure internationality and internationalisation of higher education institutions! Indicators and key figures*. Gütersloh: Centre for Higher Education Development.

Chen, C.-G., Zeng, M.-C., Wen, D.-M., Weng, L.-X., & Yu, Z. (2009). The establishment of indicator system for the evaluation of internationalisation of reserch universities in China. *Peking University Education Review, 7*(4), 116–135 (in Chinese).

Chin, J. M.-C., & Ching, G. S. (2009). Trends and indicators of Taiwan's higher education internationalization. *Asia-Pacific Education Researcher, 18*(2), 185–203.

DAAD. (2010). *internationalität an deutschen Hochschulen - Konzepte und Erhebung von Profildaten*. German: German Academic Exchange Service (DAAD).

Furushiro, N. (2006). *Developing evaluation criteria to assess the internationalization of universities final report grant-in-aid for scientific research*. Osaka: Osaka University.

Gajowniczek, J., & Schlabs, T. (2013). *International medical school label methodology*. Retrieved 20 May 2014, from http://www.ims-2020.eu/downloads/FC_IMS_label_methodology.pdf.

Green, M. F. (2005). *Measuring internationalization at research universities*. Washington, DC: American Council on Education.

Horn, A. S., Hendel, D. D., & Fry, G. W. (2007). Ranking the international dimension of top research universities in the United States. *Journal of Studies in International Education, 11*(3–4), 330–358.

Knight, J., & de Wit, H. (1999). *Quality and internationalisation in higher education/Programme on institutional management in higher education*. Paris: Organisation for Economic Co-operation and Development.

Krause, K.-L., Coates, H., & James, R. (2005). Monitoring the internationalisation of higher education: Are there useful quantitative performance indicators? *International Perspectives on Higher Education, 3*, 233–253.

Managing Committee of the EMQT Project. (2011). *The outcomes of the EMQT project*. Retrieved from http://www.emqt.org/images/stories/Outcomes_of_the_EMQT_Project_Presentation.pdf.

Paige, R. M. (2005). Internationalization of higher education: Performance assessment and indicators. 名古屋高等教育研究, *5*, 99–122.

Potts, D., Ramirez, K., & Huckel, D. (2013). *CIC international learning mobility benchmark* (Public Report 2012). Studymove Sonsultants.

van den Besselaar, P., Inzelt, A., Reale, E., de Turckheim, E., & Vercesi, V. (2012). Indicators of internationalisation for research institutions: A new approach. *A report by the ESF member organisation forum on evulation: Indicators of internationalisation*. Strasbourg cedex: European Science Foundation.

van Gaalen, A. (2009). Developing a tool for mapping internationalisation: A case study. In H. de Wit (Ed.), *Measuring success in the internationalisation of higher education* (EAIE Occasional Paper No. 22, pp. 77–91). Amsterdam: European Association for International Education.

Appendix C: Descriptive Statistics of Respondents' Perceptions of the Draft Indicators

Label	Indicator	1 Not important Frequency	1 Not important Percentage (%)	2 Neutral Frequency	2 Neutral Percentage (%)	3 Somewhat important Frequency	3 Somewhat important Percentage (%)	4 Very important Frequency	4 Very important Percentage (%)	Skewness
R1	Percentage of research projects involving international partnership and collaboration	0	0.0	4	3.1	49	38.0	76	58.9	−0.782
R2	Percentage of research projects wholly funded by sources outside of host nation (incl. overseas institutions, overseas governments, and international agencies)	2	1.6	30	23.3	64	49.6	33	25.6	−0.218
R3	Number of research centers focused on international study	0	0.0	21	16.3	77	59.7	31	24.0	−0.062
R4	Number of research centers operated with international partners	1	0.8	8	6.2	65	50.4	55	42.6	−0.631
R5	Percentage of international post-doctoral researchers	3	2.3	21	16.3	55	42.6	50	38.8	−0.622
R6	Proportion of total research income generated by research involving international collaboration	2	1.6	24	18.6	57	44.2	46	35.7	−0.455
R7	Number of international conferences organized	7	5.4	17	13.2	75	58.1	30	23.3	−0.730
R8	Number of presentations in international conferences (with qualified contribution) per faculty member	6	4.7	28	21.7	57	44.2	38	29.5	−0.455
R9	Percentage of publications cited by SCI, EI, ISTP	0	0.0	23	17.8	51	39.5	55	42.6	−0.433
R10	Number of co-editorships in international journals	5	3.9	23	17.8	59	45.7	42	32.6	−0.754
R11	Number of highly cited authors (HiCi) according to *Thomson Reuters*	6	4.7	27	20.9	57	44.2	39	30.2	−0.485
R12	Percentage of patents filed outside the country	3	2.3	41	31.8	70	54.3	15	11.6	−0.082

Appendix C: Descriptive Statistics of Respondents' Perceptions ...

Label	Indicator	1 Not important Frequency	1 Not important Percentage (%)	2 Neutral Frequency	2 Neutral Percentage (%)	3 Somewhat important Frequency	3 Somewhat important Percentage (%)	4 Very important Frequency	4 Very important Percentage (%)	Skewness
S1	Percentage of international students (for degree study) on campus in total	0	0.0	5	3.9	45	34.9	79	61.2	−0.938
S2	Percentage of international undergraduate students on campus	0	0.0	11	8.5	49	38.0	69	53.5	−0.768
S3	Percentage of international master's (coursework) students on campus	0	0.0	8	6.2	56	43.4	65	50.4	−0.609
S4	Percentage of international higher degree research (HDR) students on campus	2	1.6	6	4.7	42	32.6	79	61.2	−1.443
S5	Percentage of international students by region (Europe, Africa, Asia, North America, South America, and Pacific)	0	0.0	28	21.7	44	34.1	57	44.2	−0.420
S6	Percentage of domestic students who have international study experiences (incl. exchanges and short-term programs those are no more than an academic year)	0	0.0	3	2.3	38	29.5	88	68.2	−1.170
S7	Number of incoming international students (incl. exchanges and short-term programs those are no more than an academic year)	0	0.0	4	3.1	49	38.0	76	58.9	−0.782
S8	Ratio of the outgoing domestic students to the incoming international students (no more than an academic year)	5	3.9	25	19.4	53	41.1	46	35.7	−0.566
F1	Percentage of international (by nationality) faculty members (full-time equivalent FTE)	1	0.8	12	9.3	57	44.2	59	45.7	−0.178
F2	Number of international visiting scholars for academic purposes	1	0.8	10	7.8	61	47.3	57	44.2	−0.680

Label	Indicator	1 Not important Frequency	1 Not important Percentage (%)	2 Neutral Frequency	2 Neutral Percentage (%)	3 Somewhat important Frequency	3 Somewhat important Percentage (%)	4 Very important Frequency	4 Very important Percentage (%)	Skewness
F3	Percentage of faculty (FTE) who were awarded their highest academic qualification by an institution abroad	6	4.7	15	11.6	69	53.5	39	30.2	−0.777
F4	Percentage of faculty (FTE) proficient in a language other than the primary language of teaching/research	4	3.1	19	14.7	66	51.2	40	31.0	−0.607
F5	Percentage of faculty (FTE) who have at least one-year overseas experience (excl. degree study)	3	2.3	18	14.0	63	48.8	45	34.9	−0.617
F6	Percentage of faculty (FTE) who hold a visiting lectureship abroad	3	2.3	25	19.4	70	54.3	31	24.0	−0.369
F7	Percentage of faculty (FTE) who had international experience for academic purposes in the past academic year	4	3.1	31	24.0	66	51.2	28	21.7	−0.288
C1	Number of subjects offering foreign language studies	6	4.7	21	16.3	67	51.9	35	27.1	−0.606
C2	Number of subjects involving a partner in other countries	4	3.1	13	10.1	58	45.0	54	41.9	−0.899
C3	Number of programs available through online learning modes	14	10.9	37	28.7	55	42.6	23	17.8	−0.240
C4	Number of programs available for offshore delivery	10	7.8	41	31.8	49	38.0	29	22.5	−0.157
C5	Number of subjects offered in a foreign language	15	11.6	20	15.5	48	37.2	46	35.7	−0.670
C6	Number of programs with a mandatory period abroad	5	3.9	37	28.7	54	41.9	33	25.6	−0.207
C7	Number of subjects on foreign countries/cultures/societies	3	2.3	23	17.8	69	53.5	34	26.4	−0.423

Appendix C: Descriptive Statistics of Respondents' Perceptions …

Label	Indicator	1 Not important Frequency	1 Not important Percentage (%)	2 Neutral Frequency	2 Neutral Percentage (%)	3 Somewhat important Frequency	3 Somewhat important Percentage (%)	4 Very important Frequency	4 Very important Percentage (%)	Skewness
C8	Number of joint degree programs (Bachelor, Master's, and PhD) collaborated with overseas higher education institutions	2	1.6	11	8.5	59	45.7	57	44.2	−0.825
C9	Number of students registered in subjects taught in a foreign language	11	8.5	28	21.7	64	49.6	26	20.2	−0.470
C10	Number of students registered in programs provided via online learning modes	22	17.1	65	50.4	33	25.6	9	7.0	0.363
C11	Number of students who attend joint degree programs collaborated with overseas higher education institutions	4	3.1	24	18.6	68	52.7	33	25.6	−0.455
E1	Number of memberships in international organizations and consortia	5	3.9	14	10.9	75	58.1	35	27.1	−0.747
E2	Number of overseas partners with whom at least one academic activity (mobility, program, research) has taken place	3	2.3	11	8.5	52	40.3	63	48.8	−1.035
E3	Percentage of partnerships by region (Europe, Africa, Asia, North America, South America, Pacific)	4	3.1	20	15.5	46	35.7	59	45.7	−0.812
E4	Proportion of international (by nationality) alumni relative to the total number of alumni	3	2.3	18	14.0	62	48.1	46	35.7	−0.629
E5	Percentage of alumni working overseas	5	3.9	28	21.7	57	44.2	39	30.2	−0.439
G1	Percentage of international staff (by nationality) in institutional senior management team	10	7.8	42	32.6	61	47.3	16	12.4	−0.201

Label	Indicator	1 Not important Frequency	1 Not important Percentage (%)	2 Neutral Frequency	2 Neutral Percentage (%)	3 Somewhat important Frequency	3 Somewhat important Percentage (%)	4 Very important Frequency	4 Very important Percentage (%)	Skewness
G2	Percentage of administration staff with international experience (minimum 3 months)	11	8.5	17	13.2	69	53.5	32	24.8	−0.746
G3	Percentage of administration staff proficient in more than one working language	5	3.9	14	10.9	76	58.9	64	26.4	−0.744
G4	Percentage of administration staff who have participated in international exchange programs	8	6.2	25	19.4	74	57.4	22	17.1	−0.569
G5	Percentage of total budget available (excluding personnel costs) for internationalization activities	4	3.1	9	7.0	59	45.7	57	44.2	−1.041
G6	Funding for international visiting scholars	1	0.8	21	16.3	66	51.2	41	31.8	−0.339
G7	Funding to support the international mobility of students	0	0.0	6	4.7	52	40.3	71	55.0	−0.718
G8	Funding for international research projects	1	0.8	8	6.2	57	44.2	63	48.8	−0.815
G9	Number of scholarships for international students (all degree levels)	3	2.3	12	9.3	57	44.2	57	44.2	−0.905
G10	Number of scholarships for international post-doctoral researchers	1	0.8	27	20.9	59	45.7	42	32.6	−0.280
G11	Percentage of library collection in other languages	9	7.0	30	23.3	66	51.2	24	18.6	−0.428
G12	Number of participations in fairs abroad	16	12.4	39	30.2	57	44.2	17	13.2	−0.218
G13	Number of languages in which the university Web site can be read	10	7.8	31	24.0	60	46.5	28	21.7	−0.392
G14	Number of committee activities in international professional associations	11	8.5	37	28.7	61	47.3	20	15.5	−0.280

Descriptive Statistics of Respondents' Perceptions of the Draft Indicators (Feasibility)

Label	Indicator	−1 Infeasible Frequency	−1 Infeasible Percentage (%)	0 Unknown Frequency	0 Unknown Percentage (%)	1 Feasible Frequency	1 Feasible Percentage (%)	Skewness
R1	Percentage of research projects involving international partnership and collaboration	0	0.0	9	7.0	120	93.0	−3.417
R2	Percentage of research projects wholly funded by sources outside of host nation (incl. overseas institutions, overseas governments, and international agencies)	2	1.6	24	18.6	103	79.8	−1.898
R3	Number of research centers focused on international study	3	2.3	18	14.0	108	83.7	−2.397
R4	Number of research centers operated with international partners	0	0.0	16	12.4	113	87.6	−2.308
R5	Percentage of international post-doctoral researchers	2	1.6	18	14.0	109	84.5	−2.407
R6	Proportion of total research income generated by research involving international collaboration	6	4.7	30	23.3	93	72.1	−1.533
R7	Number of international conferences organized	2	1.6	18	14.0	109	84.5	−2.407

Label	Indicator	−1 Infeasible Frequency	−1 Infeasible Percentage (%)	0 Unknown Frequency	0 Unknown Percentage (%)	1 Feasible Frequency	1 Feasible Percentage (%)	Skewness
R8	Number of presentations in international conferences (with qualified contribution) per faculty member	8	6.2	25	19.4	96	74.4	−1.692
R9	Percentage of publications cited by SCI, EI, ISTP	0	0.0	26	20.2	103	79.8	−1.506
R10	Number of co-editorships in international journals	0	0.0	39	30.2	90	69.8	−0.871
R11	Number of highly cited authors (HiCi) according to *Thomson Reuters*	0	0.0	39	30.2	90	69.8	−0.871
R12	Percentage of patents filed outside the country	2	1.6	68	52.7	59	45.7	−0.806
S1	Percentage of international students (for degree study) on campus in total	0	0.0	3	2.3	126	97.7	−6.401
S2	Percentage of international undergraduate students on campus	0	0.0	6	4.7	123	95.3	−4.358
S3	Percentage of international master's (coursework) students on campus	0	0.0	5	3.9	124	96.1	−4.836
S4	Percentage of international higher degree research (HDR) students on campus	0	0.0	5	3.9	124	96.1	−4.836
S5	Percentage of international students by region (Europe, Africa, Asia, North America, South America, and Pacific)	1	0.8	10	7.8	118	91.5	−3.544

Appendix C: Descriptive Statistics of Respondents' Perceptions ...

Label	Indicator	−1 Infeasible Frequency	−1 Infeasible Percentage (%)	0 Unknown Frequency	0 Unknown Percentage (%)	1 Feasible Frequency	1 Feasible Percentage (%)	Skewness
S6	Percentage of domestic students who have international study experiences (incl. exchanges and short-term programs those are no more than an academic year)	1	0.8	5	3.9	123	95.3	−5.256
S7	Number of incoming international students (incl. exchanges and short-term programs those are no more than an academic year)	0	0.0	7	5.4	122	94.6	−3.982
S8	Ratio of the outgoing domestic students to the incoming international students (no more than an academic year)	2	1.6	27	20.9	100	77.5	−1.697
F1	Percentage of international (by nationality) faculty members (full-time equivalent FTE)	0	0.0	14	10.9	115	89.1	−2.547
F2	Number of international visiting scholars for academic purposes	6	4.7	20	15.5	103	79.8	−2.080
F3	Percentage of faculty (FTE) who were awarded their highest academic qualification by an institution abroad	5	3.9	22	17.1	102	79.1	−2.005
F4	Percentage of faculty (FTE) proficient in a language other than the primary language of teaching/research	9	7.0	33	25.6	87	67.4	−1.317
F5	Percentage of faculty (FTE) who have at least one-year overseas experience (excl. degree study)	7	5.4	28	21.7	94	72.9	−1.595

Label	Indicator	−1 Infeasible Frequency	−1 Infeasible Percentage (%)	0 Unknown Frequency	0 Unknown Percentage (%)	1 Feasible Frequency	1 Feasible Percentage (%)	Skewness
F6	Percentage of faculty (FTE) who hold a visiting lectureship abroad	6	4.7	45	34.9	78	60.5	−0.943
F7	Percentage of faculty (FTE) who had international experience for academic purposes in the past academic year	6	4.7	36	27.9	87	67.4	−1.274
C1	Number of subjects offering foreign language studies	1	0.8	20	15.5	108	83.7	−2.144
C2	Number of subjects involving a partner in other countries	1	0.8	23	17.8	105	81.4	−1.893
C3	Number of programs available through online learning modes	1	0.8	37	28.7	91	70.5	−1.088
C4	Number of programs available for offshore delivery	4	3.1	44	34.1	81	62.8	−0.958
C5	Number of subjects offered in a foreign language	7	5.4	25	19.4	97	75.2	−1.740
C6	Number of programs with a mandatory period abroad	8	6.2	40	31.0	80	62.8	−1.094
C7	Number of subjects on foreign countries/cultures/societies	5	3.9	22	17.1	102	79.1	−2.005
C8	Number of joint degree programs (Bachelor, Master's, and PhD) collaborated with overseas higher education institutions	1	0.8	15	11.6	113	87.6	−2.693
C9	Number of students registered in subjects taught in a foreign language	3	2.3	31	24.0	95	73.6	−1.502
C10	Number of students registered in programs provided via online learning modes	2	1.6	62	48.1	65	50.4	−0.269

Appendix C: Descriptive Statistics of Respondents' Perceptions ...

Label	Indicator	−1 Infeasible Frequency	−1 Infeasible Percentage (%)	0 Unknown Frequency	0 Unknown Percentage (%)	1 Feasible Frequency	1 Feasible Percentage (%)	Skewness
C11	Number of students who attend joint degree programs collaborated with overseas higher education institutions	0	0.0	30	23.3	99	76.7	−1.281
E1	Number of memberships in international organizations and consortia	4	3.1	12	9.3	113	87.6	−2.954
E2	Number of overseas partners with whom at least one academic activity (mobility, program, research) has taken place	4	3.1	8	6.2	117	90.7	−3.511
E3	Percentage of partnerships by region (Europe, Africa, Asia, North America, South America, Pacific)	2	1.6	13	10.1	114	88.4	−3.011
E4	Proportion of international (by nationality) alumni relative to the total number of alumni	2	1.6	24	18.6	103	79.8	−1.898
E5	Percentage of alumni working overseas	10	7.8	31	24.0	88	68.2	−1.355
G1	Percentage of international staff (by nationality) in institutional senior management team	6	4.7	28	21.7	95	73.6	−1.629
G2	Percentage of administration staff with international experience (minimum 3 months)	9	7.0	26	20.2	94	72.9	−1.598
G3	Percentage of administration staff proficient in more than one working language	5	3.9	24	18.6	100	77.5	−1.880

Label	Indicator	−1 Infeasible Frequency	−1 Infeasible Percentage (%)	0 Unknown Frequency	0 Unknown Percentage (%)	1 Feasible Frequency	1 Feasible Percentage (%)	Skewness
G4	Percentage of administration staff who have participated in international exchange programs	9	7.0	29	22.5	91	70.5	−1.472
G5	Percentage of total budget available (excluding personnel costs) for internationalization activities	7	5.4	27	20.9	95	73.6	−1.642
G6	Funding for international visiting scholars	6	4.7	34	26.4	89	69.0	−1.356
G7	Funding to support the international mobility of students	0	0.0	17	13.2	112	86.8	−2.203
G8	Funding for international research projects	1	0.8	21	16.3	107	82.9	−2.056
G9	Number of scholarships for international students (all degree levels)	1	0.8	17	13.2	111	86.0	−2.449
G10	Number of scholarships for international post-doctoral researchers	2	1.6	32	24.8	95	73.6	−1.410
G11	Percentage of library collection in other languages	3	2.3	42	32.6	84	65.1	−1.006
G12	Number of participations in fairs abroad	4	3.1	33	25.6	92	71.3	−1.415
G13	Number of languages in which the university Web site can be read	3	2.3	32	24.8	94	72.9	−1.450
G14	Number of committee activities in international professional associations	3	2.3	49	38.0	77	59.7	−0.748

Appendix D: Review Form for the Project 'A Set of Indicators for Measuring University Internationalization Across National Boundaries'

The draft indicator set

Dimension	Element	Indicator
Research	Internationally cooperative research programs	R1: Percentage of research projects involving international partnership and collaboration
	Internationally focused research centers	R4: Number of research centers operated with international partners
	International researchers	R5: Percentage of international post-doctoral researchers
	Internationally acknowledged research achievements	R9: Percentage of publications cited by SCI, EI, ISTP
Student	International students	S1: Percentage of international students (for degree study) on campus in total
	Mobility of students	S6: Percentage of domestic students who have international study experiences (incl. exchanges and short-term programs those are no more than an academic year)
Faculty	International profile of the faculty team	F1: Percentage of international (by nationality) faculty members (full-time equivalent FTE)
	International perspective and experience of faculty	F5: Percentage of faculty (FTE) who have at least one-year overseas experience (excl. degree study)
Curriculum	Courses with an international components	C2: Number of subjects involving a partner in other countries
	Joint degree programs	C8: Number of joint degree programs (Bachelor, Master's and PhD) collaborated with overseas higher education institutions
	Students' participation in international studies	C11: Number of students who attend joint degree programs collaborated with overseas higher education institutions

Appendix D: Review Form for the Project …

Dimension	Element	Indicator
Engagement	International network and partnership	E2: Number of overseas partners with whom at least one academic activity (mobility, program, research) has taken place
	International presence of alumni	E4: Proportion of international (by nationality) alumni relative to the total number of alumni
Governance	Human resources for international activities	G3: Percentage of administration staff proficient in more than one working language
	Financial support for internationalization	G7: Funding to support the international mobility of students
	International presence	G12: Number of participations in fairs abroad or G13: Number of languages in which the university website can be read

Q1: In your view, is it feasible to collect the data of the indicator F5: 'percentage of faculty (FTE) who have at least one-year overseers experience (excl. degree study)'?

Q2: Which one do you think is better to measure the element of international presence of a university?

　A. G12 'Number of participations in fairs abroad'
　B. G13 'Number of languages in which the university website can be read'

Q3: Do you think it is feasible to collect data of the indicator S6: 'Percentage of domestic students who have international study experiences (incl. exchanges and short-term programs those are no more than an academic year)' if the scope of international academic experience is extended to include international conference, competitions and filed works?

Q4: Do you think it is feasible to collect data of the two indicators: R9 'Percentage of publications cited by SCI, EI, ISTP' and G7 'Funding to support the international mobility of students'?

Q5: Do you have any other comments on the draft indicators (e.g., if any of the indictors you think may produce confusion in data collection)?

　Thank you very much for your time and valuable opinion.

Index

A

academic colonization 284
Academic Cooperation Association 4
Academic Ranking of World Universities (ARWU) 11
accountability 3, 4, 25, 73, 261, 286
approaches used to design educational indicators 82
 framework approach 82
 model approach 82
assessment of internationalization. *See* measurement of university internationalization
Association of Southeast Asian Nations (ASEAN) 5
Australia 11, 155, 189, 282
 Australian Universities International Directors' Forum (AUIDF) 158
 international links 157
 measuring internationalization performance 173
 the third most prevalent destination for foreign students 156
 world-class universities (WCU) 160

B

benchmarking 3, 5

C

Certificate for Quality in Internationalization (CeQuInt) 5
China 11, 111, 192, 196, 279
 Chinese body and Western use 198
 Confucianism 111

332 Index

Contemporary Regulation on Operation of Higher Education Institutions in Cooperation with Foreign Partners 113
Implementation Measures for Regulations on Chinese-Foreign Cooperation in Running Schools 114
Learn the techniques of the Barbarians in order to control the Barbarians 111
measurements for university internationalization 124
Notice of Strengthening Degree-Granting Management in Activities Concerning Operation of Institutions in Cooperation with Foreign Partners 113
One Belt, One Road initiative 115
Opium Wars (1840-42) 197
Regulations on Chinese-Foreign Cooperation in Running Schools 114
the Republican Era 112
Chi-Square test 245
Committee on Institutional Cooperation (CIC) 75
competitiveness 1
cross-border measurement(s) 256, 258
cross-cultural understanding 187, 275
cultural capital 277
cultural carriers 277
cultural self-awareness. *See* Fei, Xiao tong

D
Delphi method 85

dissemination of knowledge 200

E
emerging economies 43
Erasmus Mobility Quality Tools (EMQT) 5
European countries 5, 52

F
feasibility 215, 230
Fei, Xiao tong 284
flagship research universities 185

G
Gamma correlation 226
global awareness 275
global citizenship 273
globalization 22, 32, 274

H
higher education institutions (HEIs). *See* universities
homogenization 259

I
indicators 7, 9, 87, 95, 97, 125, 147, 174, 177, 211
　appropriateness 147
　availability 250
　feasibility 151
　quantitative 254
institutional capacity and reputation 123
Institutional characteristics 199

Institutional Management in Higher Education 4
intercultural competence 273
international curriculum 213
internationalization of higher education 1, 30
  Africa 30
  curricula 1, 52, 93
  Eastern Asia 30
  engagement 1
  international perspective of faculty members 92
  international profile of the faculty team 92
  Latin America 30
  learning 51
  research 1, 51, 93
  service 53
  strategies 7
  student mobility 90
  teaching 51
  university governance 1, 50, 90
International Medical School 2020 5
the International Office (IO) 118
international partnerships and collaboration 213
International Quality Review Program (IQRP) 4
international staff recruitment and management 213
international student recruitment 213
international student services 213
international values 275

K
Key Performance Indicators (KPIs) 174. *See also* key performance targets

key performance targets 173. *See also* Key Performance Indicators (KPIs)
Knight, Jane 2, 4, 9, 37, 55, 189, 203
knowledge economy 273
Kruskal-Wallis test 12, 241

L
league tables 3, 142, 235, 287. *See also* rankings

M
management-by-results (MBR) 288
Mann–Whitney U tests 12, 244
Mapping and Profiling Internationalization (IMPI) 5
Marginson, Simon 38, 157, 189
Massive Open Online Course (MOOC) 116
measurement of university internationalization 2, 201, 204
  components 6
  construct of 6
  dimension of 13
measuring university internationalization 73
  Asian countries 76
  Australia 75
  European countries 75
  United Kingdom (UK) 75
  United States 74
mobility of students and scholars 1
monitoring and assessing university internationalization performance. *See* measuring university internationalization
'mushrooming effect' 7

N

national competitiveness 136
national context 195
New Public Management (NPM) 26, 73
non-parametric tests 245

O

One Belt one Road initiative 280
ontological shock 277, 283

P

performance evaluation 125
performance management 288
performance measurement 73
the pursuit of academic excellence 186

Q

questionnaire survey 211

R

rankings 3, 24, 25, 27, 29, 45, 79, 80, 161, 287, 288. *See also* league tables
  Academic Ranking of World Universities (ARWU) 25
  QS Stars 25
  Times Higher Education (THE) World University Rankings 25
regionalization 23, 275
the role and goals of higher education 39

S

Science Citation Index (SCI) 116
self-evaluation 79
Singapore 11, 135, 195, 279
  city-state 196
  education hubs 136, 138, 139, 279
  entrepreneurial education 142
  entrepreneurship 144
  global citizenship 136
  'Global Schoolhouse' (GS) initiative 136
  institutionalization 144
  Program for Leadership in University Management (PLUM) 146
  soft power 136
skewness 213
slowbalization 274
social equity 285
statistics about internationalization performance 125
student exchanges 213

U

universities 1
universities' social mission 273
university internationalization 8, 29, 203. *See also* internationalization of higher education
  approach to 56
  components of 49, 89, 165, 187
  culture 262
  curriculum 221
  definition of 203
  dimensions of 89, 120, 165, 187

elements of 204
engagement 223
faculty 218
governance 223
a holistic approach to 191
ideologies of 46, 162
international perspective of faculty members 92
international profile of the faculty team 92
international staff recruitment and management 127, 213
international student recruitment 127, 213
international student services 213
learning 51
meaning of 32
motivation for 39, 189
rationales for 13
research 216
service 53
strategies for 13, 48
student 218
student mobility 90
teaching 51
university governance 1, 22, 26, 29, 90, 190

W

world-class universities (WCU) 27, 115, 186, 200

Printed in the United States
By Bookmasters